Prayer Book Studies
Volume Six

Trial-use Eucharist, Daily Office and
Pastoral Offices, Issues 21-24

Edited by
Derek A. Olsen

Copyright © 2026 The Domestic and Foreign Missionary Society of the Protestant Episcopal Church in the United States of America

The English text of the liturgies presented in this book is in the public domain and is freely available for quotation without restriction.

Unless otherwise noted, the Scripture quotations are from New Revised Standard Version Bible, copyright © 1989 National Council of the Churches of Christ in the United States of America. Used by permission. All rights reserved worldwide.

Seabury Books
19 East 34th Street
New York, NY 10016
www.churchpublishing.org

Seabury Books is an imprint of Church Publishing Incorporated.

Cover design by Newgen
Typeset by Integra Software Services Pvt. Ltd.

ISBN 978-1-64065-936-0 (paperback)
ISBN 978-1-64065-937-7 (hardback)
ISBN 978-1-64065-938-4 (eBook)

Library of Congress Control Number: 2025945264

CONTENTS

Introduction vii

Prayer Book Studies 21: The Holy Eucharist

Preface 3

Introduction 7
The First Service 9
The Second Service 13
An Order for Celebrating The Holy Eucharist 16
Conclusion 19

Appendices 20
Appendix 1: A note on the "ICET" Texts 20
Appendix 2: The Structure and Contents of The Eucharistic
 Liturgy and the Daily Office 22
Appendix 3: Schedule of Variations and Substitutions in the
 Liturgy of the Lord's Supper Authorized by Vote of Special
 General Convention II, 1969 26
Appendix 4: Concerning the Agapé 30
Bibliography 31

The Holy Eucharist: First Service 32
Concerning the Celebration 32
The Proclamation of the Word of God 34
The Prayers 35
The Celebration of the Holy Communion 38
Other forms of the great Thanksgiving 42
The Decalogue 44
An Exhortation 45
A Penitential Order 47

The Holy Eucharist: Second Service 49
Concerning the Celebration 49
The Proclamation of the Word of God 51
The Nicene Creed 52
The Prayers 53
The Celebration of the Holy Communion 54
Another form of the great Thanksgiving 59

An Order for Celebrating the Holy Eucharist 60
Eucharistic Prayers 61
Forms of Intercession 68
Suggested Offertory Sentences 81
Proper Prefaces 81
Additional Directions and Suggestions 86

Prayer Book Studies 22: The Daily Office

Preface 93

Introduction 96
The Background 96
The Proposals of Prayer Book Studies VI 98
The Present Situation 98
The Basic Rationale 99
The Core—Psalter and Readings from Scripture ... 100
The Rest of the Office 106
Other Offices and Devotions 113
An Order of Prayer for Noonday 113
An Order of Prayer for the Close of Day 114
The Daily Devotions 115
Conclusion 116
Appendix: A Note on the ICET Texts 116

Morning and Evening Prayer 118
Concerning The Service 118
Morning and Evening Prayer: First Order 119

Additional Directions and Suggestions for First Order and Second Order 127

Morning and Evening Prayer: Second Order 129

[Music for Preces and Suffrages] 137
The Invitatory Antiphons 144
Sentences for Seasons and Other Occasions .. 145

Canticles for use after the Reading of the Scriptures ... 146

An Order of Service for Noonday or Other Times ... 159

An Order of Service for the Close of Day (Compline) ... 160

Daily Devotions for Individuals and Families ... 165
In The Morning ... 166
At Noon ... 167
At the Close of Day ... 167

Prayer Book Studies 23: The Psalter
PART I

Introduction ... 171

Concerning the Recitation of the Psalms ... 177

The Psalter: Part I ... 178
A Selection of the Most Frequently Appointed Psalms ... 178

Prayer Book Studies 24: Pastoral Offices

Preface ... 241

Introduction ... 245
The Celebration and Blessing of a Marriage ... 246
A Thanksgiving for the Birth of a Child ... 249
A Form of Commitment to Christian Service ... 250
The Ministration to the Sick and Suffering ... 251
The Reconciliation of a Penitent ... 254
Anointing with Oil and the Laying on of Hands ... 255
The Order for Private Communions ... 256
Prayers for the Dying ... 256
The Order for the Burial of the Dead ... 257

The Celebration and Blessing of a Marriage ... 260
The Marriage ... 262
The Blessing of the Marriage ... 263
At the Eucharist: The Blessing of the Marriage ... 265

A Thanksgiving for the Birth of a Child ... 267

A Form of Commitment to Christian Service ... 269

The Ministration to the Sick and Suffering ... 270
Part I. The Ministry of the Word ... 270
Part II. Confession and Absolution ... 275

Part III. Anointing or Laying on of Hands 276
Part IV. The Communion of the Sick 276

The Reconciliation of a Penitent 277
The Absolution 278
Form of Absolution by a Deacon or Lay Person 278

The Anointing of the Sick 278
The Anointing 279
The Laying on of Hands 279
A Form for the Blessing of Oil 279

The Order for Private Communions 280
The Absolution 281
At the Offertory and Consecration 281
The Ministration of the Sacrament 286

Prayers for the Dying 286
A Prayer for a Person near Death 286
Litany for the Dying 287
A Commendation at the Time of Death 288
A Commendatory Prayer 288

The Order for the Burial of the Dead 289
First Service 289
From the Old Testament 291
From the Epistles 292
The Gospel 295
At the Eucharist 298
At the Grave 299
The Words of Committal 300
Additional Prayers, and Canticles 300
The Consecration of a Grave 303
Second Service 304
From the Old Testament 305
From the Epistles 306
The Gospel 309
At the Eucharist 312
At the Grave 313
The Words of Committal 314
Additional Prayers and Canticles 315
The Consecration of a Grave 318

INTRODUCTION

The Series as a Whole

The *Prayer Book Studies* (PBS) series documents the 26-year process of study and conversation that led to the adoption of the American 1979 Book of Common Prayer. It falls broadly into two parts, distinguished by the use of Roman numerals and Arabic numerals. PBS I-XVII were published by the members of the Standing Liturgical Commission between 1950 and 1966 to communicate research and draft liturgies leading toward a revision process; PBS 18-29 were published by the various drafting committees between 1970 and 1976 once the revision process was formally begun and the earlier drafts were being transformed into new usable liturgies leading up to the adoption of the new prayer book in 1979. Finally, PBS 30 and its commentary were added in 1989 to discuss inclusive and expansive language for God for further liturgical efforts.

Context of these Studies

These studies belong to the second series of *Prayer Book Studies*, those using Arabic numerals for their numbering (PBS 18-29), and that followed the kickoff of a formal revision process with the 1967 General Convention. Within these eleven studies, the first seven (PBS 18-24), containing the most critical materials for public worship and pastoral use, were all published in 1970. The rites within these studies, shorn of their exposition, would be printed as *Services for Trial Use*, also known as "the Green Book." The next four (with two supplements) were published in 1973. These would be collected with the preceding materials into *Authorized Services 1973*, also known as "the Zebra Book" for its striped cover. The final study in this second series (PBS 29) is the sole publication in 1976 introducing the complete set of new rites to The Episcopal Church.

In contrast with the first series, a wide range of voices are brought into the conversation as both drafters and readers. The preface to the first of the new studies, PBS 18, describes the processes followed by the Standing Liturgical Commission, the drafting committees, reader-consultants, and the Editorial Committee, and should be consulted for full details.

At the same time, the timeline for completing these studies and their liturgies was greatly compressed. While some work on the First Series had been ongoing since the publication of the 1928 *Book of Common Prayer*, all of the work here–building on and informed by the work of the First Series–had to occur at lightning speed.

One telltale sign of the haste and subsequent disorganization present within this period is the wide range of formatting choices between the studies issued in this period. The choices of fonts for text and headings, the formatting of headings, and the presence or absence of color are entirely inconsistent between studies, leading to an impression of speed and chaos across the material.

Finally—and contributing even more to the pressure on the committees—all of the rites appear in contemporary language (now known as Rite II) rather than the Elizabethan/Jacobean idiom that had been used for all of the preceding liturgical work. Several rites, of course, appear in both (Rites I and II).

These Studies

PBS 21

The first study of this volume on the Eucharist is now the third attempt to craft a satisfactory Eucharistic rite agreeable to the church as a whole. This is the first effort that includes a multiplicity of Eucharistic prayers, and several of the prayers, with emendations, will be incorporated into the new prayer book. The table of contents here may be unintentionally misleading; there is a "First Service," a "Second Service," and an "Order for Celebrating the Holy Eucharist." A reader familiar with the 1979 prayer book might assume that these represent Rite I, Rite II, and the loose framework sometimes referred to as "Rite III." The first two assumptions are correct, and the Eucharistic prayers found there are very close to the 1979's prayer book's Rite I, Prayer II, Rite II, and Prayer A, respectively. However, the "Order" contains, not a Eucharistic prayer outline or required pieces, but four complete Eucharistic Prayers. The first two, A and B, contain elements that will be combined into the 1979's Rite II, Prayer B; the third, C, is substantially the 1979's Rite II, Prayer C; the fourth, D, has no relation to the 1979's book's Rite II, Prayer D and does not appear to have left a lasting impression.

PBS 22

The second study on the Daily Office contains many changes from the rite in PBS VI. Chief among them is the shift to an identical structure for both Morning and Evening Prayer. Hence, this study does not offer distinct Morning and Evening services, but a single service in two Orders (Rite I and II, respectively) that point to both morning and evening options. Noon Prayer and Prayer at the Close of Day are included, as are three Daily Devotions–there is no evening form here. Also lacking from this study is a new Daily Office Lectionary which is promised in 1973 and which would be delivered in PBS 27.

PBS 23

The third study contains 71 of the most commonly appointed Psalms. The first series never considered a revision of the psalter, but the shift to contemporary language liturgies demanded it.

PBS 24

The fourth study gathers together all of the pastoral offices into a single gathering. Perhaps the most significant change here–apart from the adoption of contemporary language–is the separation of various elements of the visitation of the sick into separate and distinct rites. The classical prayer book visitation did have the odor of a "last rites" service about it; wishing to dispel that perception, portions like reconciliation, anointing, and prayers for the sick became their own rites set apart from end-of-life ministrations.

PRAYER BOOK STUDIES 21:
THE HOLY EUCHARIST

1970

PREFACE

In September 1967, the General Convention approved a Plan for the Revision of the Book of Common Prayer and designated the Standing Liturgical Commission as the instrument of revision. At the same time, the General Convention authorized the trial use for the Triennium 1967-1970, of *The Liturgy of the Lord's Supper*, a revision of the service of Holy Communion prepared by the Standing Liturgical Commission.[1] The coincidence of these two events confronted the Commission with both a challenge and an opportunity.

It might have been considered logical for the Commission to proceed with the revision of other parts of the Prayer Book, while suspending action on the revision of the service of Holy Communion until all the results of trial use, obtained through lay and clergy questionnaires and by direct correspondence were in, and had been sorted, tabulated, and analyzed. The Commission decided, however, to proceed simultaneously with the conduct and evaluation of the trial use of *The Liturgy of the Lord's Supper* and with the further revision of the eucharistic liturgy. The Commission is satisfied that it made the right decision.

The preliminary results of trial use indicated clearly that there was within the Church a considerable amount of suspicion about the purpose of Prayer Book revision. The suspicion expressed itself in some of the answers to the questionnaires designed by the Commission, in the Church press, and in the vehemence of the language used by some correspondents in commenting on *The Liturgy of the Lord's Supper*. Without analyzing the reactions in detail, one motif stood out clearly: a sizeable body of Churchmen simply did not believe that the Commission meant it when it said that trial use was precisely what it claimed to be, namely, the testing and evaluation of a new rite in situations of actual worship. Many people seemed to think that trial use was a public relations device designed to sell "the new service". Many were not convinced that their views would be taken into account if they ran counter to what were assumed to be the views of the Standing Liturgical Commission.

The Drafting Committee on the Holy Eucharist, set up by the Standing Liturgical Commission under the Revision Plan, established as its first priority the task of responding promptly to criticisms that had been made by giving attention to such variations and changes as were shown to be desirable through actual

---

1. Prayer Book Studies XVII, *The Liturgy of the Lord's Supper*, New York: The Church Pension Fund, 1966. (Contained in Volume 4 of this edition.)

experience in trial use. The Schedule of Variations and Substitutions proposed by the Drafting Committee was approved by the Standing Liturgical Commission early in 1969, and was adopted by Special General Convention II at South Bend, Indiana, in September 1969.[2]

At the same time, the Drafting Committee proceeded with its study of the liturgical needs of the Church as revealed in trial use, and with the drafting of several services designed to meet these needs. In this work, the Committee and the Commission itself were greatly assisted by the 260 Consultants appointed under the Revision Plan, and by the Chairmen and members of Diocesan Liturgical Commissions. Their criticisms, comments, and suggestions made an invaluable contribution to the development of the rites presented in this Study.

The Drafting Committee on the Holy Eucharist consisted of the following:[3]

The Right Reverend Jonathan G. Sherman, member of the Standing Liturgical Commission and Chairman of the Drafting Committee;

The Right Reverend Lyman C. Ogilby;

The Very Reverend Henry N. Hancock;

The Very Reverend Charles U. Harris;

The Reverend Alfred R. Shands III;

The Reverend Carroll E. Simcox;

The Reverend James P. Morton;

The Reverend Jules L. Moreau;

The Reverend David E. Babin;

Miss Marianne H. Micks;

Mr. Francis F. Bowman, Secretary.

The Reverend Leo Malania, Co-ordinator for Prayer Book Revision, participated *ex officio* in all meetings of the Committee, and the Committee was especially fortunate in having the assistance at several meetings of the Reverend H. Boone Porter, Jr., and of Captain Howard Galley and Sister Brooke Bushong, both of the Church Army in the U.S.A., and both of them members of the Co-ordinator's staff.

The Committee was also fortunate to have the assistance at most of its meetings of the Venerable Frederic P. Williams and the Reverend Norman C. Mealy, members of the Joint Commission on Church Music, who made an invaluable

---

2. The text of the Schedule as approved by the General Convention is reproduced for the record on pages 26-29. Additional copies may be obtained from the Office of the Co-ordinator for Prayer Book Revision, 815 Second Avenue, New York, N.Y. 10017.

3. The Reverend Nathan A. Scott was appointed member of the Drafting Committee, but the pressure of other duties made it impossible for him to attend any of its meetings. The Rev. Alfred Shands resigned from the Committee on February 25, 1970. Dean Marianne Micks was prevented from attending the last two sessions.

contribution by their assessment of the musical possibilities of the material under consideration, and by noting the Proper Prefaces.

The Standing Liturgical Commission desires to record its own deep sorrow and that of members of the Drafting Committee over the death on March 24, 1970, of the Very Reverend Henry N. Hancock, Dean of St. Mark's Cathedral, Minneapolis, Minnesota. Dean Hancock made a distinguished contribution to the work of the Drafting Committee. He was a fine Christian, a faithful Priest, and a generous and loyal colleague.

In the course of its work, the Drafting Committee received thousands of comments and suggestions, not only from the Consultants of the Commission and the Chairmen of Diocesan Liturgical Commissions, but also from many lay persons, reflecting the widest range and variety of points of view. To all of them the Commission expresses its sincere appreciation.

To the Dean, the Faculty, and the student body of Seabury-Western Theological Seminary at Evanston, Illinois, the Drafting Committee owes a debt of deep gratitude for their unfailing hospitality, and their warm interest in its work. All the meetings of the Committee, from the first meeting in 1967 to the final session in March 1970, were held there. Seabury-Western became virtually the home of the Drafting Committee.

The Commission desires also to express its appreciation to the Editorial Committee for its careful and painstaking review of this Study;[4] and to Mr. Alston Purvis for the typographical design of this publication.

In presenting to the Episcopal Church and to the entire Christian community this Study and the rites and texts included therein, the Standing Liturgical Commission expresses the hope that its work on the Holy Eucharist may be found worthy of being approved for trial use by the General Convention. The Commission hopes that such trial use, if authorized, will be conducted in a spirit of reverent and sincere devotion to our Lord; and that all Christians, whatever their own ecclesiastical affiliation, will assist in the further development of this central service of Christian worship by making known their views and suggestions, either to local Diocesan Liturgical Commissions or to the Standing Liturgical Commission, at 815 Second Avenue, New York, N.Y. 10017.

The Commission assures all who will take the trouble to respond that their communications will be acknowledged and will receive thoughtful consideration. The Commission thanks in advance all who may accept this invitation.

THE STANDING LITURGICAL COMMISSON

Chilton Powell, *Chairman*
John W. Ashton

---

4. The Editorial Committee is constituted as follows: The Reverend Robert W. Estill, Chairman; the Reverend Donald L. Garfield, the Reverend Canon Charles M. Guilbert, the Reverend H. Boone Porter, Jr., and the Reverend Massey H. Shepherd, Jr., members; and Captain Howard Galley, C.A., and the Reverend Leo Malania, Co-ordinator for Prayer Book Revision, members *ex officio*.

Dupuy Bateman, Jr.
James D. Dunning
Robert W. Estill
William C. Frey
Charles M. Guilbert, *Secretary*
Mrs. Richard Harbour
Joseph M. Harte
Louis B. Keiter
H. Boone Porter, Jr.
Charles P. Price
Massey H. Shepherd, Jr., *Vice Chairman*
Jonathan G. Sherman
Charles W. F. Smith
Bonnell Spencer, O.H.C.
Albert R. Stuart.
Leo Malania, *Co-ordinator*

Introduction

The service of Holy Communion in the Book of Common Prayer adopted in 1928 has served the Church well for more than four decades as the center of its liturgical worship. The Anglican tradition of uniformity in worship, dating from the Prayer Books of 1549 and 1552, has been expressed in our attachment to the 1928 rite as the norm throughout the American Church. Yet, any Episcopalian who has moved from one part of this country to another, or who has visited and worshiped with congregations other than his own, is aware of the fact that even the structure of the 1928 rite lends itself to wide variety in celebration. Some of the variety is distinctly within the spirit of that rite, but much of it is a frank attempt to go beyond 1928 in any one of a number of different directions. Some of these variations have attempted to assimilate the Prayer Book service to other traditional rites, while others have sought to incorporate new perspectives and new insights into eucharistic worship. The distance between the two *Prayer Book Studies IV* and *XVII*[5] prepared by the Standing Liturgical Commission in 1953 and 1966 respectively is an indication of the rapidity with which seemingly assured historical results are superseded.

The need for a revision of the 1928 rite was eloquently and persuasively set forth in *Prayer Book Studies IV* more than fifteen years ago.[6] *Prayer Book Studies XVII* no longer found it necessary to plead for revision, but instead, relied upon a simplified expression of principle: "Any adequate revision must be sufficiently imaginative regarding the various ways and the various settings in which the liturgy is celebrated in our congregations."[7]

The Liturgy of the Lord's Supper presented in *Prayer Book Studies XVII* was an important step in a process of revision intended to re-order the basic structure of eucharistic worship, so as to conform it to the shape of the liturgy as the early Church celebrated it. Trial use of this liturgy evoked that variety of response which is characteristic of a living and worshiping Church: enthusiastic support balanced by deep-seated objection; acceptance of the rite as a good first step toward much more drastic revision, countered by reluctance to admit any, even minute, alteration of either text or rubric in the 1928 Prayer Book. Nevertheless, the response to *The Liturgy of the Lord's Supper* was generally favorable, and acceptance of its structure was almost unanimous.

---

5. *The Eucharistic Liturgy* (Prayer Book Studies IV), Standing Liturgical Commission of the Episcopal Church, New York: Church Pension Fund, 1953. *The Liturgy of the Lord's Supper* (*Prayer Book Studies XVII*), New York: Church Pension Fund, 1966. The latter was authorized for trial use by the General Convention of 1967.

6. *Prayer Book Studies IV*, Vol. 1, pp. 223-228.

7. *Prayer Book Studies XVII*, Introduction, Vol. 4, p. 226.

While there appeared, however, to be general agreement about the structure or outline of the service, there was at the same time a good deal of disagreement about whether or not the language of 1928 ought to be altered; and if so, how far. Opinion ranged all the way from wanting nothing other than traditional Prayer Book language to wanting no specific words prescribed at all, so long as the basic elements of Eucharist were included. A substantial segment of opinion was quite favorable, however, to a combination of the dignity of the 1928 rite's locution with those new dimensions that marked *The Liturgy of the Lord's Supper*.

Recognizing that no single rite can satisfy both caution about any revision whatsoever and desire for complete freedom to compose all prayers, the Standing Liturgical Commission has charted a new course. It now offers for the Episcopal Church's responsible experimentation two complete Eucharistic rites and an order of service for use in circumstances other than regular parish celebrations. In all of them continuity with Christian tradition is maintained by preserving the structure of the rite.

The first of these Services preserves the language of 1928 so far as was deemed advisable. It also recognizes the positive features[8] of the Eucharistic Prayer of *The Liturgy of the Lord's Supper* by permitting it as an alternative in this rite. In addition, a short form of the revised 1928 Prayer of Consecration is provided for use when necessary.

The second rite, using the 1967 Liturgy as a starting point, responds to the frequently expressed criticism that that rite came to rest between the tendencies toward contemporaneity and traditionalism. Although this Service chooses the direction of contemporaneity, it maintains a link with its parent rite by allowing the alternative use of the 1967 Eucharistic Prayer in a form congruent with the rest of the Service in employing the pronoun "you" in divine address.

The additional Order is fundamentally an outline of the elements considered necessary for celebrating the Eucharist. It permits a wide latitude in the choice of forms for these elements, so as to express the unique concerns of the specific community doing the liturgy. Since, however, the Eucharistic Prayer is the corporate responsibility of the Church, specific limitation is placed on the freedom of this Order by prescribing the use of one of several Eucharistic Prayers.

Each of these forms of service demonstrates that it is principally the structure that unifies the several rites and holds them within the compass of the Church at worship. Each of them accepts three basic elements in eucharistic worship: a) a form of proclamation of the Word of God by readings from Scripture, which may be elaborated by preaching and other media of communication; b) a prayer of intercession, which gathers together the worshiping community's concerns and focuses its attention upon the mission and ministry of the Church as a thankful

---

8. *Prayer Book Studies XVII.* Introduction, Vol. 4, pp. 253-254

congregation; c) the Liturgy of the Table which intends to do again what the Church affirms its Lord to have done before his death.

The English Prayer Book of 1662 placed the intercession within the Liturgy of the Table, and since that time most Anglican liturgies have maintained this arrangement. One of the great gains of the 1967 *Liturgy of the Lord's Supper* was its clear distinction among the three elements mentioned; thus it overcame what to many, if not all, students of liturgy was an unfortunate confusion in the rites which followed 1662.

Since all the forms of service presented in this study exhibit the same structure, this could certainly be recognized as acquiescence in the desire for uniformity. If indeed the words employed, and even the forms of prayers, are highly divergent among these services, at least it will be clear from a careful look at their outlines that each intends to do the same thing.

In our ecumenical encounters with Churches of entirely different traditions, as well as in our inter-Anglican exchanges, we have come to appreciate the effectiveness as well as the beauty of services often very different from our own. In them, we have also been able to understand structural similarity even where few verbal contacts were perceptible.

The First Service

Perhaps the most important observation to be made about this Service is that it casts substantially the entire 1928 rite within the framework which is now recognized by all Provinces of the Church as both ancient and fundamental to eucharistic worship. Once this principle was accepted as basic, the actual achievement of it required some slight relocation of certain elements of the service. Yet all such relocation has been done, not merely as a matter of expediency, but in accordance with the criteria of good liturgical usage. The framework is further clarified by the insertion of titles and sub-titles, to point up the basic divisions and to note transitions from part to part, a practice initiated in *Prayer Book Studies IV*[9] and continued in the 1967 *Liturgy of the Lord's Supper*.

Following an introduction with the *Gloria in excelsis* as its climax, the service proceeds with (a) The Proclamation of the Word of God, beginning with a Salutation and the Collect of the Day, incorporating readings from Scripture, the Sermon, and the Creed, and ending, if desired, with an act of penitence; (b) The Prayers, comprising an expanded form of what we have come to know as the Prayer for the Church, and an alternate place for the Confession and Absolution in one of two forms; (c) The Celebration of the Holy Communion, in which the fourfold action of Offertory, Thanksgiving, Breaking of the Bread, and Communion is placed. If the brief conclusion, culminating in the Blessing and

---

9. *Prayer Book Studies IV*, Vol. 1, pp. 233-234.

Dismissal, and the introduction are construed as separate parts, it would be possible to speak of five divisions, although this point need not be labored.

This basic pattern corresponds to that set forth by the Inter-Anglican Liturgical Consultation in Toronto in 1963, as a guide for liturgical revision throughout the Anglican Communion.[10] Substantially the same outline was recently reaffirmed at the direction of the Lambeth Conference of 1968.[11]

The Confession and Absolution may be used before the Service, where the penitential act would form an introduction to worship, much as they do in the longer form of Morning Prayer, or in one of two other places: immediately following the Proclamation of the Word, as a response to it; or immediately before the Peace, in preparation for the Offertory. Two briefer forms of Confession and Absolution are provided: one from the Communion of the Sick,[12] somewhat revised; the other adapted from that proposed by the British Joint Liturgical Group.[13]

Two major changes have been introduced in the order of the Proclamation of the Word of God. The first — widely approved in trial use —is the placing of the Sermon immediately after the Gospel, where it may be more closely related to the Scripture lessons. The reason for this sequence is amply discussed in *Prayer Book Studies XVII*.[14] The second major change, in response to many requests, is the permission to use the Order of Morning or Evening Prayer as the Proclamation of the Word of God, provided that it always include a lesson from the Gospel.

Two points are to be stressed in connection with the Nicene Creed: when, and in what form, it is to be used. *The Liturgy of the Lord's Supper*, recognizing a growing custom, prescribed the Creed only on Sundays and other festivals and made it optional on other occasions. The First Service makes the same provision. The wording of the Creed is, however, a more complex problem. The Standing Liturgical Commission, after responsible historical research, could possibly produce a felicitous and accurate translation of this Creed. To do so, however, would fail to take into account the work being done cooperatively among the various Christian bodies, our own included, through the agency of the International Consultation on English Texts.[15]

The Nicene Creed is the corporate confession of the Church's faith. It seems logical, therefore, that whenever the Creed is recited it should be in a widely-accepted form. The ICET version restores the first person plural of the original

---

10. Reprinted in *Prayer Book Studies XVII*, Vol. 4, pp. 261-263.

11. This document is reprinted in full on pages 22-26 of this book.

12. Book of Common Prayer, page 323.

13. *The Daily Offices by the Joint Liturgical Group*, edited by the Rev. Canon R.C.D. Jasper, London: S.P.C.K., 1968; page 77.

14. *Prayer Book Studies* XVII, Vol. 4, p. 242.

15. A note on the ICET will be found on pages 20-22 of this book.

text, and in this, and several other respects, follows the translation proposed by the Standing Liturgical Commission in 1967. With regard to the procession of the Holy Spirit, the International Consultation placed the phrase "and the Son" in parentheses, leaving it to the participating Church bodies whether to use this phrase or to omit it. The Standing Liturgical Commission reaffirms the position it adopted in the 1967 *Liturgy of the Lord's Supper*, and recommends that this phrase be omitted in "recognition of the fact that it was not originally in the Creed, and is therefore not truly ecumenical."[16] Along the same line of reasoning, "holy" has been restored to the group of adjectives describing the Church.

The Prayer for the Church has been dissociated from the Offertory and placed between the Proclamation of the Word and the Liturgy of the Table. This relocation necessitated changes in the wording of the first paragraph; it also gave opportunity to respond to many pleas to broaden the scope of this prayer, so that it might take a larger account of the Church's responsibility for the world in which it lives and to which it has a mission. The new bidding for this prayer expresses that extension of compass. This becomes even more evident in the change of one paragraph and the inclusion of one more. The prayer for "Christian Rulers" has been broadened to include all who bear the authority of government throughout the world, and has been given a new location immediately preceding a petition for good stewardship of God's creation.

Congregational participation in this prayer is facilitated by making it possible for a member or members of the congregation to read one or all of the paragraphs of this prayer, and by the provision of an optional response for the whole congregation after each paragraph.

Trial use of *The Liturgy of the Lord's Supper* revealed that for many worshipers the most unsatisfactory part of that rite was The Prayer of Intercession, even though the litany form of the prayer was generally welcomed. It is impossible to assign any one cause for this dissatisfaction. The Commission responded to negative reactions by proposing to Special General Convention II, in September 1969, a variation in the manner of saying this Prayer, by permitting the omission of the purpose clauses, and by providing an alternative Prayer of Intercession. The generally favorable response to these proposals confirms the impression that a major problem with The Prayer of Intercession was its lack of variety and flexibility. Accordingly, the Commission now offers seven prayers of intercession, in various forms, which may be used in place of the Prayer for the Church and the World. Some of these are primarily intended for use with the First Service, addressing God in the second person singular. All of the Prayers, however, may be used in both the First and Second Service, by a relatively simple substitution of "thou" for "you" and vice versa, and by a corresponding adjustment, where necessary, in the form of the verbs.

---

16. *Prayer Book Studies XVII*, Vol. 4, pp. 242-243.

Following the lead of *The Liturgy of the Lord's Supper*, the two rubrics in the 1928 Prayer Book permitting a form of the service without the celebration of the Eucharist have been revised and incorporated in this Service, so that a complete liturgy of the Proclamation of the Word including a Sermon, a form of Confession and Absolution, together with a form of Intercession and the Lord's Prayer, and concluding with the Peace or the Grace or a Blessing, may be employed where circumstances dictate it. When a priest is not available, it will be possible to use this form of the service omitting the Absolution and the Blessing. Thus a completely workable form of Sunday morning worship for small missions and other types of congregations is made possible within the spirit of this liturgy.

Adhering to the ecumenically agreed structure, the Offertory begins the action which is centered on the Table. It may be preceded by the Peace. Provision has been made for a deacon to prepare the elements. The rubrics envisage lay persons bringing forward the bread and wine; and a deacon receiving them, preparing the paten and chalice, and placing them on the holy Table.

Then, when all has been prepared for the Thanksgiving over the elements, the Priest takes his position at the Table, as president of the eucharistic fellowship. The *Sursum Corda* and the Thanksgiving (Prayer of Consecration) follow the order and phraseology of the 1928 Prayer Book.

A shortened form of the Thanksgiving is provided as an alternative. It is based on the form for the Communion of the Sick in the present Prayer Book and on the form in *A Prayer Book for the Armed Forces*.[17] On occasions when brevity is imperative, this form may be used without detracting from the parts deemed necessary for an adequate celebration. As indicated above, the Canon of the 1967 *Liturgy of the Lord's Supper* may also be used as an alternative.

The only things specifically new in this part of the service are the provision for the Breaking of the Bread before the distribution of Communion, the permissive use of the anthem "Christ our Passover . . .", and an option for using the Peace immediately before Communion. The place of the Breaking of the Bread after the Lord's Prayer is not particularly startling, however, since this has been done in the past, either as a practical measure when large wafers or a loaf have been used, or as a symbolic act to emphasize the participation of all the faithful in the one bread (1 Corinthians 10:17). Likewise, as a means of exemplifying this participation, the Prayer after Communion may be said by the congregation with the Celebrant. The Prayer of Humble Access has been revised and made optional.

By making some parts of this Service optional and allowing the substitution of briefer forms for some other portions, the Commission has devised a rite within the spirit of 1928 and in the pattern of 1967, useful on a variety of occasions.

---

17. Book of Common Prayer, page 323. *A Prayer Book for the Armed Forces*, New York: The Seabury Press, 1967; pages 20-21.

It will be noticed with regard to the rubrics, that they are intended to facilitate the performance of the Service and to point directions in which it may go, rather than to inhibit movement by legalistic restrictions. Accordingly, all of the rubrics have been carefully constructed to give a clear outline of the rite, to allow for a variety of circumstances and number of participating ministers, while at the same time emphasizing the actions essential to each section. While the distinction between mandatory rubrics and permissive rubrics remains, the former, describing what is to be done, are expressed in simple declarative sentences in the indicative mode, while options are still indicated by the permissive "may". One significant purpose of this re-working is to recapture the living and responsive character of corporate worship as celebrated by a congregation aware of its joyful privilege to be thankful.

The Second Service

Among the responses to the trial use of *The Liturgy of the Lord's Supper* there was one clear note from many who welcomed it and used it diligently, that a rite which intended to be contemporary could not continue with integrity to use archaic expressions, and in particular such forms as "thee" and "thou" in addressing God. This objection pointed directly to the problem involved in revising time-honored texts, and thus the whole question of phraseology was brought to the fore. Having decided to provide the First Service in response to those to whom the words of the 1928 Prayer Book were especially dear, the Liturgical Commission embarked upon the more thorough revision desired by an increasing segment of the Episcopal Church, and made more compelling as a result of more frequent participation in ecumenical gatherings. The Second Service is marked by a more contemporary style of speech, while retaining a clear and traditional structure.

This Service, like the First, follows the pattern of the 1967 *Liturgy of the Lord's Supper*. The opening expresses our approach to the worship of God the Father, through the mediation of Jesus Christ, in the fellowship of the Holy Spirit. The slight amount of change in wording necessitated by the pronominal alteration in addressing God can be seen in the Collect for Purity (which is optional). The *Gloria in excelsis* (which is provided for use on festal occasions) is the version made by the International Consultation on English texts. The opening part of the service is concluded with the Gloria or one of the alternatives for it.

The Proclamation of the Word of God begins with the Salutation by the presiding Minister, followed by the Collect of the Day, and, like the First Service, it allows for one or two lessons to precede the Gospel, with psalms, hymns, or anthems between them. The Gospel is directly followed by the Sermon. The Nicene Creed is recited on Sundays and other feasts, and the ICET text is used.

In the place of a prescribed Prayer of Intercession, there appears an extended rubric, listing the normative topics of corporate intercession of the Church. The list is a minimum for regular parish petitions. It is a nucleus which requires expansion and elaboration. For this purpose, seven forms of common intercessory prayers are provided. These are grouped together on pages 68-81.

These forms may be used with the First as well as the Second Service. They include two versions of an ancient litany: one is adapted directly from its Eastern form, which is basic to the Liturgy of the Greek Orthodox Church; the other is based on a skillful western adaptation.[18] Both forms (Intercessions I and V) incorporate more current concerns, yet preserve the structure and, it is hoped, the spirit of this ancient litany. The second of the intercessions is an open form consisting of biddings followed by silence, during which members of the congregation are free to express their own personal needs and petitions for the concern and attention of the entire worshiping body. The next prayer, more structured, is cast in dialogue form, the leader stating the subject of the petition, and the people responding with the intention.[19] The fourth form is an adaptation of the Prayer of Intercession in the English Second Series Liturgy.[20] The sixth is the solemn biddings and Collects from the Good Friday Liturgy prepared by the Standing Liturgical Commission for *The Church Year* (*Prayer Book Studies 19*). The collection ends with a form based on the alternative litany approved by Special General Convention II in 1969, but with the people's responses taking the form of petitions complementary to the leader's, each pair constituting a related whole.

Several of the intercessions include a penitential petition or petitions to be read when a confession of sin is not used. In turn, this petition may be omitted when a confession is used in the celebration. Petitions which are not required to be used at every celebration have been marked with an asterisk.

The variety of prayers of intercession, ranging from the most ancient to more contemporary and open forms, and including two based on intercessions devised by sister Churches of the Anglican Communion, should go far to meet the needs of times and occasions. It is hoped that the regular use of all these forms will deepen and enrich worship in our Church, and perhaps open new perspectives to the meaning of intercession and the mission of the Church.

The Prayers are followed by the greeting of Peace between the Celebrant and the congregation, and it is again recommended that it be followed by an exchange of greetings among the ministers and the people, in order that the corporate quality of the eucharistic offering be emphasized. Placed at this point, the Peace expresses the spirit of reconciliation among the followers of Christ in obedience

---

18. Brightman, F. E., *Liturgies Eastern and Western*, Oxford: Clarendon Press, 1896, 1965; Vol. I, pages 362-363, 388 ff. Oración de los Fieles, recomendada para los días más solemnes, en *Santa Misa, Acción de Gracias de la Comunidad Cristiana*, New York: Pro Musica Press, 1965; pages 16-19.

19. This form is based on one of the litanies in the New Zealand. Experimental Liturgy, 1966; quoted in *Modern Anglican Liturgies, 1958-1968*; Edited by Colin O. Buchanan, London: Oxford University Press, 1968; pages 334-335.

20. Quoted in *Modern Anglican Liturgies*, pages 132-133.

to the Dominical command: "First be reconciled to thy brother, and then come and offer thy gift" (Matthew 5:24).

The celebration of the Eucharist begins with the Offertory, and proceeds in a quite familiar way. Again, it is strongly recommended that deacons and others be involved in this ceremony, stressing the roles of the various members of the congregation, each in his order.[21] The Great Thanksgiving begins, as is customary, with the *Sursum Corda*, also an ICET text, as is the *Sanctus* and the Lord's Prayer. To the Proper Prefaces, three new Prefaces have been added for use on Sundays after Pentecost (not, however, for use on the succeeding weekdays). One celebrates the Creation, another the Resurrection, and the third, the work of the Spirit in Baptism, thus expressing the three basic themes of the Lord's Day. In addition, the enrichment of Proper Prefaces already accomplished by the 1967 *Liturgy of the Lord's Supper* has been preserved. The Preface culminates in the *Sanctus*, to which the *Benedictus qui venit* has been restored.[22] The version used is that of the ICET.

The giving of thanks for Creation and Redemption leads into the familiar words concerning the Bread and the Wine. At this point, the congregation joins the Priest in an acclamation of God's mighty acts in Christ. This constitutes the liturgical *anamnesis*. The Priest then proceeds with an invocation and a concluding doxology, to which the people respond with a clearly audible *Amen*. In place of this prayer, a slightly revised version of the Canon of the 1967 *Liturgy of the Lord's Supper* may be substituted. It has been altered mainly in respect of the pronouns and verbs of the divine address to achieve concord with the remainder of the Service.

As in the First Service, the Breaking of the Bread follows the Lord's Prayer, after which "Christ our Passover" is sung or said.

The invitation to Communion follows: "The Gifts of God for the People of God". Alternative forms of invitation are given in the Additional Directions. Alternate words of administration have also been provided.

The familiar Prayer after Communion is rich in the imagery of the sixteen-century authors of the Prayer Book, but it translates into modern English only with difficulty. Therefore, in addition to this ancient prayer, somewhat altered, there is provided one that emphasizes the mission of the worshiping community to "go forth". The Blessing is optional, followed by a Dismissal which recalls that of the 1967 *Liturgy of the Lord's Supper*, but is more brief and direct. Two further options are provided. In each case, the response is "Thanks be to God."

---

21. See page 12 above.

22. The adding of this verse from Psalm 118 to the text of the *Sanctus* is characteristic of almost all Christian liturgies, Catholic and Protestant. It is analogous to the Synagogue custom of adding to the *Kedushah* (*Sanctus*) the words "Blessed be the glory of the Lord from his place" (Ezekiel 3:12); and "The Lord shall reign for ever and ever" (Exodus 15:18).

This Second Service introduces a large measure of flexibility into a firm structure virtually identical with that of the First. Both are recognizably derived from the 1967 *Liturgy of the Lord's Supper*. The freer composition of prayers accomplished by some rephrasing, some rendering into more contemporary modes of language, and some extension of scope, is a reflection of the experience of Christians who have been nurtured on the Book of Common Prayer. It is hoped that the Second Service achieves what so many correspondents and critics have asked for: contemporaneity, flexibility, and clarity, combined with that dignity which is so vital an ingredient in the liturgical tradition of the Anglican Communion.

An Order for Celebrating The Holy Eucharist

One of the most perplexing questions about liturgy is, "What is absolutely necessary?" Another way of asking it is, "How much of what we have done in this setting is essential, and how much is simply helpful or explanatory?" At base, it is the question which faces any worshiping community, and certainly vexes any group charged with planning the liturgy for a given occasion. If one compares the Communion of the Sick (BCP, pages 321-323) with the Holy Communion intended for public worship, the question is faced concretely. The priest who schedules a celebration of the liturgy in a downtown parish church at noontime, trying to accommodate busy people on their lunch hour, knows the difficulty of providing an adequate service without taking an undue amount of time. The Book of Common Prayer seems to take little account of any public worship that is not set in the leisurely context of a Sunday morning. Historically, of course, there is reason for this, since Sunday mornings were traditionally given over almost entirely to worship in the parish church.

Summer camp and similar experiences have frequently pointed up the incongruity of sixteenth-century English custom and language with the "here-ness and now-ness" of such occasions. While some groups, such as those in detention camps during World War II, were deprived of the Book of Common Prayer and were forced to improvise as best they could, other groups have felt it not only necessary, but salutary, to improvise in order to bring spontaneity to worship. The fundamental problem with which all such worshiping groups have been faced is similar. Regardless of whether it is out of necessity or out of desire, the experience of constructing a liturgy is a rewarding one. Nevertheless, there still exists a certain degree of uncertainty as to what constitutes a proper eucharistic celebration. From what we are able to glean about the life of the Church in the earliest centuries, it is quite clear that freedom to improvise within a more or less stable framework was common. This observation leads us to a question which is posed for us by Christians in non-liturgical Churches: "What virtue is there in adhering to the same formula of words each time we make Eucharist?"

The Liturgical Movement has made us deeply aware of the wide variety of liturgical services that have been celebrated with the basic intention of following the command in the narrative of the Last Supper, "Do this for the remembrance of me."[23] The fundamental criterion for evaluating the adequacy of these various services depends upon the definition of the word "this" in that command. Is nothing more needed than to -give thanks over a loaf and a cup? How may we best relate that action to the life, death, and resurrection of Jesus Christ? It is by way of attempting to answer this question in a quite contemporary setting that the Liturgical Commission includes in this study An Order for Celebrating the Holy Eucharist.

The need for such an Order has been made urgent by the growth within the Church itself, and especially on the overlapping peripheries of many Churches, of groups of people of varying size and character, who are searching for a living experience of worship outside of what, to them at least, appears as a rigid institutional framework. Such groups are not limited to young people, although the young have been most vocal in their demands for freedom and spontaneity in worship. Less publicized, but equally important, perhaps, for the longer range renewal of the Church, are study groups consisting of professional people who are interested in discovering the relevance of the Gospel to their secular concerns, groups of young married couples who are seeking a more mature restatement of the religious principles on which they were brought up as children, and similar *ad hoc* gatherings of adults.

These groups may engage for several weeks in an intensive study of one of the Gospels, or of some aspect of the Bible, or of some questions of theology. They may then break up and regroup in some other framework. They may or may not consist of regular churchgoers. But one thing they seem to have in common—the desire to relate their secular lives to the transcendent, to experience the worship of God as an intimate personal and group happening. The existence and the needs of such groups cannot be ignored. To let them drift on their own without guidance is to deepen their alienation.

It is not only with these widespread needs in view, but also to meet the more conventional needs of house Communions, the Communion of shut-ins, celebrations at summer camps and other informal occasions, that the Standing Liturgical Commission proposes this Order for the thoughtful consideration of the Church and for responsible trial use.

The Order is designed for groups, because Eucharist is made only by an assembly, however small. The Christian Church is community; it is more than a random gathering of people. It is a group of people who by their incorporation

---

23. 1 Corinthians 11:24. No single word in English—remembrance, recall, memorial—can render satisfactorily the connotation of the Greek *anamnesis*—the bringing into the living present of an action, which while accomplished in the past, points to the future, and remains outside of time.

into the Christian Church affirm a certain confession of faith which is pre-eminently set out in the Scriptures. Hence, the reading of Scripture, the Gospel at the very least, reminds this gathering of what it is. How should it respond to being recalled to the ground of its being? To a certain extent, of course, the words used for such response will be determined by the language used in the version of Scripture from which the reading is taken. But, as we are being reminded constantly by psychologists, communication is not limited to verbal expression: gesture, song, the strumming of a guitar, silence itself, or a combination of actions, can express an attitude and convey meaning. Just as it is impossible to legislate or dictate freedom, so it is equally impossible to direct how response should be made.

As has already been stated, prayer for the world and the Church forms a significant part of eucharistic worship. In this Order, those who plan the service are free to design or choose such prayers as seem suitable to the occasion. Christian concern may invite the world to write the agenda. The daily newspaper itself is a potential intercession list.

As we come to the Liturgy of the Table, we emphasize once again our unity and mutual interdependence by the exchange of the Peace. Then we proceed to the offering of bread and wine and other gifts. The Eucharistic Prayer, from the simplest to the most elaborate forms in traditional liturgies, is man's response to the basic acts of God for which we are thankful as Christians. Mindful, however, that this narrative thanksgiving has a historical dimension that completes and fulfills itself in the "now", the Commission provides a choice of four prayers, adapted from the many which have been developed experimentally in particular settings and for particular groups. It is understood, of course, that any of the Eucharistic Prayers from the First and Second Services may also be used.

There may indeed be occasions when none of these will seem to be right for that moment. As other forms are evolved under controlled conditions, they may be commended to the Church for use in this Order, and thus the celebration of the Eucharist may be kept intimate and spontaneous without sacrificing that vital link with the past which binds the worshiping community across time.

The notice in the rubric on page 60 emphasizes that the celebration is not intended to be a casual improvisation. The filling-in of the outline of the service must grow out of the experience of the group. If it is to be that particular group's distinctive expression, it must embody the thoughtful contribution of the group. Under competent leadership, the group discusses, decides, and plans the selection of readings, and the use of other art forms. The intention is that every participant should understand what takes place and why. This may involve a depth of liturgical and theological discussion unusual for most of our parishes. But without such preparation, the celebration is likely to be little more than a stunt.

It cannot be stressed too strongly that this Order is not intended to displace the regular celebration of the authorized complete rites. It would be a gross travesty were a priest and a few acolytes to prepare the celebration in accordance with this Order, and then spring it on an unprepared congregation.

Each of the four Eucharistic Prayers given in this Order has its own distinctive quality. Each includes a thanksgiving to God the Father for some aspect of creation, culminating in a thanksgiving for the gift of his only-begotten Son Jesus Christ. A recital of the words of institution follows, with an invocation and oblation, climaxing in a doxology to the Father, through the Son, in the unity of the Holy Spirit.

It is not necessary to give a detailed analysis of each prayer. A careful reading will bring out their distinctive features. Attention may be drawn to the third Eucharistic Prayer. It is fuller and more elaborate than the others, and it allows the congregation to participate by appropriate responses, each of them thoroughly biblical both in content and in wording.

The fourth prayer permits the celebrant to draw up his own formulation of the thanksgiving to the Father. Headings are provided to ensure that the Thanksgiving will be adequate. But here also the intention is not to encourage an improvisation on the spur of the moment, but rather to provide the outline for a careful preparation of the content of the Thanksgiving.

The breaking of the Bread, and the sharing of the Bread and the Cup in communion, are indeed the culmination of the action; but an important aspect of this liturgy, as of any other, would be lost, were it not dramatized in some way that the worship of the community has its issue in sending the worshipers back into the world. A dismissal like that in the First or Second Service, the familiar blessing, or the Grace, or some other form will make this point clear. Once again, to dictate or direct would intrude upon the creative and responsive quality implied by this Order.

On occasion, as the rubrics suggest, the eucharistic celebration may be followed by a meal or *Agapé*: A note on the *Agapé* will be found on pages 30-31.

Conclusion

One important emphasis about these proposals must be made. In offering these additional forms for the celebration of the Holy Eucharist, and given the continuing availability of the 1928 rite in its Prayer Book form as well as of the 1967 *Liturgy of the Lord's Supper*, the Commission is not envisioning the formation of partisan groups within the Episcopal Church, each of which would become advocates of one particular form of service. Far from it! Each of the services is as completely and truly a Eucharist as any of the others, or as any other authorized liturgy of the Church that has been celebrated in its history.

The Commission offers these services for the whole Church, and not for separate parts of it. This implies a certain responsibility on the part of all types of congregation—from the homogeneous parish in a stable community to an *ad hoc* gathering of Christians in the most uncommon circumstances—to make use of all the orders, to study them thoroughly, to consider them thoughtfully, and to experiment reverently with each of them.

In the response to trial use during the past triennium, we have sensed a considerable tension between the traditional and the new. To us, this means that the Church is on the move. While parts of the Church may be moving at differing speeds, parts with differing intensity of response to what is encountered, it is the whole Church, nevertheless, that endeavors earnestly to plot its course in the direction pointed by the Christ it confesses. This is as it should be, for as the Epistle to the Hebrews reminds us, we are a pilgrim Church, and it is both the joy and the agony of the pilgrim that he may never settle permanently at any stopping place. It is a long distance from Judea in the first century to America in the twentieth, but to absolutize any era in theology or liturgy, even our own, is to deny that pilgrim life which the Church is called upon to live.

Appendices

Appendix 1: A note on the "ICET" Texts

When the Roman Catholic Church decided at the Second Vatican Council to translate its liturgy into contemporary vernaculars, it seemed to many an opportune time for an ecumenical endeavor to develop common texts for those liturgical formularies which all English-speaking Christians use in their corporate worship. The initiative for such an endeavor was taken by members of the Lutheran Church —Missouri Synod, who called an informal meeting of representatives of the liturgical commissions of the Lutheran, Roman Catholic, Episcopal, and Presbyterian Churches in the United States.

Out of this meeting was formed a group known as the Consultation on Common Texts. During the years 1967-69, the group held several meetings in Chicago and Washington, and produced new versions in contemporary English of the Lord's Prayer, the Nicene and Apostles' Creeds, the Gloria in excelsis, and the Sanctus. Though the group itself was an informal and unofficial one, it was, nonetheless, made up of official representatives from the Inter-Lutheran Commission on Worship, the Bishops' Committee on Liturgy of the Roman Catholic Church in America, and the Commission on Worship of the Consultation on Church Union (including two members of the Standing Liturgical Commission of the Episcopal Church).

The texts of this group were sent to the liturgical commissions of the various Churches for their comments and suggestions; and early drafts of these texts were included in *An Order of Worship for the Proclamation of the Word of God and the Celebration of the Lord's Supper* (Cincinnati: Forward Movement Publications, 1968), sponsored by the Consultation on Church Union.

Meanwhile the International Committee on English in the Liturgy (ICEL) — an official body of the Roman Catholic Church charged with producing vernacular versions of the revised Roman liturgy for use in all. English-speaking countries—invited members of the American group, and scholars from the several Churches of the British Isles to meet in London in the spring of 1969. This new body, the International Consultation on English Texts (ICET), met again in London in the fall of 1969 and in the spring of 1970.[24]

The proposals of ICET have now been published in a booklet, *Prayers We Have in Common* (London: Geoffrey Chapman; Philadelphia: Fortress Press, 1970); and the several Churches of the English-speaking world are invited to use these texts on an experimental basis in the new liturgies which many of them are preparing. The International Consultation itself neither has, nor claims to have, the authority to put any of these texts into use. It fully recognizes that this is the responsibility of the official agencies which the Churches have for providing or recommending new liturgies for their own constituencies.

The texts in *Prayers We Have in Common* are grouped in two categories. Category A consists of those texts which have gone through several stages, having been revised in the light of criticisms and suggestions from individuals and members of worship commissions in all parts of the world. Further revision of texts in this category will not be considered until after a two or three-year period of experimental use. These are the texts of the Lord's Prayer, the two Creeds, the Gloria in excelsis, the Sanctus and Benedictus, and the Gloria Patri. The texts in Category B are those now being reviewed for possible further revision. These include the *Sursum Corda*, the *Agnus Dei*, and the Canticles of the Daily Office.

The texts of Category A have been accepted for use by the Roman Catholic Committee (except for the Lord's Prayer and the Apostles' Creed). The Inter-Lutheran Commission on Worship has accepted them for their new rite which is soon to be published; and the United Presbyterian Church, U.S.A., has them under consideration in their work of revising *The Book of Common Worship*. Among Anglicans, the Liturgical Commissions of the Church of England and of the Episcopal Church in the United States have acted to include them in their proposed services in contemporary English; and other Anglican provinces will be considering them in the near future. In those Protestant Churches which

---

24. The International Consultation on English Texts consists of members drawn from the official liturgical or worship commissions of the following Churches: 1) The Roman Catholic Church—members of the Advisory Committee of its International Committee on English in the Liturgy, including representatives from England, Ireland, the United States, Canada, and Australia; 2) The Anglican Churches—representatives of the liturgical commissions of the Church of England, the Episcopal Church of Scotland, the Church of Ireland, the Church in Wales, and the Episcopal Church in the United States; 3) The Inter-Lutheran Commission on Worship, which comprises members of the Lutheran Church of America, the American Lutheran Church, and the Lutheran Church—Missouri Synod; and 4) The (Presbyterian) Church of Scotland; and the English Methodist, Presbyterian, Congregational, and Baptist Churches.

require no official or synodical action to authorize texts, a number of pastors have already introduced these new versions to their congregations. Within a few years we should know whether the new texts have "caught on" and whether they are serving the ecumenical purpose for which they are intended.

Additional Note. The Standing Liturgical Commission of the Episcopal Church has decided to put the new texts in all proposed services that use contemporary English. But the new version of the Nicene Creed will be printed in all services, whether in traditional or contemporary style. The *filioque* clause ("and the Son"), however, has been omitted, as in the *Liturgy of the Lord's Supper*, since it is not part of the original Greek text. The International Consultation was unanimous in its opinion that the *filioque* clause should be optional, and that the several Churches might include it or exclude it without any question regarding their orthodoxy.

Appendix 2: The Structure and Contents of The Eucharistic Liturgy and the Daily Office

A document prepared for the Liturgical Conference held in connection with the Lambeth Conference of 1968 by the Right Reverend Leslie Brown and the Reverend Canon Ronald C. D. Jasper.

The Lambeth Conference of 1958 passed a Resolution (76) which reads: "The Conference requests the Archbishop of Canterbury, in co-operation with the Consultative Body, to appoint an Advisory Committee to prepare recommendations for the structure of the Holy Communion service which could be taken into consideration by any Church or Province revising its Eucharistic rite, and which would both conserve the doctrinal balance of the Anglican tradition and take account of present liturgical knowledge." No action was taken on this Resolution until the Liturgical Consultation held after the Anglican Congress in Toronto in August 1963 when four people (Archbishop Clark, Primate of Canada; Bishop Sansbury of Singapore; Dr. Massey Shepherd of PECUSA; and Archbishop Brown of Uganda) were appointed to draw up a document suggesting a basic shape or pattern for eucharistic liturgies. The document was circulated to Metropolitans and Liturgical Consultants in March 1965, but it was not studied or used widely.

The Liturgical Consultation held in London after the Lambeth Conference in August 1968 requested Dr. Brown (now Bishop of St. Edmundsbury and Ipswich) and Dr. Jasper to undertake a revision of the document in the light of the considerable experience of liturgical revision since 1958, in consultation with the other scholars originally concerned. At the same time it was agreed that a similar document should be prepared on the structure of the Daily Office. After due consideration, however, it was thought wise to discuss both questions in a single document. There is nowadays a desire to relate more closely the Daily Office and the Eucharist. Such an arrangement is desirable not only on weekdays, but on Sundays, in those congregations which do not have the Eucharist as their principal act of worship. In many Churches of the Anglican Communion this is the case not from choice, but from necessity, because the number of priests is inadequate. This point is considered in the suggestions made in this document. Sections 1-3 could be used, with little modification, as a Daily Office or a Sunday service without eucharistic celebration: and it could be used either in the morning or in the evening. Experience has already proved this to be a perfectly satisfactory arrangement in a number of places.

Attention should be drawn to the fact that the 1958 Resolution referred specifically to the structure of the Holy Communion service. We have therefore concerned ourselves primarily with this aspect in this document: but it is very obvious that the problems of language will also play a large part in the work of liturgical revision for some time to come. There is clearly a desire to use more contemporary forms in all Churches, as the work of the International Consultation on English Texts indicates. This in itself poses a whole range of new questions, both practical and technical. We believe, however, that the search for contemporary liturgical language should be pursued vigorously; and provided there is a willingness to regard experimental texts as expendable, there is no reason why there should not emerge in the foreseeable future liturgical forms which are truly relevant to the situations in which they are used.

Finally, we wish to emphasize that, although we have considered very carefully the comments and criticisms of the scholars whom we have consulted and have made several amendments to this document in the light of them, we alone bear the responsibility for what is written here.

Leslie St. Edmundsbury and Ipswich
Ronald Jasper

The Eucharistic Liturgy and the Daily Office

In the full Eucharistic rite we identify a number of basic elements in the celebration:

1. The Preparation.
2. The Ministry of the Word.
3. The Prayers.
4. The Offertory.
5. The Thanksgiving over Bread and Wine.
6. The Breaking of the Bread.
7. The Communion.
8. The Dismissal.

1. **The Preparation**
   a. The celebrant greets the congregation. This greeting could have reference to the season (e.g. at Easter—V. The Lord is risen. R. Alleluia. Indeed he is risen.)
   b. An act of praise and adoration. The *Gloria in Excelsis* is very suitable; or a psalm or a hymn (optional on weekdays).
   c. A confession of sins, with absolution or prayer for forgiveness (optional on weekdays). Alternatively, this might be placed with the prayers (No. 3) after the Ministry of the Word.
2. **The Ministry of the Word**
   a. Scripture Readings, including Psalms. Three lessons should be provided, from the Old Testament, Epistles and Gospels; although it is likely that in many cases only two of the three readings will be used. These readings can be interspersed with psalms, canticles or hymns.
   b. Sermon (optional on weekdays).
   c. Creed—either the Nicene Creed or the Apostles' Creed (optional).
3. **The Prayers**
   a. Intercessions with thanksgivings. These may be offered in many forms. A litany form allowing for extemporary prayer and congregational participation is widely appreciated.
   b. A confession of sins, with absolution or prayer for forgiveness—if not used in the Preparation (1) (optional on weekdays).
   c. The Peace.

These first three elements of the Service may be used alone, as one of the Daily Offices: and especially when used on Sundays they may be supplemented with an act of Thanksgiving and Dedication and the Lord's Prayer before the Pax. In this case the first half of the 1662 Blessing might be regarded as an appropriate form for the Pax. When using these elements as either the Morning or the Evening Office, care should be taken to ensure a systematic use of psalmody and a variety of canticles. Psalmody, canticles and lessons should be used in both the Daily Offices, although not necessarily in equal proportions; and care should be taken to avoid unnecessary duplication of material.

4. **The Offertory**

A sentence which looks forward to the eucharistic action may be used: but care should be taken not to give any impression that the Offertory is an act of oblation in itself.

5. **The Thanksgiving over Bread and Wine**

   The basic elements and progression of this eucharistic prayer are:

   a. *Sursum Corda.*
   b. The proclamation and recital of the mighty acts of God in creation, redemption and sanctification.
   c. The Narrative of the Institution.
   d. The anamnesis of the work of Christ in Death, Resurrection and Ascension "until He come". It is recognized that this is the most difficult section of the prayer in view of the different doctrinal emphases which are expressed and recognized within the Anglican Communion. The whole concept of anamnesis is, however, so rich in meaning that it should not be impossible to express it in such a way that the needs of everyone are met. Whatever language is adopted should, however, avoid any idea of a propitiatory sacrifice or a repetition of Christ's sacrifice. The "once for all" character of His work must not be obscured.
   e. The prayer that through the sharing of the bread and wine and through the power of the Holy Spirit we may be made one with our Lord and so renewed in the Body of Christ.

   The whole prayer is rightly set in the context of praise, e.g. *Sursum Corda* and *Sanctus*.

6. **The Breaking of the Bread**

   This may be done in silence or may be accompanied by suitable words (e.g., 1 Corinthians 10 vv 16-17).

7. **The Communion**

   a. The Communion Devotions. These must not be elaborate or distracting from the main action of the liturgy. The basic devotion can be the Lord's Prayer alone, the doxology of which suitably expresses the element of praise at this point.
   b. The Communion.
   c. The post-communion devotion. This may take the form of a prayer or/ and a hymn or canticle of thanksgiving and dedication: but whatever material is used should make the point clear that God's people are to witness and serve as the body of Christ in the world, strengthened by His grace and looking forward to the fulfillment of His promise.

8. **The Dismissal**

   It may be found appropriate, as a concession to people's traditional expectation at this point, or for the benefit of non-communicants who are present, to associate a blessing with the actual words of dismissal. It is desirable, however, and certainly logical, that no further devotions should follow the dismissal. This is the final action in the rite.

Appendix 3: Schedule of Variations and Substitutions in the Liturgy of the Lord's Supper Authorized by Vote of Special General Convention II, 1969

The General Convention of 1967 authorized for trial use *The Liturgy of The Lord's Supper, The Celebration of Holy Eucharist, and Ministration of Holy Communion* (*Prayer Book Studies XVII*, The Church Pension Fund, 1967). The results of trial use, while still preliminary and incomplete, have clearly identified several major areas of concern and a few passages which seemed to be obscure. Acting in response to the suggestions of both lay persons and clergymen, conveyed through Questionnaires and in direct correspondence, the Standing Liturgical Commission recommended that the following variations and substitutions be made even before the end of the triennium.

Special General Convention II, meeting in South Bend in September 1969, has approved these recommendations. The following changes should therefore be made in the copies of the texts now in use. All references to page numbers are to the *pew edition* (not *Prayer Book Studies XVII*) published by The Church Pension Fund.

1. **The Penitential Order**

    [*The following rubrics replace the last rubric on page 19.*]

    The Penitential Order is a normal part of the service, but it may be omitted on appropriate occasions.

    The Order may be said at any of the following places: (1) Before the service; (2) Immediately following the Summary of the Law; (3) Before the Prayer of Intercession (If The Peace is exchanged at this point, it will follow the Penitential Order).

    If there is no Communion, the phrase in the Invitation, "draw near with faith to receive the Holy Sacrament, and", shall be omitted. "The Comfortable Words" may be used or omitted.

2. **The Peace**

    [*The following rubrics and directions are to be inserted on page 9.*]

    The Peace may be exchanged at any one of the following places: (1) Immediately before the Collect for Purity; (2) Immediately before the Prayer of Intercession; (3) Between the Prayer of Intercession and the Offertory; (4) Immediately before the administration of Communion, before or after the sentence of invitation; (5) At the conclusion of the service, following the dismissal.

The formula on page 9 is traditional; but in the exchange of the Peace among the People, any appropriate greeting in the Name of the Lord is allowable.

Although it is desirable that some manual act accompany the exchange, the form and manner of such acts, if any, are not prescribed.

3. **The Old Testament Lesson and The Epistle**

[*The following rubric is to be inserted between the two headings above on page 6.*]

A Lesson from the Old Testament may be read before the Epistle or instead of it.

4. **The Sermon**

[*The following rubric is to be inserted under the heading above, on page 7.*]

A Psalm or Hymn may be said or sung before and after the Sermon.

5. **The Prayer of Intercession**

[*Replace the rubric immediately above this heading on page 9, with the following rubrics and text.*]

The Deacon or Priest, or some other person or persons appointed, shall lead the People in a prayer of intercession using one of the following:

1. The Prayer of Intercession as it appears on pages 9 to 12; *provided*, that if the Penitential Order has been used, the penitential suffrage on page 11 may be omitted;
2. The Prayer of Intercession on pages 9 to 12, but omitting all purpose clauses beginning with the word "that";
3. The following **Alternative Prayer of Intercession**, it being understood that (a) Special intentions may be introduced in any suffrage with the words, "and especially for . . ."; (b) A brief silence may be observed within any suffrage, preferably before the words "We pray to thee."

In Peace let us pray to the Lord:

For all people in their daily life and work, (especially for . . .),
We pray to thee.

Lord, hear our prayer.

For our families, friends and neighbors, and for those who are alone,
We pray to thee.

Lord, hear our prayer.

For those who serve our community, state, and nation,
We pray to thee.

Lord, hear our prayer.

For those who work for justice, freedom and peace among the nations,
We pray to thee.

Lord, hear our prayer.

For our just and proper use of the natural riches of the world,
We pray to thee.

Lord, hear our prayer.

For all who are in danger, sorrow, need, sickness, or any other trouble,
We pray to thee.

Lord, hear our prayer.

For the victims of hunger, fear, injustice, and oppression,
We pray to thee.

Lord, hear our prayer.

For all who minister to the suffering, the friendless, and the needy,
We pray to thee.

Lord, hear our prayer.

For those who proclaim the Gospel, and for all who seek the truth,
We pray to thee.

Lord, hear our prayer.

For the unity and peace of all Christian people,
We pray to thee.

Lord, hear our prayer.

For Bishops and other Ministers, and all who serve thee in thy Church,
We pray to thee.

Lord, hear our prayer.

(Here opportunity may be given to the members of the congregation to ask the prayers and share the thanksgiving of those present.)

For all who have departed this life,
We pray to thee.

Lord, hear our prayer.

We give thanks for all thy saints and servants in time past (especially N. . . . whom we honor this day). Grant us, we pray thee, to share with them thine everlasting kingdom.
Lord, hear our prayer.

Lord, forgive us our sins.
And amend our lives according to thy Word. Amen.

6. **The Breaking of the Bread**

[*The following rubric and text are to be inserted after the first rubric under the above heading on page 16.*]

Then shall be sung or said the following Anthem, or some other proper Hymn:

(Alleluia) Christ our passover is sacrificed for us:
Therefore let us keep the feast. (Alleluia)

Blessed is He who comes in the Name of the Lord.
Hosanna in the highest.

From Ash Wednesday until Easter Even, Alleluia shall be omitted.

7. **The Invitation to Communion**

[*Add the following rubric immediately after the invitation on page 17.*]

Instead of "Holy Things for the People of God", the Priest may say, "The Gifts of God for the People of God: . . .". After this, the Priest shall make his own communion.

8. **The Dismissal**

[*Add the following rubric at the bottom of page 18.*]

In place of the foregoing, the following procedure may be used: The Priest, or the Bishop if he is present, may bless the People, and the Priest or the Deacon shall dismiss them as follows:

Go forth into the world in peace, rejoicing in the power of the Spirit.
Thanks be to God.

THE STANDING LITURGICAL COMMISSION

Appendix 4: Concerning the *Agapé*

The *agapé* or "love feast" is a very ancient custom of the Church, and derives from the Jewish custom of holding brotherhood meals—*chaburoth*—on significant occasions.

In the earliest decades of Christian history, it appears that the celebration of the Eucharist frequently took place in the context of such a meal, the sharing of the Eucharistic Bread and Cup being understood as the cause and sign of that unity in Christ which the participants expressed by joining in a meal together.

With the passage of time and for several reasons—1 Corinthians 11:17-34 may perhaps be a clue to one of them—the Eucharistic celebration was separated from the common meal. The Liturgy of the Word, an adaptation of the synagogue service, came to precede the celebration. This sequence of Word followed by Sacrament remains the order of service we are familiar with today.

The *agapé* itself continued for generations as a separate observance, the void left by the removal of the Eucharistic action being filled by starting the meal with the ceremonial sharing of "blessed" bread. This was bread over which a brief blessing or grace had been recited, but which was carefully distinguished from the Bread of the Eucharist. This blessing was of exactly the same kind as that used by private persons, or by individuals eating alone, and it did not, of course, contain the words spoken by our Lord at the Last Supper. The serving of wine at these church suppers, while it seems to have been usual, was not considered essential to the occasion. Customarily, the supper concluded with the singing of psalms and other songs, and with prayers appropriate to the time of day.

Recent years have seen a widespread revival of interest in the *agapé*, and much experimentation with varying forms of it, ranging from formal suppers on festal occasions (patterned on the order described in the preceding paragraph) to the simple sharing of bread and wine in an atmosphere of spontaneous festivity and celebration.

Regrettably, one byproduct of these otherwise laudable experiments has been to cause confusion and misunderstanding. It has not always been clearly understood by the participants that while the sharing of bread and wine in *agapé* clearly demonstrates the unity and togetherness of the participants, the Eucharist has as its purpose a further and more radical dimension: the anamnesis of the Lord. The Eucharist celebrates not only the unity of those present, but the unity in Christ of the whole Church at all times and in all places, and is the effectual proclamation of his death and resurrection.

In introducing the rubric at the bottom of page 61 in the order of service, the Standing Liturgical Commission calls the Church's attention to the entire propriety, on occasion, of celebrating the Eucharist as the prelude to a common meal, but with the clear understanding that no part of the consecrated Bread and Wine is subsequently to be put to common use. If any remains, it is to be consumed before the meal begins. A brief blessing over the bread to be eaten at the meal might then follow, spoken by one of the participants, or said by all. This blessing could be worded in such a way as to relate the Bread of the Eucharist to the bread of the common table. A similar blessing might be said over the container of wine.

A final note: If, when there is no Eucharist, it is desired to offer a blessing over wine as well as the bread at the beginning of the meal, it is suggested that the wine blessing come first, in order that any possible confusion with the Eucharist be minimized.

Bibliography

Prayer Book Studies XVII (The Church Pension Fund, 1966) provided an extensive and useful bibliography on various aspects of liturgical revision and reform. This current Study depends upon *Prayer Book Studies XVII* in many ways, and the reader is referred to its bibliography. Most of the following books have been published since 1966, and are suggested for general reading. The list has been compiled with a view to providing additional materials suitable as resources for parishes, study groups, and individuals.

Babin, David E. *The Celebration of Life: Our Changing Liturgy.* New York: Morehouse-Barlow; 1969.
— *An Introduction to The Liturgy of the Lord's Supper.* New York: Morehouse-Barlow; 1968.
Buchanan, Colin O. ed. *Modern Anglican Liturgies 1958-1968.* London: Oxford University Press; 1968.
— *A Guide to Second Series Communion Service.* (Prayer Book Reform Series). London: Church Book Room Press; 1966.
Davies, J. G. *Worship and Mission.* Philadelphia: Association Press; 1966.
Dewitt, John. *Making a Community Out of A Parish.* Washington: The Liturgical Conference; 1967.
Experiment and Liturgy. The Anglican Church of Canada, Toronto; 1969.
Garfield, Donald A. ed. *Towards A Living Liturgy.* New York: Church of St. Mary the Virgin; 1969.
— *Worship in Spirit and Truth.* New York: Jarrow Press; 1970.
Hovda, Robert W., and Huck, Gabe. *There's No Place Like People.* Washington: The Liturgical Conference; 1969.
Hovda, Robert W. *Manual of Celebration.* Washington: The Liturgical Conference; 1970.
Kilpatrick, G. D. *Remaking the Liturgy.* Philadelphia: Fontana Press; 1967.
Kirby, John C. ed. *Words and Action: New Forms of the Liturgy.* Toronto: The Anglican Church of Canada; 1969.
Micks, Marianne H. *The Future Present.* New York: The Seabury Press; 1970.
Porter, H. Boone, Jr. *Growth and Life in the Local Church.* New York: Seabury Press; 1968.
Rivers, Clarence. *Celebration.* New York: Herder and Herder; 1969.
Schauer, Blase. *The Experimental Liturgy Book.* New York; Herder and Herder; 1969.
Schmemann, Alexander. *The World As Sacrament.* New York: Darton, Longman and Todd; 1968.
Shepherd, Massey H., Jr. *The Reform of Liturgical Worship.* New York: Seabury Press; 1960.
Spielman, Richard M. *History of Christian Worship.* New York; Seabury Press; 1966.
Stevik, Daniel B. *Language in Worship.* New York: The Sea-bury Press; 1970.
White, James F. *The Worldliness of Worship.* New York: Oxford University Press; 1967.

The Holy Eucharist
THE LITURGY FOR THE PROCLAMATION OF THE WORD OF GOD AND CELEBRATION OF THE HOLY COMMUNION
First Service

Concerning the Celebration

The Holy Eucharist is the principal act of Christian worship on the Lord's Day.

At all celebrations of the Liturgy, it is fitting that the presiding Minister, whether bishop or priest, be assisted by other priests, and by deacons and lay persons.

When the Bishop is present, it is his prerogative as the chief sacramental minister of the Diocese to be the principal celebrant at the Lord's Table, and to preach the Gospel.

It is appropriate that other priests present stand with the presiding Minister at the altar, and join with him in the consecration of the gifts, in breaking the Bread, and in distributing Communion.

A deacon, when present, should read the Gospel and lead the prayer of Intercession. Deacons should also serve at the Lord's Table, preparing and placing on it the elements of bread and wine, and assisting in the ministration of the Sacrament to the People. In the absence of a deacon, his duties may be performed by an assisting priest.

Lay persons appointed by the presiding Minister should normally be assigned the reading of the Lessons which precede the Gospel; and in the absence of a deacon, they may lead the intercession.

The Order for Morning or Evening Prayer may be used in place of all that precedes the Offertory, provided that a Lesson from the Gospel is always included and that the Intercession conforms to the directions on page 68.

Additional Directions and Suggestions for the Ministers will be found on page 86 ff.

THE HOLY EUCHARIST
First Service

A Psalm, Hymn, or Anthem may be sung during the entrance of the Ministers.

The People being assembled, the Priest, standing, says

Almighty God, unto whom all hearts are open, all desires known, and from whom no secrets are hid: Cleanse the thoughts of our hearts by the inspiration of thy Holy Spirit, that we may perfectly love thee, and worthily magnify thy holy Name; through Christ our Lord. *Amen.*

Then the Ten Commandments (page 44) may be said, or the following

Hear the words of our Lord Jesus Christ:

Thou shalt love the Lord thy God with all thy heart, and with all thy soul, and with all thy mind. This is the first and great commandment. And the second is like unto it; Thou shalt love thy neighbor as thyself. On these two commandments hang all the Law and the Prophets.

Here is sung or said

Lord, have mercy upon us.		Kyrie eleison.
Christ, have mercy upon us.	*or*	*Christe eleison.*
Lord, have mercy upon us.		Kyrie eleison.

or this

Holy God,
Holy and Mighty,
Holy Immortal One,
Have mercy upon us.

When appointed, the following Hymn or some other song of praise is sung or said, all standing

GLORY BE TO GOD ON HIGH,
    and on earth peace, good will towards men.
We praise thee, we bless thee,
    we worship thee,
    we glorify thee,
    we give thanks to thee for thy great glory,
O Lord God, heavenly King, God the Father Almighty.
O Lord, the only-begotten Son, Jesus Christ;
O Lord God, Lamb of God, Son of the Father,
    that takest away the sins of the world,
    have mercy upon us.
Thou that takest away the sins of the world,
    receive our prayer.
Thou that sittest at the right hand of God the Father,
    have mercy upon us.
For thou only art holy;
thou only art the Lord;
thou only, O Christ,

with the Holy Ghost,
art most high in the glory of God the Father. Amen.

The Proclamation of the Word of God

The presiding Minister says to the People

	The Lord be with you
Answer	And with thy spirit.
Priest	Let us pray.

The Collect of the Day

The People respond Amen.

The Lessons

The People sit. One or two Lessons, as appointed, are announced and read. [See page 87 for forms for announcing and ending Epistles and other Lessons.]

A Psalm, Hymn, or Anthem may follow each Lesson.

Then, all standing, the Deacon or a priest reads the Gospel, first saying

THE HOLY GOSPEL of our Lord Jesus Christ according to _____.

The People respond   Glory be to thee, O Lord.

At the end of the Gospel, the Deacon says

The Gospel of the Lord.

The People respond   Praise be to thee, O Christ.

The Sermon

On Sundays and other festivals there follows, all standing

The Nicene Creed[25]

We believe in one God,
    the Father, the Almighty,
    maker of heaven and earth,
    of all that is seen and unseen.

---

25. This translation of the Creed has been adopted by the International Consultation on English Texts, ICET, and is recommended for experimental use in all Orders of the Eucharist. See the information on page 20.

We believe in one Lord, Jesus Christ,
    the only Son of God,
    eternally begotten of the Father,
    God from God, Light from Light,
    true God from true God,
    begotten, not made, one in Being with the Father.
    Through him all things were made.
    For us men and for our salvation
        he came down from heaven
    by the power of the Holy Spirit
        he was born of the Virgin Mary, and became man.
    for our sake he was crucified under Pontius Pilate;
        he suffered, died, and was buried.
        On the third day he rose again
            in fulfillment of the Scriptures;
        he ascended into heaven
            and is seated at the right hand of the Father.
    He will come again in glory to judge the living and the dead,
        and his kingdom will have no end.

We believe in the Holy Spirit, the Lord, the giver of life, who proceeds from the Father.
    With the Father and the Son he is worshiped and glorified.
He has spoken through the Prophets.
    We believe in one holy catholic and apostolic Church.
    We acknowledge one baptism for the forgiveness of sins.
    We look for the resurrection of the dead,
        and the life of the world to come. Amen.

The version of the Creed in the Book of Common Prayer may be used in place of the preceding.

A confession of sin may be said here (pages 37 or 47).

The Prayers

Intercession is offered according to the following form, or according to one of those provided on pages 68-81.

The Deacon, or some other person appointed, says

Let us pray for Christ's Church and the world.

After each paragraph of this prayer, the People may make an appropriate response as directed by the Minister.

Almighty and everliving God, who hast taught us to make prayers, and supplications, and to give thanks for all men: Receive these our prayers which we offer unto thy Divine Majesty, beseeching thee to inspire continually the Universal Church with the spirit of truth, unity, and concord; and grant that all those who do confess thy holy Name may agree in the truth of thy holy Word, and live in unity and godly love.

Give grace, O heavenly Father, to all Bishops and other Ministers, [especially _____], that they may, both by their life and doctrine, set forth thy true and lively Word, and rightly and duly administer thy holy Sacraments.

And to all thy People give thy heavenly grace; and especially to this congregation here present; that, with meek heart and due reverence, they may hear, and receive thy holy Word; truly serving thee in holiness and righteousness all the days of their life.

We beseech thee also, to rule the hearts of those who bear the authority of government in this and every land, [especially _____], and to lead them to wise decisions and right actions for the welfare of mankind, and for the peace of the world.

Grant to all people, Lord, the will and the wisdom to be good stewards of the riches of creation, that we neither selfishly waste nor wantonly destroy thy handiwork.

And we most humbly beseech thee, of thy goodness, O Lord, to comfort and succor all those who, in this transitory life, are in trouble, sorrow, need, sickness, or any other adversity, [especially _____].

And we also bless thy holy Name for all thy servants departed this life in thy faith and fear, [especially _____], beseeching thee to grant them continual growth in thy love and service, and to give us grace so to follow their good examples, that with them we may be partakers of thy heavenly kingdom.

Grant these our prayers, O Father, for Jesus Christ's sake, our only Mediator and Advocate. Amen.

If there is no celebration of the Communion, or if a priest is not available, the Service is concluded as directed on page 87.

Confession of Sin

The Deacon or Priest says the following, or the Exhortation on page 45.

Ye who do truly and earnestly repent you of your sins, and are in love and charity with your neighbors, and intend to lead the new life, following the commandments of God, and walking from henceforth in his holy ways; Draw near with faith, and make your humble confession to Almighty God, devoutly kneeling.

The People kneel. A period of silence may be kept; after which one of the Ministers leads the People in this General Confession:

Father almighty, Lord of heaven and earth:
We confess that we have sinned against thee
    in thought, word, and deed.
Have mercy upon us, O God,
    according to thy loving-kindness;
In thy great goodness,
    do away our offences,
    and cleanse us from our sins;
For Jesus Christ's sake. Amen.

or this

Almighty God, Father of our Lord Jesus Christ, Maker of all things, Judge of all men:

We acknowledge and bewail our manifold sins and wickedness, Which we, from time to time, most grievously have committed, By thought, word, and deed, against thy Divine Majesty, Provoking most justly thy wrath and indignation against us.

We do earnestly repent, And are heartily sorry for these our misdoings; The remembrance of them is grievous unto us; The burden of them is intolerable.

Have mercy upon us, Have mercy upon us, most merciful Father: for thy Son our Lord Jesus Christ's sake, Forgive us all that is past; And grant that we may ever hereafter, Serve and please thee in newness of life;

To the honor and glory of thy Name; Through Jesus Christ our Lord. Amen.

The Minister may then say

Hear the Word of God to all who truly turn to him:

Come unto me, all ye that travail and are heavy laden, and I will refresh you [*St. Matthew 11:28*]

God so loved the world, that he gave his only-begotten Son, to the end that all that believe in him should not perish, but have everlasting life. [*St. John 3:16*]

This is a true saying, and worthy of all men to be received, That Christ Jesus came into the world to save sinners. [*1 Timothy 1:15*]

If any man sin, we have an Advocate with the Father, Jesus Christ the righteous; and he is the perfect offering for our sins, and not for ours only, but for the sins of the whole world. [*1 St. John 2:1-2*]

The Bishop, if he is present, or the Priest, stands and says this Absolution:

Almighty God, our heavenly Father, who of his great mercy hath promised forgiveness of sins to all those who with hearty repentance and true faith turn unto him; Have mercy upon you; pardon and deliver you from all your sins; confirm and strengthen you in all goodness; and bring you to everlasting life; through Jesus Christ our Lord. *Amen.*

The Peace

Here (or at one of the other places suggested on page 88), the Priest may say to the People

    The Peace of the Lord be always with you.

Answer And with thy spirit.

Then the Ministers and People may greet one another in the Name of the Lord.

The Celebration of the Holy Communion

The Priest, standing at the Holy Table, begins the Offertory with this or some other Sentence of Scripture:

Ascribe to the Lord the honor due his name; bring offerings and come into his courts. (*Psalm 96:8*)

During the Offertory, a Psalm, Hymn, or Anthem may be sung.

Representatives of the Congregation bring the People's offerings of bread and wine, and money or other gifts, to the Deacon or Priest. The People stand while the offerings are presented and placed on the Altar.

The Great Thanksgiving

The People remain standing. The Priest faces them, and sings or says

    The Lord be with you
People And with thy spirit.
Priest Lift up your hearts.
People We lift them up unto the Lord.
Priest Let us give thanks unto our Lord God.
People It is meet and right so to do.

Then, facing the Holy Table, the Priest proceeds

It is very meet, right, and our bounden duty, that we should at all times, and in all places, give thanks unto thee, O Lord, Holy Father, Almighty, Everlasting God.

On all Sundays, and on other occasions when a Proper Preface is appointed, it is sung or said here.

Therefore with Angels and Archangels, and with all the company of heaven, we laud and magnify thy glorious Name; evermore praising thee, and saying,

Priest and People

HOLY, HOLY, HOLY, Lord God of Hosts:
Heaven and earth are full of thy glory.
Glory be to thee, O Lord Most High.

Here may be added

Blessed is He that cometh in the Name of the Lord:
Hosanna in the highest!

The People may kneel.

Then the Priest continues

All glory be to thee, Almighty God, our heavenly Father, for that thou, of thy tender mercy, didst give thine only Son Jesus Christ to suffer death upon the Cross for our redemption; who made there, by his one oblation of himself once offered, a full, perfect, and sufficient sacrifice for the sins of the whole world; and did institute, and in his holy Gospel command us to continue, a perpetual memory of that his precious death and sacrifice, until his coming again:

> *At the following words concerning the Bread, the Priest is to hold it, or lay his hand upon it. And at the words concerning the Cup, he is to hold, or lay his hand upon, the Cup and any other vessel containing wine to be consecrated.*

For in the night in which he was betrayed, he took bread; and when he had given thanks, he brake it, and gave it to his disciples, saying, "Take, eat: This is my Body which is given for you. Do this in remembrance of me."

Likewise, after supper, he took the cup; and when he had given thanks, he gave it to them, saying, "Drink this, all of you: For this is my Blood of the New Covenant, which is shed for you, and for many, for the remission of sins. Do this, as oft as ye shall drink it, in remembrance, of me."

Wherefore, O Lord and heavenly Father, we, thy humble servants, do celebrate and make here before thy Divine Majesty, with these thy holy Gifts, which we now offer unto thee, the memorial thy Son hath commanded us to make; having in remembrance his blessed passion and precious death, his mighty resurrection and glorious ascension; rendering unto thee most hearty thanks for the innumerable benefits procured unto us by the same.

And we most humbly beseech thee, O merciful Father, to hear us; and, of thy almighty goodness, vouchsafe to bless and sanctify, with thy Word and Holy Spirit, these Gifts of bread and wine; that we, receiving them according to thy Son our Savior Jesus Christ's holy institution, may be partakers of his most blessed Body and Blood.

And we earnestly desire thy fatherly goodness, mercifully to accept this our sacrifice of praise and thanksgiving; most humbly beseeching thee to grant that, by the merits and death of thy Son Jesus Christ, and through faith in his blood, we and all thy whole Church, may obtain remission of our sins, and all other benefits of his passion.

And here we offer and present unto thee, O Lord, ourselves, our souls and bodies, to be a reasonable, holy, and living sacrifice unto thee; humbly beseeching thee, that we, and all others who shall be partakers of this Holy Communion, may worthily receive the most precious Body and Blood of thy Son Jesus Christ, be filled with thy grace and heavenly benediction, and made one body with him, that he may dwell in us, and we in him.

And although we are unworthy, through our manifold sins, to offer unto thee any sacrifice; yet we beseech thee to accept this our bounden duty and service; not weighing our merits, but pardoning our offences:

Through Jesus Christ our Lord; by whom, and with whom, in the unity of the Holy Ghost, all honor and glory be unto thee, O Father Almighty, world without end.

Amen.

And now, as our Savior Christ hath taught us, we are bold to say,

People and Priest

Our Father, who art in heaven,
    hallowed be thy Name,
    thy kingdom come,
    thy will be done,
        on earth as it is in heaven.
Give us this day our daily bread.
And forgive us our trespasses,
    as we forgive those who trespass against us.
And lead us not into temptation,
    but deliver us from evil.
For thine is the kingdom, and the power, and the glory,
    for ever and ever. Amen.

The Breaking of the Bread

A period of silence is kept, during which the Priest breaks the consecrated Bread.

Then may be sung or said

(Alleluia.) Christ our Passover is sacrificed for us: *Therefore let us keep the feast. (Alleluia.)*

From Ash Wednesday until Easter Eve, Alleluia is omitted; and may be omitted at other times except during Easter Season.

The following prayer may be said:

We do not presume to come to this thy Table, O merciful Lord, trusting in our own righteousness, but in thy manifold and great mercies. We are not worthy so much as to gather up the crumbs under thy Table. But thou art the same Lord whose property is always to have mercy. Grant us therefore, gracious Lord, so to partake of the Body and Blood of thy dear Son Jesus Christ, that we may be cleansed from all our sins, and may evermore dwell in him, and he in, us. *Amen.*

The Ministers receive the Sacrament in both kinds, and then immediately deliver it to the People.

The Bread and the Cup are given to the communicants with these words, or with the words on pages 88-89:

The Body of our Lord Jesus Christ, which was given for thee, preserve thy body and soul unto everlasting life. Take and eat this in remembrance that Christ died for thee, and feed on him in thy heart by faith, with thanksgiving.

The Blood of our Lord Jesus Christ, which was shed for thee, preserve thy body and soul unto everlasting life. Drink this in remembrance that Christ's Blood was shed for thee, and be thankful.

During the ministration of Communion, Psalms, Hymns, or Anthems may be sung.

After Communion the Priest says

Let us pray.

He then says this prayer. The People may repeat it with him.

Almighty and everliving God, we most heartily thank thee, For that thou dost feed us in these holy mysteries, With the spiritual food of the most precious Body and Blood of thy Son our Savior Jesus Christ:

And dost assure us thereby of thy favor and goodness toward us; And that we are very members incorporate in the mystical body of thy Son, The blessed company of all faithful people; And are also heirs, through hope, of thine everlasting kingdom.

And we humbly beseech thee, O heavenly Father, So to assist us with thy grace, That we may continue in that holy fellowship, And do all such good works as thou hast prepared for us to walk in:

Through Jesus Christ our Lord, To whom, with thee and the Holy Ghost, be all honor and glory, world without end. Amen.

The Bishop, if present, or the Priest, gives the blessing

The Peace of God, which passeth all understanding, keep your hearts and minds in the knowledge and love of God, and of his Son Jesus Christ our Lord: And the Blessing of God Almighty, the Father, the Son, and the Holy Ghost, be amongst you, and remain with you always. *Amen.*

or

The Blessing of God Almighty, the Father, the Son, and the Holy Spirit, be upon you, and remain with you for ever. *Amen.*

The Deacon (or Priest) may then dismiss the People

Go forth into the world,
rejoicing in the power of the Spirit.
Thanks be to God.

or

Go in peace to love and serve the Lord.
Thanks be to God.

or

Let us go forth in the Name of Christ.
Thanks be to God.

Other forms of the great Thanksgiving

which may be used in place of the Prayer in the preceding Rite.

I

[From the Liturgy of the Lord's Supper, 1967.]

After the Sursum Corda *and* Sanctus, *the Priest continues*

All glory be to thee, Almighty God, Holy Father, Creator of heaven and earth, who didst make us in thine own image: And when we had fallen into sin, thou of thy tender mercy didst give thine only-begotten Son Jesus Christ, to take our nature upon him, and to suffer death upon the Cross for our redemption: Who made there, by his one oblation of himself once offered, a full and perfect sacrifice for the whole world; And instituted and commanded us to continue this perpetual memorial of his precious death and sacrifice, until his coming again.

At the following words concerning the Bread, the Priest is to hold it, or lay his hand upon it. And at the words concerning the Cup, he is to hold or lay his hand upon, the Cup and any other vessel containing wine to be consecrated.

For in the night in which he was betrayed, he took bread; and when he had given thanks to thee, he broke it, and gave it to his disciples, and said, "Take, eat: This is my Body which is given for you. Do this in remembrance of me." In the same way also, after supper, he took the cup; and when he had given thanks, he gave it to them and said, "Drink this, all of you: For this is my Blood of the New Covenant, which is poured out for you and many for the forgiveness of sins. Do this, as often as you drink it in remembrance of me."

Wherefore, O Lord and Holy Father, we thy people do celebrate here before thy Divine Majesty, with these thy holy Gifts, which we offer unto thee, the memorial of the blessed Passion and precious Death of thy dear Son, his mighty Resurrection and glorious Ascension, looking for his Coming again in power and great glory, And herewith we offer and present unto thee, O Lord, ourselves, which is our bounden duty and service. And we entirely desire thy fatherly goodness mercifully to accept, through the eternal mediation of our Savior Jesus Christ, this our sacrifice of praise and thanksgiving.

We pray thee, gracious Father, of thine almighty power, to bless and sanctify us and these holy Mysteries with thy Life-giving Word and Holy Spirit. Fill with thy grace all who partake of the Body and Blood of our Lord Jesus Christ. Make us one Body, that he may dwell in us and we in him. And grant that with boldness we may confess thy Name in constancy of faith, and at the last Day enter with all thy saints into the joy of thine eternal kingdom:

Through the same Jesus Christ our Lord; by whom, and with whom, and in whom, in the unity of the Holy Spirit all honor and glory be unto thee, O Father Almighty, world without end.

Amen.

II

After the Sursum Corda *and* Sanctus, *the Priest continues*

All glory be to thee, Almighty God, our heavenly Father, for that thou, of thy tender mercy, didst give thine only Son Jesus Christ to suffer death upon the Cross for our redemption; who made there by his one oblation of himself once offered, a full, perfect, and sufficient sacrifice for the sins of the whole world; and did institute, and in his holy Gospel command us to continue, a perpetual memory of that his precious death and sacrifice, until his coming again.

At the following words concerning the Bread, the Priest is to hold it, or lay his hand upon it. And at the words concerning the Cup, he is to hold, or lay his hand upon, the Cup and any other vessel containing wine to be consecrated.

For in the night in which he was betrayed, he took bread; and when he had given thanks, he brake it, and gave it to his disciples, saying, "Take, eat: This is my Body, which is given for you. Do this in remembrance of me."

Likewise, after supper, he took the cup; and when he had given thanks, he gave it to them, saying, "Drink this, all of you: For this is my Blood of the New Covenant, which is shed for you, and for many, for the remission of sins. Do this, as oft as ye shall drink it in remembrance of me."

Wherefore, O Lord and heavenly Father, we, thy humble servants, do celebrate and make here before thy Divine Majesty, with these thy holy Gifts, which we now offer unto thee, the memorial thy Son hath commanded us to make; having in remembrance his blessed passion and precious death, his mighty resurrection and glorious ascension; rendering unto thee most hearty thanks for the innumerable benefits procured unto us by the same.

And we most humbly beseech thee, O merciful Father, to hear us; and, of thy almighty goodness, vouchsafe to bless and sanctify, with thy Word and Holy Spirit, these Gifts of bread and wine; that we, receiving them according to thy Son our Savior Jesus Christ's holy institution, may be partakers of his most blessed Body and Blood.

And we earnestly desire thy fatherly goodness, mercifully to accept this our sacrifice of praise and thanksgiving; and to accept us, our souls and bodies, in union with our Savior Jesus Christ, a reasonable, holy, and living sacrifice unto thee; beseeching thee to make us one body with him, that he may dwell in us, and we in him:

Through Jesus Christ our Lord; by whom, and with whom, in the, unity of the Holy Ghost, all honor and glory be unto thee, O Father Almighty, world without end.

Amen.

The Decalogue

The Ten Commandments with their responses may be substituted for the Summary of the Law, or may precede it, the People kneeling.

God spake these words, and said:
I am the Lord thy God; Thou shalt have none other gods but me.
Lord, have mercy upon us, and incline our hearts to keep this law.

Thou shalt not make to thyself any graven image, nor the likeness of any thing that is in heaven above, or in the earth beneath, or in the water under the earth; thou shalt not bow down to them, nor worship them.
Lord, have mercy upon us, and incline our hearts to keep this law.

Thou shalt not take the Name of the Lord God in vain.
Lord, have mercy upon us, and incline our hearts to keep this law.

Remember that thou keep holy the Sabbath-day.
Lord, have mercy upon us, and incline our hearts to keep this law.

Honor thy father and thy mother.
Lord, have mercy upon us, and incline our hearts to keep this law.

Thou shalt do no murder.
Lord, have mercy upon us, and incline our hearts to keep this law.

Thou shalt not commit adultery.
Lord, have mercy upon us, and incline our hearts to keep this law.

Thou shalt not steal.
Lord, have mercy upon us, and incline our hearts to keep this law.

Thou shalt not bear false witness against thy neighbor.
Lord, have mercy upon us, and incline our hearts to keep this law.

Thou shalt not covet
Lord, have mercy upon us, and incline our hearts to keep this law.

> *The Minister may then proceed directly to the Hymn, "Glory be to God on High", or to the Salutation and Collect of the Day.*

An Exhortation

> *which may be used in whole or in part, either during the Liturgy or at other times. In the absence of a deacon or priest, this Exhortation may be read by a lay person. The People stand or sit.*

Beloved in the Lord:
Our Savior Christ, on the night before he suffered, established the Sacrament of his Body and Blood: as a sign and pledge of his love, for the continual remembrance of the sacrifice of his death, and for a spiritual sharing in his life. For in those holy Mysteries we are made one with Christ, and Christ with us; we are made one body in him, and fellow-members one of another.

Having in mind, therefore, his great love for us, and in obedience to his command, his Church renders to Almighty God our heavenly Father never-ending thanks:

for the creation of the world,
for his continual providence over us,
for his love for all mankind, and

for the redemption of the world by our Savior Christ, who took upon himself our flesh, and humbled himself even to death on the Cross, that he might make us the children of God by the power of the Holy Spirit, and exalt us to everlasting life.

But if we are to share rightly in the celebration of those holy Mysteries, and be nourished by that spiritual Food, we must remember the dignity of that holy Sacrament. I therefore call upon you to consider how Saint Paul exhorts all persons to prepare themselves carefully before eating of that Bread and drinking of that Cup.

For as the benefit is great, if with penitent hearts and living faith we receive the holy Sacrament; so is the danger great, if we receive it improperly, not recognizing the Lord's Body. Judge yourselves therefore, my brothers, lest you be judged by the Lord.

Examine your lives and conduct by the rule of God's commandments, that you may perceive wherein you have offended in what you have done or left undone, whether in thought, word, or deed. And acknowledge your sins before Almighty God, with full purpose of amendment of life, being ready to make restitution for all injuries and wrongs done by you to others; and also being ready to forgive those who have offended you, in order that you yourselves may be forgiven. And then, being reconciled with your brothers, come to the banquet of that most heavenly Food.

And if in your own preparation, you cannot quiet your conscience, but need help and counsel, then go to a discreet and understanding Priest, and open your grief to him: that you may receive the benefit of Absolution and spiritual counsel and advice; to the removal of scruple and doubt, the assurance of pardon, and the strengthening of your faith.

To Christ our Lord who loves us, and washed us in his own blood, and made us a kingdom of priests to serve his God and Father: to him be glory in the Church evermore. Through him let us offer continually the sacrifice of praise which is our bounden duty and service, and, with faith in him, come boldly before the Throne of grace [and humbly confess our sins to Almighty God].

A Penitential Order

This Order may be used immediately before the Liturgy (in which case the Collect for Purity is to be omitted), or as a separate service.

When used separately, a Sermon or the Exhortation on page 45 may follow the Sentences; and then, after the confession of sin, the service may be concluded with suitable prayers, and the Grace.

The Minister begins with this Sentence:

Grace to you and peace from God our Father and the Lord Jesus Christ. [*Philippians 1:2*]

He then adds one or more of the following:

If we say that we have no sin, we deceive ourselves, and the truth is not in us. But if we confess our sins, God, who is faithful and just, will forgive our sins and cleanse us from all unrighteousness. [*1 John 1:8-9*]

Since we have a great high priest who has passed through the heavens, Jesus, the Son of God, let us with confidence draw near to the throne of grace, that we may receive mercy and find grace to help in time of need. [*Hebrews 4:14*]

Jesus said,
The first commandment is this: "Hear, O Israel: The Lord your God is the only Lord. Love the Lord your God with all your heart, with all your soul, with all your mind, and with all your strength."
The second is this: "Love your neighbor as yourself." There is no other commandment greater than these.
[*Mark 12:29-31*]

Then follows a confession of sin.

Confession of Sin

[For use with the First Service]

The Minister says

Let us confess our sins against God and our neighbor.

A period of silence may be observed. Minister and People

Most merciful God,
we confess that we have sinned against thee
in thought, word and deed:

we have not loved thee with our whole heart;
we have not loved our neighbors as ourselves.
We pray thee of thy mercy
>   forgive what we have been,
>   amend what we are,
>   direct what we shall be;

that we may delight in thy will,
and walk in thy ways,
through Jesus Christ our Lord. Amen.

or

Father almighty, Lord of heaven and earth:
We confess that we have sinned against thee
>   in thought, word, and deed.

Have mercy upon us, O God,
>   according to thy loving-kindness;

In thy great goodness,
>   do away our offences,
>   and cleanse us from our sins;

for Jesus Christ's sake. Amen.

The Bishop, if present, or the Priest stands and says

The Almighty and merciful Lord grant you Absolution and Remission of all your sins, true repentance, amendment of life, and the grace and consolation of his Holy Spirit. *Amen.*

Confession of Sin

[For use with the Second Service]

The Minister says

Let us confess our sins against God and our neighbor.

A period of silence may be observed. Minister and People

Most merciful God,
we confess that we have sinned against you
in thought, word and deed:
we have not loved you with our whole heart;
we have not loved our neighbors as ourselves.
We pray you of your mercy
>   forgive what we have been,

amend what we are,
    direct what we shall be;
that we may delight in your will,
and walk in your ways,
through Jesus Christ our Lord. Amen.

The Bishop, if present, or the Priest stands and says

Almighty God have mercy on you, forgive you all your sins, through our Lord Jesus Christ; strengthen you in all goodness, and by the power of the. Holy Spirit, keep you in eternal life. *Amen.*

The Holy Eucharist
THE LITURGY FOR THE PROCLAMATION OF THE WORD OF GOD
Second Service

Concerning the Celebration

The Holy Eucharist is the principal act of Christian worship on the Lord's Day.

At all celebrations of the Liturgy, it is fitting that the presiding Minister, whether bishop or priest, be assisted by other priests, and by deacons and lay persons.

When the Bishop is present, it is his prerogative as the chief sacramental minister of the Diocese to be the principal celebrant at the Lord's Table, and to preach the Gospel.

It is appropriate that other priests present stand with the presiding Minister at the altar, and join with him in the consecration of the gifts, in breaking the Bread, and in distributing Communion.

A deacon, when present, should read the Gospel and lead the Prayer of Intercession. Deacons should also serve at the Lord's Table, preparing and placing on it the elements of bread and wine, and assisting in the ministration of the Sacrament to the People. In the absence of a deacon, his duties may be performed by an assisting priest.

Lay persons appointed by the presiding Minister should normally be assigned the reading of the Lessons which precede the Gospel; and in the absence of a deacon, they may lead the intercession.

The Order for Morning or Evening Prayer may be used in place of all that precedes the Offertory, provided that a Lesson from the Gospel is always included and that the Intercession conforms to the directions on page 68.

Additional Directions and Suggestions for the Ministers will be found on page 86.

THE HOLY EUCHARIST
Second Service

A Psalm, Hymn, or Anthem may be sung during the entrance of the Ministers.

The People being assembled, and all standing, the Priest says

Blessed be God: Father, Son, and Holy. Spirit.

People

And blessed be his Kingdom, now and for ever. Amen.

From Easter Day through the Day of Pentecost, in place of the above, he says

	Alleluia! Christ is risen.
People	The Lord is risen indeed. Alleluia!

The Priest may say

Almighty God, to you all hearts are open, all desires known, and from you no secrets are hid: Cleanse the thoughts of our hearts by the inspiration of your Holy Spirit, that we may perfectly love you, and worthily magnify your holy Name; through Christ our Lord. *Amen.*

When appointed, the following Hymn[26] or some other song of praise is sung or said, all standing

GLORY TO GOD IN THE HIGHEST,
 and peace to his people on earth.
Lord God, heavenly King,
almighty God and Father,
 we worship you, we give you thanks,
 we praise you for your glory.
Lord Jesus Christ, only Son of the Father,
Lord God, Lamb of God,
you take away the sin of the world:
 have mercy on us;

---

26. An ICET text. See the note on pages 20-22.

you are seated at the right hand of the Father:
    receive our prayer.
For you alone are the Holy One,
you alone are the Lord,
you alone are the Most High,
    Jesus Christ,
      with the Holy Spirit,
      in the glory of God the Father. Amen.

On other occasions the following is used

Lord, have mercy.		Kyrie eleison.
Christ, have mercy.	*or*	*Christe eleison.*
Lord, have mercy.		Kyrie eleison.

    or this

Holy God,
Holy and Mighty,
Holy Immortal One,
Have mercy upon us.

The Proclamation of the Word of God

The presiding Minister says to the People

	The Lord be with you.
Answer	And also with you.
Priest	Let us pray.

The Collect of the Day

The People respond Amen.

The Lessons

The People sit. One or two Lessons, as appointed, are announced and read. [See page 87 for forms for announcing and ending Epistles and other Lessons.]

A Psalm, Hymn, or Anthem may follow each Lesson.

Then, all standing, the Deacon or a priest reads the Gospel, first saying

THE HOLY GOSPEL of our Lord Jesus Christ according to _____.

The People respond   Glory to you, Lord Christ.

At the end of the Gospel, the Deacon says

The Gospel of the Lord.

The People respond   Praise to you, Lord Christ.

The Sermon

On Sundays and other festivals there follows, all standing

The Nicene Creed

We believe in one God,
> the Father, the Almighty,
> maker of heaven and earth,
> of all that is seen and unseen.

We believe in one Lord, Jesus Christ,
> the only Son of God,
> eternally begotten of the Father,
> God from God, Light from Light,
> true God from true God,
> begotten, not made, one in Being with the Father.
> Through him all things were made.
> For us men and for our salvation
>> he came down from heaven
> by the power of the Holy Spirit
>> he was born of the Virgin Mary, and became man.
> For our sake he was crucified under Pontius Pilate;
>> he suffered, died, and was buried.
>> On the third day he rose again
>>> in fulfillment of the Scriptures;
>> he ascended into heaven
>>> and is seated at the right hand of the Father.
> He will come again in glory to judge the living and the dead,
> and his kingdom will have no end.

We believe in the Holy Spirit, the Lord, the giver of life, who proceeds from the Father.
> With the Father and the Son he is worshiped and glorified.

He has spoken through the Prophets.
We believe in one holy catholic and apostolic Church.
We acknowledge one baptism for the forgiveness of sins.
We look for the resurrection of the dead,
    and the life of the world to come. Amen.

A confession of sin may be said here, or after the Intercession.

Confession of Sin

The Minister says
Let us confess our sins against God and our neighbor.

A period of silence may be observed.

Minister and People

Most merciful God,
we confess that we have sinned against you
in thought, word and deed:
we have not loved you with our whole heart;
we have not loved our neighbors as ourselves.
We pray you for your mercy
    forgive what we have been,
    amend what we are,
    direct what we shall be;
that we may delight in your will,
and walk in your ways,
through Jesus Christ our Lord. Amen.

The Bishop, if present, or the Priest stands and says

Almighty God have mercy on you, forgive you all your sins, through our Lord Jesus Christ; strengthen you in all goodness, and by the power of the Holy Spirit, keep you in eternal life. *Amen.*

The Prayers

Here Prayer is offered with intercession for

The Universal Church and all its members
The Nation and all in authority
The welfare of the world
The concerns of the local community

Those who suffer and those in any trouble

The departed (with commemoration of a saint when appropriate)

See pages 68-81 for various forms of Intercession.

The Peace

Here (or at one of the other places suggested on page 88), the Priest may say to the People

    The Peace of the Lord be always with you.
Answer And also with you.

Then the Ministers and People may greet one another in the Name of the Lord.

If there is no celebration of the Communion, or if a priest is not available, the Service is concluded as directed on page 87.

The Celebration of the Holy Communion

The Priest, standing at the Holy Table, begins the Offertory with this or some other Sentence of Scripture:

Ascribe to the Lord the honor due his Name; bring offerings and come into his courts. [*Psalm 96:8*]

Representatives of the Congregation bring the People's offerings of bread and wine, and money or other gifts, to the Deacon or Priest. The People stand while the offerings are presented and placed on the Altar.

The Great Thanksgiving

The People remain standing. The Priest faces them, and sings or says

Priest	The Lord be with you.
People	And also with you.
Priest	Lift up your hearts.
People	We lift them up to the Lord.
Priest	Let us give thanks to the Lord our God.
People	It is right to give him thanks and praise.

Then, facing the Holy Table, the Priest proceeds

It is right, and a good and joyful thing, always and everywhere to give thanks to you, Father Almighty, Creator of heaven and earth:

On all Sundays, and on other occasions when a Proper Preface is appointed, it is sung or said here.

Therefore we praise you,
joining our voices with angels and archangels
and with all the company of heaven,
who for ever sing this hymn
to proclaim the glory of your Name:

Priest and People

Holy, holy, holy Lord, God of power and might,
heaven and earth are full of your glory.
    Hosanna in the highest.
Blessed is he who comes in the name of the Lord.
    Hosanna in the highest.

The People may kneel.

Then the Priest continues

Holy and gracious Father,
in your infinite love you made us for yourself;
and when we fell into sin
and became subject to evil and death,
you, in your mercy, sent Jesus Christ,
your only and eternal Son,
to share our human nature,
to live and die as one of us
to reconcile us to you,
the God and Father of all.

He stretched out his arms upon the Cross,
and offered himself, in obedience to your will,
a perfect sacrifice for all mankind.

At the following words concerning the Bread, the Priest is to hold it, or lay his hand upon it. And at the words concerning the Cup, he is to hold, or lay his hand upon, the Cup and any other vessel containing wine to be consecrated.

On the night he was handed over to suffering and death,
our Lord Jesus Christ took bread;
and when he had given thanks to you,
he broke it, and gave it to his disciples,
and said, "Take this and eat it:

This is my Body, which is given for you.
Do this for the remembrance of me."

After supper he took the cup of wine;
and when he had given thanks, he gave it to them,
and said, "Drink this, all of you:
This is my Blood of the new Covenant,
which is shed for you and for many
for the forgiveness of sins.
Whenever you drink it, do this for the remembrance of me."

Priest and People

Christ has died,
Christ is risen,
Christ will come again.

The Priest continues

We celebrate the memorial of our redemption, O Father,
in this sacrifice of praise and thanksgiving,
and we offer you these Gifts.
Sanctify them by your Holy Spirit
to be for your people the Body and Blood of your Son,
the holy food and drink of new and unending life in him.
Sanctify us also
that we may faithfully receive this holy Sacrament,
and serve you in unity, constancy, and peace;
and at the last day bring us with all your saints
into the joy of your eternal kingdom.

All this we ask through your Son Jesus Christ:
By him, and with him, and in him,
in the unity of the Holy Spirit
all honor and glory is yours, Almighty Father,
now and for ever.

Amen.

As our Savior Christ has taught us, we now pray,

People and Priest

Our Father in heaven,
    holy be your Name,

your kingdom come,
your will be done,
    on earth as in heaven.
Give us today our daily bread.
Forgive us our sins
    as we forgive those who sin against us.
Do not bring us to the test
    but deliver us from evil.
For the kingdom, the power, and the glory are yours
    now and for ever. Amen.

The Breaking of the Bread

A period of silence is kept, during which the Priest breaks the consecrated Bread.

Then may be sung or said

(Alleluia.) Christ our Passover is sacrificed for us: *Therefore let us keep the feast. (Alleluia.)*

From Ash Wednesday until Easter Eve, Alleluia is omitted; and may be omitted at other times except during Easter Season.

Facing the People, the Priest says the following Sentence of Invitation:

The Gifts of God for the People of God.

He may add: Take them in remembrance that Christ gives himself for you, and feed on him in your hearts by faith, with thanksgiving.

The Ministers receive the Sacrament in both kinds, and then immediately deliver it to the People.

The Bread and the Cup are given with these words, to which the communicant may respond, Amen.

The Body [Blood] of our Lord Jesus Christ keep you in everlasting life.

or this

The Body of Christ, the Bread of heaven.
The Blood of Christ, the Cup of salvation.

During the ministration of Communion, Psalms, Hymns, or Anthems may be sung.

After Communion, the Priest says

Let us pray.

People and Priest

Eternal God, Heavenly Father,
you have accepted us as living members of your Son
    our Savior Jesus Christ,
and you have fed us with spiritual food
    in the Sacrament of, his Body and Blood.
Send us now into the world in peace,
    and grant us strength and courage
    to love and serve you
    with gladness and singleness of heart. Amen.

or this

Almighty and everliving God,
you have fed us with the spiritual food
    of the most precious Body and Blood
    of your Son, our Savior Jesus Christ;

You have assured us, in these holy Mysteries,
    that we are living members
    of the Body of your Son,
    and heirs of your eternal kingdom.

And now, Father, send us out
    to do the work you have given us to do,
To love and serve you
    as faithful witnesses of Christ our Lord.

To him, to you, and to the Holy Spirit,
    be honor and glory now and for ever. Amen.

The Bishop, if present, or the Priest, may bless the People.

The Deacon (or Priest) may dismiss them with these words

Go forth into the world,
rejoicing in the power of the Spirit.
Thanks be to God.

or

Go in peace to love and serve the Lord.
Thanks be to God.

or

Let us go forth in the Name of Christ.
Thanks be to God.

Another form of the great Thanksgiving

[Based on the Liturgy of the Lord's Supper, 1967]

After the Sursum Corda *and* the Sanctus, *the Priest continues*

All glory is yours, Almighty God, Holy Father:
You made us in your own image;
and when we had fallen into sin,
you gave your only-begotten Son Jesus Christ,
to take our nature upon him,
and to suffer death upon the Cross for our redemption.
He made there, by his one oblation of himself,
a full and perfect sacrifice for the whole world;
And instituted and commanded us to continue
this memorial of his precious death and sacrifice,
until his coming again.

At the following words concerning the Bread, the Priest is to hold it, or lay his hand upon it. And at the words concerning the Cup, he is to hold, or lay his hand upon, the Cup and any other vessel containing wine to be consecrated.

For in the night in which he was betrayed, he took bread;
and when he had given thanks to you,
he broke it, and gave it to his disciples, and said,
"Take, eat: This is my Body which is given for you.
Do this in remembrance of me."

After supper, he took the cup;
and when he had given thanks, he gave it to them and said,
"Drink this, all of you: For this is my Blood of the New Covenant
which is poured out for you and for many
for the forgiveness of sins.
Do this, as often as you drink it, in remembrance of me."

Therefore, O Lord and Holy Father, we your people
celebrate here before your Divine Majesty,

with these holy Gifts which we offer to you,
the memorial of the blessed Passion
and precious Death of your dear Son,
his mighty Resurrection and glorious Ascension,
looking for his Coming again in power and great glory.
And with these Gifts, O Lord, we offer to you ourselves,
for this is our duty and service.
And we pray you, in your goodness and mercy, to accept,
through the eternal mediation of our Savior Jesus Christ,
this our sacrifice of praise and thanksgiving.

Gracious Father, in your almighty power,
bless and sanctify us and these holy Mysteries
with your Life-giving Word and Holy Spirit;
fill with your grace all who partake
of the Body and Blood of our Lord Jesus Christ;
make us one Body that he may dwell in us and we in him.
And grant that with boldness
we may confess your Name in constancy of faith,
and at the last Day enter with all your Saints
into the joy of your eternal kingdom:

Through Jesus Christ our Lord,
by whom, and with whom, and in whom,
in the unity of the Holy Spirit
all honor and glory is yours,
O Father Almighty,
now and for ever.

Amen.

An Order For Celebrating The Holy Eucharist

which may be used on occasions other than the principal service on Sundays and other feasts of our lord

ORDER OF THE CELEBRATION

This order requires for its effective use careful preparation by all the worshippers so that all may understand what takes place and their own part in the celebration.

The use of silence, movement, and music will depend on the nature of the particular occasion.

THE PEOPLE AND PRIEST

gather in the lord's name

proclaim and respond to the word of god

> *the proclamation and response may include, in addition to a reading from the gospel, other readings, song, talk, dance, instrumental music, other art forms, silence.*

pray for the world and the church

exchange the peace

prepare the table

> *some of those present prepare the table; the bread, the cup of wine, and other offerings, are placed upon it.*

make eucharist

> *the great thanksgiving is said by the priest in the name of the gathering, using one of the eucharistic prayers provided. In the course of the prayer, he takes the bread and cup into his hands, or places his hand upon them.*
>
> *the people respond—amen!*

break the bread

eat and drink together

> *the body and blood of the lord are shared in a reverent manner; after all have received, any of the sacrament that remains is then consumed.*
>
> *When a common meal or* agapé *accompanies the celebration, it follows here.*

Eucharistic Prayers

In making Eucharist, the Priest uses one of the Eucharistic Prayers from the First or Second Service, or one of the following.

A

After a suitable invitation by the Priest, and a response by the People, the Priest gives thanks as follows:

We give thanks to you, O God our Creator;
You are worthy of praise from every creature you have made.
For in these last days you have sent your only Son
to be the Savior and Redeemer of the world.
In him, you have forgiven our sins,
and made us worthy to stand before you
In him, you have brought us out of darkness into light
out of error into truth,
out of death into life.

On the night he was handed over to suffering and death,
our Lord Jesus Christ took bread;
and when he had given thanks to you,
he broke it, and gave it to his disciples,
and said, "Take this and eat it:
This is my Body, which is given for you.
Do this for the remembrance of me."

After supper he took the cup of wine,
and when he had given thanks, he gave it to them,
and said, "Drink this, all of you:
This is my Blood of the new Covenant,
which is shed for you and for many
for the forgiveness of sins.
Whenever you drink it, do this for the remembrance of me."

Remembering his death and resurrection,
we offer in thanksgiving this Bread and this Cup.
And we pray you to send your Holy Spirit
upon this Offering and upon your People,
to change us, and to make us one in your kingdom.
To you be praise and honor and worship
through your Son Jesus Christ
with the Holy Spirit
for ever and ever.

Amen.

B

After a suitable invitation by the Priest, and a response by the People, the Priest gives thanks as follows:

We give you thanks, O Father,
for the goodness and love
which you have made known to us in creation,
in the calling of Israel,
in the words of the prophets,
and, above all, in Jesus your Son:

Who, on the night before he died for us,
took bread and gave thanks;
he broke it and gave it to his disciples, and said
"This is my body which is for you
do this for my memorial."
In the same way,
he took the cup after supper and said
"This cup is the new Covenant in my Blood.
Whenever you drink it,
do this for my memorial."

Remembering now his suffering and death,
and celebrating his resurrection,
and looking for his coming again
to fulfill all things according to your will,
we ask you, Father,
through the power of the Holy Spirit,
to accept and bless these Gifts.
Make us one with your Son in his sacrifice,
that his life may be renewed in us.

And therefore, Father, through Jesus your Son,
in whom we have been accepted and made your children,
by your life-giving Spirit
we offer our grateful praise and say:

People and Priest

Our Father . . .

C

In the following Prayer, the italicized lines are spoken by the People.

The Lord be with you.
And also with you.

Lift up your hearts.
We lift them up to the Lord.

Let us give thanks to the Lord our God.
Let us praise him for his goodness now and for ever.

God of all power, Ruler of the Universe,
you are worthy of glory and praise.
Glory to you for ever and ever.

At your command all things came to be,
the vast expanse of interstellar space,
galaxies, suns, the planets in their courses,
and this fragile earth, our island home:
By your will they were created and have their being.

From the primal elements you brought forth the race of man,
and blessed us with memory, reason, and skill;
you made us the rulers of creation.
But we turned against you, and betrayed your trust;
and we turned against one another.
Have mercy, Lord, for we are sinners in your sight.

Again and again, you called us to return.
Through prophets and sages you revealed your righteous Law;
and in the fullness of time, you sent your only Son,
born of a woman, to fulfill your Law,
to open for us the way of freedom and peace.
By his blood, he reconciled us.
By his wounds, we are healed.

[And, therefore, we praise you,
joining with the heavenly chorus,
with prophets, apostles, and martyrs,
and with men of every generation
who have looked to you in hope:
to proclaim with them your glory,
in their unending hymn:

Priest and People

Holy, holy, holy Lord, God of power and might,
heaven and earth are full of your glory.
Hosanna in the highest.
Blessed is he who comes in the name of the Lord.
Hosanna in the highest.]

The Priest continues

And so, Father, we who have been redeemed by him,
and made a new people by water and the Spirit,
now bring before you these gifts.
Sanctify them by your Holy Spirit
to be for us the Body and Blood
of Jesus Christ our Lord.

On the night he was betrayed,
he took bread, said the blessing,
broke the bread, and gave it to his friends,
and said, "Take this and eat it.
This is my Body, which is given for you.
Do this for the remembrance of me."

In the same way, after supper, he took the cup,
and said "Drink of this, all of you.
This is my Blood of the new Covenant,
which is poured out for you and for all mankind
for the forgiveness of sins.
Whenever you drink it, do this for the remembrance of me."

Priest and People

When we eat this Bread
and drink this Cup,
we show forth your death, Lord Christ,
until you come in glory.

Priest

Lord God of our Fathers,
God of Abraham, Isaac, and Jacob,
God and Father of our Lord Jesus Christ:
open our eyes to see your hand at work in the world about us.
Deliver us from the presumption of coming to this Table

for solace only, and not for strength;
for pardon only, and not for renewal.
Let the grace of this Holy Communion
make us one body, one spirit in Christ,
that we may worthily serve the world in his name.
Risen Lord, be known to us in the breaking of the Bread.

Accept these prayers and praises, Father,
through Jesus Christ, our great High Priest,
to whom with you and the Holy Spirit,
your Church gives honor, glory, and worship,
from generation to generation.

    Amen.

D

Priest	The grace of our Lord Jesus Christ and the love of God and the fellowship of the Holy Spirit be with you all.
or	The Lord be with you.
People	And also with you.
Priest	Lift up your hearts.
People	We lift them up to the Lord.
Priest	Let us give thanks to the Lord our God.
People	It is right to give him thanks and praise.

The Priest begins the Prayer with these or similar words:

Father, we thank you and we praise you . . .

He gives thanks for God's work in Creation and his revelation of himself to men.

He may recall before God the particular occasion being celebrated.

He may incorporate or adapt the Proper Preface of the day.

[If the Sanctus is to be included he leads into it with these or similar words:

And so we join the saints and angels in proclaiming your glory as we sing (say),

Holy, holy, holy Lord . . .

Here he praises God for the salvation of the world through Jesus Christ our Lord.

He then continues with these words

And so, Father, we bring you these gifts.
Sanctify them by your Holy Spirit
to be for your People the Body and Blood
of Jesus Christ our Lord.

On the night he was betrayed,
he took bread, said the blessing,
broke the bread, and gave it to his friends,
and said, "Take this and eat it.
This is my Body, which is given for you.
Do this for the remembrance of me."

In the same way, after the supper, he took the cup,
and said "Drink of this, all of you.
This is my Blood of the new Covenant,
which is poured out for you and for all men
for the forgiveness of sins.
Whenever you drink it, do this for the remembrance of me."

Father, we now celebrate the memorial of your Son.
By means of this holy Bread and Cup,
we show forth the sacrifice of his death
and proclaim his resurrection
until he comes again.

Gather us by this Holy Communion
into one Body in your Son Jesus Christ.
Make us a living sacrifice of praise.

By him, and with him, and in him,
in the unity of the Holy Spirit
all honor and glory is yours,
Almighty Father,
now and for ever.

Amen.

Forms of Intercession

Prayer is offered with intercession for

The Universal Church and all its members
The Nation and all in authority
The welfare of the world
The concerns of the local community
Those who suffer and those in any trouble
The departed (with commemoration of a saint when appropriate)

If a confession of sin is not said at the service, a form of Intercession containing a penitential petition should be chosen. [For example: I, V, or VII.]

The Priest may introduce the Prayers with a sentence of invitation related to the Season or the Proper of the Day.

When a briefer form of Prayer is desired, some or all of the petitions marked with an asterisk may be omitted.

I

Deacon or other leader

With all our heart and with all our mind, let us pray to the Lord, saying, "Lord, have mercy".

* For the peace from above, for the loving kindness of God, and for the salvation of our souls,
let us pray to the Lord.

> *Lord, have mercy.*

For the peace of the world, for the welfare of the holy Church of God, and for the unity of all mankind,
let us pray to the Lord.

> *Lord, have mercy.*

For our Bishop, and for all the clergy and people, let us pray to the Lord.

> *Lord, have mercy.*

For our President, for the leaders of the nations, and for all in authority,
let us pray to the Lord.

> *Lord, have mercy.*

For this city (*town, village,* . . .), for every city and community, and for those who live in them,
let us pray to the Lord.
Lord, have mercy.

* For seasonable weather, and for an abundance of the fruits of the earth,
let us pray to the Lord.
Lord, have mercy.

* For the good earth which God has given us, and for the wisdom and will to conserve it,
let us pray to the Lord.
Lord, have mercy.

* For those who travel on land, on water, in the air, or through outer space,
let us pray to the Lord.
Lord, have mercy.

For the aged and infirm, for widows and orphans, and for the sick and the suffering,
let us pray to the Lord.
Lord, have mercy.

For the poor and the oppressed, for prisoners and captives, and for all who remember and care for them,
let us pray to the Lord.
Lord, have mercy.

For all who have died in the hope of the resurrection, and for all the departed,
let us pray to the Lord.
Lord, have mercy.

* For deliverance from all danger, violence, oppression, and degradation,
let us pray to the Lord.
Lord, have mercy.

* For the absolution and remission of our sins and offenses,
let us pray to the Lord.
Lord, have mercy.

* That we may end our lives in faith and hope, without suffering and without reproach,
let us pray to the Lord.
Lord, have mercy.

* Defend us, deliver us, and in *thy* compassion protect us, O Lord, by *thy* grace.
Lord, have mercy.

In the Communion of Saints, let us commend ourselves, and one another, and all our life, to Christ our God.

To thee, O Lord our God.

A brief silence is then observed.

The Priest concludes with the following or some other prayer:

Lord Jesus Christ: who *hast* given us grace at this time with one accord to make our common supplication; and *hast* promised that when two or three are agreed together in *thy* Name *thou wilt* grant their requests; Fulfill now, O Lord, our desires and petitions, as may be best for us; granting us in this world knowledge of *thy* truth, and in the world to come life everlasting; through *thy* mercy, O Christ, to whom with the Father and the Holy Spirit be honor and glory for ever and ever. *Amen.*

II

In the course of the silence after each bidding, the People offer their own prayers, either silently or aloud.

I ask your prayers for God's people throughout the world: for our Bishop(s) _____; for this gathering; and for all ministers and people.
Pray, brothers, for the Church.

Silence

I ask your prayers for peace among men; for goodwill among nations; and for the well-being of all people.
Pray, brothers, for justice and peace.

Silence

I ask your prayers for the poor, the sick, the hungry, the oppressed, and those in prison.
Pray, brothers, for those in any need or trouble.

Silence

I ask your prayers for all who seek God, or a deeper knowledge of him.
Pray, brothers, that they may find and be found of him.

Silence

I ask your prayers for the departed [especially _____].
Pray, brothers, for those who have died.

Silence

Members of the congregation may ask the prayers or the thanksgiving of those present.

* I ask your prayers for . . .

* I ask your thanksgiving for . . .
Give thanks, brothers, for God's great goodness.

Silence

Praise God for those in every generation in whom Christ has been honored [especially _____ whom we remember today]. And pray that we may have grace to glorify Christ in our own day.

Silence

The Priest adds a concluding collect.

III (Traditional Form)

After the Priest's invitation to prayer, the Leader and People pray responsively.

Father, we pray for thy holy Catholic Church:
That we all may be one.

Grant that every member of the Church may truly and humbly serve thee:
That thy Name may be glorified by all people.

We pray for all Bishops, Priests and Deacons:
That they may be faithful stewards of thy holy mysteries.

We pray for all who govern and hold authority in the nations of the world:
That there may be peace and justice among men.

May we seek to do thy will in all that we undertake:
That we may be blest in all our works.

Have compassion on those who suffer from any grief or trouble:
That they may be delivered from their distress.

Grant rest eternal to the departed:
Let light perpetual shine upon them.

We praise thee for all thy saints who have entered into joy:
May we also come to share in thy heavenly kingdom.

Let us pray in silence for our own needs and those of others.

>   *Silence*

>   *The Priest concludes with this or some other collect:*

Almighty God, the fountain of all wisdom, who knowest our necessities before we ask, and our ignorance in asking: We beseech thee to have compassion upon our infirmities; and those things which for our unworthiness we dare not, and for our blindness cannot ask, mercifully give us for the sake of thy Son Jesus Christ our Lord. Amen.

III (Contemporary Form)

>   *After the Priest's invitation to prayer, the Leader and People pray responsively.*

Father, we pray for your holy Catholic Church:
That we all may be one.

Grant that every member of the Church may truly and humbly serve you:
That your Name may be glorified by all people.

We pray for all Bishops, Priests and Deacons:
That they may be faithful ministers of your Word and Sacraments.

We pray for all who govern and hold authority in the nations of the world:
That there may be peace and justice among men.

Give us courage to do your will in all that we undertake:
That we may be blest in all our works.

Have compassion on those who suffer from any grief or trouble:
That they may be delivered from their distress.

Give to the departed eternal rest:
Let your light shine upon them for ever.

We praise you for all your saints who have entered into joy:
May we also come to share in your heavenly kingdom.

Let us pray in silence for our own needs and those of others.

>   *Silence*

>   *The Priest concludes with this or some other collect:*

Almighty God, to whom our needs are known before we ask, help us to ask only what accords with your will; and those good things which we dare not, or in our blindness cannot ask, grant us for the sake of your Son, Jesus Christ our Lord. Amen.

IV

The Leader may expand any paragraph with specific petitions. A short period of silence follows each paragraph. The periods of silence may be concluded as follows:

Lord, in your mercy
Hear our prayer.

Let us pray for the whole Church of God in Christ Jesus, and for all men according to their needs.

Silence

Grant, Almighty God, that we who confess your Name may be united in your truth, live together in your love, and show forth your glory in the world.

Silence

Direct this and every nation into the ways of justice and peace, that we may honor all men, and seek the common good.

Silence

Save and comfort those who suffer, that they may hold to you through good and ill, and trust in your unfailing love.

Silence

Remember, Lord, those who have died in the peace of Christ, and those whose faith is known to you alone, and deal with us and them according to your great mercy.

Silence

Grant these our prayers, O merciful Father, for the sake of your Son, our Savior Jesus Christ. *Amen.*

V

Deacon or other leader

In peace, let us pray to the Lord, saying

> "Lord, have mercy"
> *or* "Kyrie eleison".

For the peace of the world, that a spirit of respect and forbearance may grow among nations and peoples, we pray to you, O Lord.

Here and after every petition the People respond:

> "Kyrie eleison".
> *or* "Lord, have mercy"

For the holy Church of God, that it may be filled with truth and love, and be found without fault at the Day of your Coming, we pray to you, O Lord.

For N. our Presiding Bishop, for N. (N.) our own Bishop(s), for all Bishops and other Ministers, and for all the holy People of God,
we pray to you, O Lord.

* For all who fear God and believe in his Christ, that our divisions may cease and all may be one as you, Lord, and the Father are one,
we pray to you, O Lord.

* For the mission of the Church, that in faithful witness it may preach the Gospel to the ends of the earth,
we pray to you, O Lord.

* For those who do not yet believe, and for those who have lost their faith, that they may receive the light of the Gospel,
we pray to you, O Lord.

For those in positions of public trust, [especially _____], that they may serve justice, and promote the dignity and freedom of all men,
we pray to you, O Lord.

* For a blessing upon the labors of men, and for the right use of the riches of creation, that mankind may be freed from famine and disaster,
we pray to you, O Lord.

For the poor, the persecuted, the sick, and all who suffer; for refugees, prisoners, and all who are in danger: that they may be relieved and protected,
we pray to you, O Lord.

For this Congregation; for those who are present, and for those who are absent, that we may be delivered from hardness of heart, and show forth your glory in all that we do,
we pray to you, O Lord.

* For our enemies and those who wish us harm; and for all whom we have injured or offended,
we pray to you, O Lord.

* For ourselves; for the forgiveness of our sins, and for the grace of the Holy Spirit to amend our lives,
we pray to you, O Lord.

For all who have commended themselves to our prayers: for our families, friends, and neighbors; that being freed from anxiety, they may live in joy, peace, and health, we pray to you, O Lord.

* For _____,
we pray to you, O Lord.

For all who have died in the faith of Christ, that, with all the saints, they may have rest in that place where there is no pain or grief, but life eternal,
we pray to you, O Lord.

Rejoicing in the fellowship of [the ever-blessed Virgin Mary, (blessed N.) and] all the saints, let us commend ourselves, and one another, and all our life to Christ our God.

To you, O Lord our God.

Silence

The Priest says this doxology:

For yours is the Majesty, O Father, Son, and Holy Spirit; yours is the kingdom and the power and the glory, now and for ever. *Amen.*

or else he concludes with this or some other prayer:

O Lord our God, accept the fervent prayers of your people; in the multitude of your mercies, look with compassion upon us and all who turn to you for help: For you are gracious, O lover of men; and to you we give glory, Father, Son, and Holy Spirit, now and for ever. *Amen.*

VI

The specific petitions that are indented may be adapted by addition or omission, as appropriate, at the discretion of the Minister. The collects which follow each period of silent prayer are customarily said by the Priest. Each collect is printed twice: first in contemporary and then in traditional language.

Deacon or other leader

Let us pray for all men everywhere according to their need, and for the people of God in every place.

Let us pray for the holy Catholic Church of Christ throughout the world; especially,

For its unity in witness and service
For all Bishops and other Ministers and the people whom they serve
For *N.*, our Bishop, and all the people of this Diocese
For all Christians in this community
For those preparing to be baptized (particularly, . . .)

that God will confirm his church in faith, increase it in love, and preserve it in peace.

Silence

Almighty and everlasting God, by whose Spirit the whole company of your faithful people is governed and sanctified: Receive our prayers which we now offer before you for all members of your holy Church, that in their vocation and ministry they may truly and devoutly serve you, to the glory of your Name; through our Lord and Savior Jesus Christ. *Amen.*

Almighty and everlasting God, by whose Spirit the whole body of the Church is governed and sanctified: Receive our supplications and prayers, which we offer before thee for all members of thy holy Church, that every member of the same, in his vocation and ministry, may truly and godly serve thee; through our Lord and Savior Jesus Christ. *Amen.*

Let us pray for all nations and peoples of the earth, and for those in authority among them; especially,

For *N.*, the President of the United States
For the Congress and the Supreme Court

> For the Members and representatives of the United Nations
> For all who serve the common good of men

that by God's help they may seek justice and truth, and live in peace and concord.

Silence

Almighty God, from whom all thoughts of truth and peace proceed: We pray you to kindle in the hearts of all men the true love of peace; and guide with your pure and peaceable wisdom those who take counsel for the nations of the earth, that in tranquillity your kingdom may go forward, until the earth is filled with the knowledge of your love; through Jesus Christ our Lord. *Amen.*

Almighty God, from whom all thoughts of truth and peace proceed: Kindle, we pray thee, in the hearts of all men the true love of peace; and guide with thy pure and peaceable wisdom those who take counsel for the nations of the earth; that in tranquillity thy kingdom may go forward, till the earth is filled with the knowledge of thy love; through Jesus Christ our Lord. *Amen.*

Let us pray for all who suffer, and are afflicted in body or in mind; especially,

> For the hungry and the homeless, the destitute and the oppressed
> For the sick, the wounded, and the crippled
> For those in loneliness, fear, and anguish
> For those who face temptation, doubt, and despair
> For prisoners and captives, and those in mortal danger
> For the sorrowful and bereaved

that God in his mercy will comfort and relieve them, and grant them the knowledge of his love, and stir up in us the will and patience to minister to their needs.

Silence

Gracious God, you see all the suffering, injustice, and misery which abound in this world. We implore you to look mercifully upon the poor, the oppressed, and all who are burdened with pain and sorrow. Fill our hearts with your compassion, and give us strength to serve them in their need, for the sake of him who suffered for us, our Savior Jesus Christ. *Amen.*

Gracious God, who seest all the suffering, injustice, and misery which abound in this world: We beseech thee to look mercifully upon the poor, the oppressed, and all who are burdened with pain and sorrow. Fill our hearts with thy compassion, and give us strength to serve them in their need, for the sake of him who suffered for us, our Savior Jesus Christ. *Amen.*

Let us pray for all who, whether in ignorance or in disbelief, have not received the gospel of Christ; especially,

For those who have never heard the word of Christ
For those who have lost their faith
For those hardened by sin or indifference
For the contemptuous and the scornful
For those who are enemies of the Cross of Christ, and persecutors of his disciples

that God will open their hearts to the truth, and lead them to faith and obedience.

Silence

Merciful God, who made all men and hate nothing that you have made; nor do you desire the death of a sinner, but rather that he should be converted and live: Have mercy upon all who know you not as you are revealed in the Gospel of your Son. Take from them all ignorance, hardness of heart, and contempt of your Word. Bring all men home, good Lord, to your fold, so that they may be one flock under the one shepherd, your Son Jesus Christ our Lord. *Amen.*

Merciful God, who hast made all men, and hatest nothing that thou hast made, nor desirest the death of a sinner, but rather that he should be converted and live: Have mercy upon all who know thee not as thou art revealed in the Gospel of thy Son. Take from them all ignorance, hardness of heart, and contempt of thy Word; and so bring them home, blessed Lord, to thy fold, that they may be made one flock under one shepherd, Jesus Christ our Lord. *Amen.*

Let us commit ourselves to our God, and pray for the grace of a holy life, that, with all who have departed this world and have died in the faith, we may be accounted worthy to enter into the fullness of the joy of our Lord, and receive the crown of life in the day of resurrection.

Silence

O God of unchangeable power and eternal light: Look favorably on your whole Church, that wonderful and sacred mystery. By the tranquil operation of your providence, carry out the work of man's salvation. Let the whole world see and know that things which were cast down are being raised up, and things which had grown old are being made new, and that all things are being renewed to the perfection of him through whom all things were made, your Son our Lord Jesus Christ, who lives and reigns with you, in the unity of the Holy Spirit, one God, for ever and ever. *Amen.*

O God of unchangeable power and eternal light: Look favorably upon thy whole Church, that wonderful and sacred mystery; and by the tranquil operation of thy providence, carry out the work of man's salvation. Let the whole world see and know that things which were cast down are being raised up, and things which had grown old are being made new, and that all things are being renewed unto the perfection of him through whom all things were made, thy Son our Lord Jesus Christ, who liveth and reigneth with thee in the unity of the Holy Spirit, one God, for ever and ever. *Amen.*

VII

The Leader and People pray responsively

In peace, we pray to you, Lord God:

For all people in their daily life and work;
For our families, friends, and neighbors, and for those who are alone.

For this community, the nation, and the world;
For all who work for justice, freedom, and peace.

For the just and proper use of your creation;
For the victims of hunger, fear, injustice and oppression.

For all who are in danger, sorrow, or any kind of trouble;
For those who minister to the sick, the friendless, and the needy.

For the peace and unity of the Church of God;
For all who proclaim the Gospel, and all who seek the Truth.

For Bishops and other Ministers, [especially for *N.* our Presiding Bishop, and *N.(N.)* our Bishop(s)];
For all who serve God in his Church.

For the special needs and concerns of this congregation.

Those present may add their own petitions.

Hear us, Lord;
For your mercy is great.

We thank you, Lord, for all the blessings of this life.

The People may add their own thanksgivings

We will exalt you, O God our King;
And praise your Name for ever and ever.

We pray for all who have died, [especially _____], that they may have a place in your eternal kingdom.

Lord, let your loving-kindness be upon them;
Who put their trust in you.

* We pray to you also for the forgiveness of our sins.

Leader and People

Have mercy upon us, most merciful Father:
In your compassion forgive us our sins,
known and unknown, things done and left undone:
And so uphold us by your Spirit
that we may live and serve you in newness of life,
to, the honor and glory of your Name.

The Priest concludes the prayers with a suitable collect.

Concerning the Collect at the Prayers

When a Collect concludes the Intercession, a suitable one is selected, such as:

a. a collect appropriate to the Season or occasion being celebrated;

b. a collect expressive of some special need in the life of the local congregation;

c. a collect for the mission of the Church;

d. a general collect such as the following:

Lord, hear the prayers of your people; and what we have asked faithfully, grant that we may obtain effectually, to the glory of your Name; through Jesus Christ our Lord. *Amen.*

Heavenly Father, you have promised to hear what we ask in the Name of your Son: We pray you, accept and fulfill our petitions, not as we ask in our ignorance, nor as we deserve in our sinfulness, but as you know and love us in your Son, Jesus Christ our Lord. *Amen.*

Almighty and eternal God, ruler of all things in heaven and earth: Mercifully accept the prayers of your people, and strengthen us to do your will; through Jesus Christ our Lord. *Amen.*

Hasten, O Father, the coming of your Kingdom; and grant that we your servants, who now live by faith, may with joy behold your Son at his coming in glorious majesty; even Jesus Christ, our only Mediator and Advocate. *Amen.*

Lord Jesus Christ, you said to your Apostles, "Peace I give to you; my own peace I leave with you": Regard not our sins, but the faith of your Church, and give to us the peace and unity of that heavenly City where, with the Father and the Holy Spirit, you live and reign now and for ever. *Amen.*

O God, you have brought us near to an innumerable company of angels, and to the spirits of just men made perfect: Grant us during our earthly pilgrimage to abide in their fellowship, and in our heavenly country to become partakers of their joy; through Jesus Christ our Lord. *Amen.*

God:
Grant to the living—grace;
to the departed—rest;
to the church, the nation, and all mankind—peace and concord;
and to us and all his servants—life everlasting. *Amen.*

Suggested Offertory Sentences

One of the following, or some other appropriate Sentence of Scripture, may be used in place of the Offertory Sentence provided in the text of the Service.

Walk in love, as Christ loved us and gave himself for us, an offering and sacrifice to God. (*Ephesians 5:2*)

I pray you brethren, by the mercies of God, to present yourselves as a living sacrifice, holy and acceptable to God, which is your spiritual worship. (*Romans 12:1*)

If you are offering your gift at the altar, and there remember that your brother has something against you; leave your gift there before the altar and go; first be reconciled to your brother, and then come and offer your gift. (*Matthew 5:23-24*)

Thine, O Lord, is the greatness, and the power, and the glory, and the victory, and the majesty. For all that is in the heaven and in the earth is thine. Thine is the kingdom, O Lord, and thou art exalted as head above all. (*1 Chronicles 29:11*)

Yours, O Lord, is the greatness, the power, the glory, the victory, and the majesty. For everything in the heaven and on earth is yours. Yours, O Lord, is the kingdom, and you are exalted as head over all. (*1 Chronicles 29:11*)

Worthy art thou, our Lord and God, to receive glory and honor and power; for thou hast created all things, and by thy will they exist and were created. (*Revelation 4:11*)

O Lord our God: you are worthy to receive glory and honor and power; because you have created all things; and by your will they were created and have their being. (*Revelation 4:11*)

or this Bidding:

Let us with gladness present the offerings and oblations of our life and labor unto the Lord.

Proper Prefaces

[Musical settings of the Prefaces will appear in the Altar Edition.]

Advent

From the First Sunday in Advent until Christmas Day, except on Saints' Days.

Traditional wording
Because thou didst send thy well-beloved Son to redeem us from sin and death, and to make us, in him, sons and heirs of everlasting life: that when he shall come again in power and great triumph to judge the world, we may without shame or fear rejoice to behold his appearing:

Contemporary wording
Because you sent your well-beloved Son to redeem us from sin and death, and to make us, in him, sons and heirs of everlasting life: that when he shall come again in power and great triumph to judge the world, we may without shame or fear rejoice to behold his appearing

Christmas

From Christmas Day until the Epiphany.

Traditional wording
Because thou didst give Jesus Christ, thine only Son, to be born for us; who, by the mighty power of the Holy Spirit, was made perfect Man of the flesh of the Virgin Mary his mother: that we, being delivered from the bondage of sin, might receive power to become the sons of God:

Contemporary wording
Because you gave Jesus Christ, your only Son, to be born for us; who, by the mighty power of the Holy Spirit, was made perfect Man of the flesh of the Virgin Mary his mother: that we, being delivered from the bondage of sin, might receive power to become the sons of God:

Epiphany

From the Epiphany until Ash Wednesday, except on Saints' Days.

Through Jesus Christ our Lord; who, in the substance of our human nature, manifested his glory: that he might bring us out of darkness into his own marvelous light:

The Incarnation

On the Feasts of the Presentation, Annunciation, Visitation, and Transfiguration.

The Holy Eucharist

Traditional wording
Because in the Mystery of the Word made flesh, thou hast caused a new light to shine in our hearts, to give the knowledge of thy glory in the face of thy Son Jesus Christ our Lord:

Contemporary wording
Because in the Mystery of the Word made flesh, you have caused a new light to shine in our hearts, to give the knowledge of your glory in the face of your Son Jesus Christ our Lord:

Lent

From Ash Wednesday until Palm Sunday, except upon the Annunciation, and major Saints' Days.

Through Jesus Christ our Lord; who was in every way tempted as we are, yet did not sin; by whose grace we are able to triumph over every evil, and to live no longer unto ourselves, but unto him who died for us and rose again:

Holy Week

From Palm Sunday through Maundy Thursday, and on Holy Cross Day.

Through Jesus Christ our Lord; who for our sins was lifted up upon the Cross, that he might draw all men to himself; who by his suffering and death became the way of eternal salvation to all who obey him:

Easter

From Easter Day until Ascension Day, except on major Holy Days.

Traditional wording
But chiefly are we bound to praise thee for the glorious Resurrection of thy Son Jesus Christ our Lord, for he is the Paschal Lamb who by his death hath overcome death, and by his rising to life again hath opened to us the way of everlasting life:

Contemporary wording
But chiefly are we bound to praise you for the glorious Resurrection of your Son Jesus Christ our Lord, for he is the Paschal Lamb who by his death has overcome death, and by his rising to life again has opened to us the way of everlasting life:

Ascension

From Ascension Day until the Day of Pentecost, except on major Holy Days.

Through thy (your) dearly beloved Son Jesus Christ our Lord; who, after his glorious Resurrection, openly appeared to all his Apostles, and in their sight was taken into heaven, to prepare a place for us: that where he is, there we might also be, and reign with him in glory:

Pentecost

> *On the day of Pentecost, and on the Feasts of the Apostles.*

Through Jesus Christ our Lord; according to whose true promise the Holy Spirit came down from heaven upon the disciples, to teach them and to lead them into all truth; giving them boldness with fervent zeal to preach the Gospel to all nations:

Trinity Sunday

Traditional wording
Whom with thy co-eternal Son and Holy Spirit we worship as one God, one Lord, in Trinity of Persons and in Unity of Being; and we celebrate the one and equal glory of thee, O Father, and of the Son, and of the Holy Spirit:

Contemporary wording
Whom with your co-eternal Son and Holy Spirit we worship as one God, one Lord, in Trinity of Persons and in Unity of Being; and we celebrate the one and equal glory, O Father, of you, and of the Son, and of the Holy Spirit:

The Lord's Day

> *For use on the Sundays after Pentecost, but not on the succeeding weekdays.*

Traditional wording
Creator of the light and source of life; who hast made us in thine image and called us to new life in Jesus Christ our Lord:

Contemporary wording
For you are the source of light and life; you made us in your image and called us to new life in Jesus Christ our Lord:

> *or this*

Through Jesus Christ our Lord, who on this day overcame death and the grave, and by his glorious resurrection opened to us the way of everlasting life:

> *or this*

Traditional wording
Who by water and the Holy Spirit hast made us a new people in Jesus Christ our Lord, to set forth thy glory in all the world:

Contemporary wording
For by water and the Holy Spirit you have made us a new people in Jesus Christ our Lord, to set forth your glory in all the world:

All Saints

On All Saints' Day and upon certain other Saints' Days.

Traditional wording
Who, in the multitude of thy saints, hast compassed us about with so great a cloud of witnesses: that we, rejoicing in their fellowship, may run with patience the race that is set before us; and, together with them, may receive the crown of glory that fadeth not away:

Contemporary wording
For in the multitude of your saints, you have compassed us about with so great a cloud of witnesses: that we, rejoicing in their fellowship, may run with patience the race that is set before us; and, together with them, may receive the crown of glory that never fades away:

Apostles and Ordinations

On Feasts of the Apostles, and at the time of conferring Holy Orders.

Through the great Shepherd of thy (*your*) flock, Jesus Christ our Lord; who after his Resurrection sent forth his Apostles to preach the Gospel, and to teach all nations; and to be with them always, even unto the end of the ages:

Baptism

For use at Baptism when there is no other Preface appointed.

Because in Jesus Christ our Lord thou hast (*you have*) received us as your children, made us citizens of your kingdom, and given us the Holy Spirit to guide us into all truth:

Marriage

Traditional wording
Because thou hast ordained the solemn covenant of love between husband and wife as a witness of the union of thy son Jesus Christ with the holy fellowship of all faithful people:

Contemporary wording
Because you have ordained the solemn covenant of love between husband and wife as a witness of the union of your son Jesus Christ with the holy fellowship of all faithful people:

Commemoration of the Dead

Through Jesus Christ our Lord; who brought to light the living hope of a blessed resurrection: that in our grief we may rejoice in full assurance of our change into the likeness of his glory:

Additional Directions and Suggestions

The Holy Table is spread with a clean white cloth during the celebration.

A Psalm, or part of a Psalm, may be sung or said at the places indicated in the Services. The addition of Gloria Patri is optional.

On occasion, and when appropriate, instrumental music may be used in place of a Psalm, Hymn, or Anthem.

The Beginning of the Service

When the Litany is sung or said immediately before the Eucharist, the Prayer of Intercession may be omitted. The Litany may be concluded with the Kyries, in which case the Eucharist begins with the Salutation and Collect of the Day.

In the First Service, the Priest may preface the Collect for Purity with an Opening Sentence from Morning or Evening Prayer.

The Decalogue (page 44) with its responses may be used before the Summary of the Law and Kyries, or in place of them.

The *Kyrie eleison*, or "Lord, have mercy", may be sung or said in three-fold, six-fold, or nine-fold form. The Trisagion, "Holy God", may be sung or said three times.

Gloria in excelsis is sung or said from Christmas Day through the Feast of the Epiphany; on Sundays from Easter Day through the Day of Pentecost, and on Ascension Day; and at other times as desired; but it is not used on the Sundays or ordinary weekdays of Advent or Lent. Te Deum laudamus is not used on the Sundays or ordinary weekdays of Lent.

The Collect of the Day is said by the Bishop or Priest presiding at the celebration. With few exceptions, there is only one Collect at this point.

Concerning the Lessons

It is desirable that the Lessons which precede the Gospel be read from a lectern.

Lessons are announced in the following manner:
"A Reading from [*Name of Book*]",
or "The Word of God, written in [*Name of Book*]",
(A citation in the following words may be added: "chapter _____, beginning at the _____ verse.")

After each Lesson, the reader may say,
"Here ends the Lesson (Reading, Epistle)."

It is desirable that the Gospel be read from the pulpit or a lectern or from the midst of the Congregation.

When a significant portion of the Congregation is composed of persons whose native tongue is other than English, the Gospel may be read in that language by a reader appointed by the Priest, either in place of, or in addition to, the Gospel in English.

A Hymn may be sung before or after the Sermon.

The Nicene Creed may be omitted, except on Sundays and major Feasts.

Directions concerning the Prayer of Intercession will be found on page 68.

The Confession of Sin

A confession of sin is a normal part of the Service, but may be omitted on appropriate occasions. It may be said before the Liturgy begins; or before or after the Prayer of Intercession. When a confession is used, the Peace should not precede it. When the Confession is omitted, a form of Intercession containing a penitential petition should be chosen.

When there is no Communion

If there is no Communion, all that is appointed through the Prayer of Intercession may be said. (The Confession of Sin under such circumstances should be said before the Service begins or before the Intercession). A Hymn or Anthem may then be sung, and the offerings of the People received. The Service may then conclude with the Lord's Prayer; and with either the Grace or a Blessing, or with the exchange of the Peace.

In the absence of a priest, all that is described above (except for the Absolution and Blessing) may be said by a deacon, or if there is no deacon, by a lay-reader specially licensed by the Bishop.

At the Peace and Offertory

The greeting, "The Peace of the Lord be always with you", is addressed to the entire assembly. In the exchange between individuals which may follow, any appropriate words of greeting may be used.

The greeting of Peace may take place:

1. Before the Offertory Sentence.
2. Before the Prayer of Intercession.
3. Before the ministration of the Sacrament (before or after the Sentence of Invitation.)

Necessary announcements may be made after the Creed, or before the Offertory (before or after the Peace), or at the end of the Service, as convenient.

It is appropriate that the Deacon and other assisting ministers make ready the Table for the celebration, preparing and placing upon it the bread and cup of wine. (In preparing the chalice it is customary to add a little water.)

Alternative Acclamations at the Great Thanksgiving

One of the following alternative acclamations may be used in the course of the Great Thanksgiving:

A. We remember his death;
   We proclaim his resurrection;
   We await his coming in glory.
B. When we eat this Bread and drink this Cup, we proclaim your death, Lord Christ, until you come in glory.

At the Breaking of the Bread

At the Breaking of the Bread, in place of "Christ our Passover", some other appropriate Anthem may be used.

If the number of communicants requires the use of additional chalices, it is convenient that Wine which had been consecrated in a flagon be poured into them at the time of the Breaking of the Bread.

At the Ministration of the Sacrament

In the First Service, at the ministration of the Sacrament, the following procedure may be used:

1. Before receiving Communion himself, the Priest says to the People:
   The Body and Blood of our Lord Jesus Christ, given for you, preserve your bodies and souls unto everlasting life. Take this in remembrance that Christ died for you, and feed on him in your hearts by faith, with thanksgiving.
2. The Gifts are then ministered with these words: The Body [Blood] of our Lord Jesus Christ. (*Amen.*)

or he may use this Invitation:

The Gifts of God for the People of God.

or this Invitation

The Gifts of God for the People of God: Take them in remembrance that Christ gives himself for you, and feed on him in your hearts by faith, with thanksgiving.

While the People are coming forward to receive Communion, the presiding Minister receives the Sacrament in both kinds. The bishops, priests, and deacons at the Holy Table then communicate, and after them the People.

Opportunity shall always be given to every communicant to receive the consecrated Bread and Wine separately. But the Sacrament may be received in both kinds simultaneously, in a manner approved by the Bishop.

When the presiding Minister is assisted by a deacon or another priest, it is customary for the President to minister the consecrated Bread and the assistant the Chalice. When several deacons or priests are present, some may minister the Bread, others the Wine, as the President may appoint.

The Consecration of Additional Elements

If the Consecrated Bread or Wine does not suffice for the number of communicants, the Priest is to consecrate more or either or both, saying,

HEAR US, O HEAVENLY FATHER, AND WITH THY (YOUR) WORD AND HOLY SPIRIT BLESS AND SANCTIFY THIS BREAD [WINE] THAT IT, ALSO, MAY BE THE SACRAMENT OF THE PRECIOUS BODY [BLOOD] OF THY (YOUR) SON JESUS CHRIST OUR LORD, WHO TOOK BREAD [THE CUP] AND SAID, "THIS IS MY BODY [BLOOD]". *Amen.*

or else he may consecrate more of both kinds, saying again the Prayer of Consecration, beginning with the words which follow the Sanctus, and ending with the Invocation.

The Ministration of Communion by a Deacon

When there is no priest available, a deacon may be appointed to distribute Holy Communion from the reserved Sacrament in the following manner:

After the Intercession (and the receiving of the People's offerings), the Deacon reverently places the holy Sacrament on the altar.

The Lord's Prayer is then said, the Deacon first saying, "Let us pray in the words which our Savior Christ has (hath) taught us."

And then, omitting the breaking of the Bread, he proceeds with what follows in the Liturgy (page 41 or 57) as far as the end of the Prayer after Communion, after which he dismisses the People.

The Conclusion of the Service

If any of the consecrated Bread or Wine remain, apart from any which may be required for the Communion of the sick or of others who for weighty cause could not be present at the celebration, the Priest (or Deacon) and other communicants shall reverently eat and drink the same, either immediately after the Communion of the People or after the Dismissal.

A hymn of praise may be sung before or after the Prayer after Communion.

From Easter Day through the Day of Pentecost, Alleluia may be added to any of the Dismissals in the following manner:

"Go in peace to love and serve the Lord. Alleluia, alleluia.
Thanks be to God. Alleluia, alleluia."

The Music of the Liturgy

In the Second Service, the texts of the Kyrie eleison, Gloria in excelsis, Nicene Creed, and Sanctus given in the Book of Common Prayer may be substituted for the ICET versions when a musical setting composed for the Prayer Book wording is being used.

Musicians are encouraged to write new music for the Services, and especially for the ICET and other next texts.

PRAYER BOOK STUDIES 22: THE DAILY OFFICE

1970

PREFACE

The first major attempt since 1928 to revise the Daily Offices was made by the Standing Liturgical Commission in 1957 with the publication of *Prayer Book Studies VI* entitled *Morning and Evening Prayer*. Since then, the process of liturgical revision has gathered momentum throughout the Anglican Communion and in all Christian Churches.

The approval by the Sixty-Second General Convention in 1967 of a Plan for the Revision of the Book of Common Prayer, under which the Standing Liturgical Commission was designated as the instrument of revision, gave an opportunity to the Commission to up-date its thinking, to benefit by the progress of revision in other Christian churches, and to make use in a systematic manner of the experience and knowledge of the 260 Consultants appointed to assist the Commission under the Revision Plan.

The use of Consultants in Prayer Book Revision was an essential feature of the Plan approved by the General Convention.

Of the total number of Consultants, 64 served on the fourteen Drafting Committees set up under the Plan. The main body of Consultants served as Readers. They received all the drafts prepared by the various committees; they studied them and made comments and suggestions. These were transmitted to the Drafting Committee concerned, and, when possible, the Consultants' suggestions were incorporated in the developing draft of the Committee. The Standing Liturgical Commission studied the Committees' drafts, and it also took into account the suggestions and comments sent in by the Reader-Consultants. The Study and the Services presented here reflect this process of Church-wide consultation.

The Standing Liturgical Commission set up fourteen Drafting Committees, and assigned to each a section of the Book of Common, Prayer for study and revision. The Drafting Committee on the Daily Offices was constituted as follows:

The Reverend Charles W. F. Smith, Member of the Commission and
    Chairman of the Drafting Committee
Mr. David Johnson

The Reverend Edward R. Hardy*
The Reverend Benjamin Minifie
Sister Mary Clare, O.S.A.*
The Reverend William Sydnor
The Reverend Paul Wessinger, S.S.J.E.*

An effort was made, within the necessary limitations of budget and distance of travel, to ensure that the Committee would be representative of a variety of interests: monastic communities, women, laymen, parish life, and biblical and liturgical scholarship.

To the many Reader-Consultants who responded to the various drafts and progress reports of the Committee, the Commission owes special thanks: as in the case of the other Drafting Committees, the Commission's work would not have been as representative of the mind of the Church, were it not for their thoughtful comments, criticisms, and suggestions.

The next stage of the work on *The Daily Offices*, subject to the continued approval of the Revision program by the General Convention, is the preparation for trial use of a daily Lectionary, to be completed by 1973.

The Committee was substantially assisted by the presence at some of its meetings of members of the joint Commission on Church Music, the Reverend Norman C. Mealy and the Reverend William B. Schmidgall, whose advice extended beyond the strictly musical aspects. The Committee was also assisted by the Reverend Charles P. Price, Chairman of the Drafting Committee on Occasional Prayers and Thanksgivings, in coordinating the overlapping tasks of the two Committees. Mr. Martens deserves the Commission's thanks for a number of helpful suggestions.

The Commission desires to place on record its appreciation of the hospitality extended to the Drafting Committee on the Daily Offices, by the Dean and Faculty of the Episcopal Theological School in Cambridge, Massachusetts, to the Warden and staff of the College of Preachers in Washington, D.C., and to the Rector of Grace Church, the Reverend Benjamin Minifie, a member of the Drafting Committee, and to Mrs. Minifie.

The process of Church-wide consultation, which is the distinctive characteristic of the present Revision Plan, does not end with the publication of *Prayer Book Studies 22*; on the contrary, it is now expanded to include all who may read this publication, whether clergymen or lay persons, whether members of the

---

* The Reverend Paul Wessinger was compelled by the pressure of other responsibilities to resign at an early stage of the work. Sister Mary Clare was then invited to join the Drafting Committee. The Reverend Dr. Hardy accepted a post with Cambridge University in 1969, but has continued to contribute by correspondence.

Episcopal Church or of another Communion. All are invited to enter this process of consultation by sending their comments to the Standing Liturgical Commission, 815 Second Avenue, New York, N.Y. 10017.

All comments will be given serious consideration, and an effort will be made to acknowledge all correspondence.

To all who may respond to this invitation, the Commission expresses in advance its sincere thanks.

THE STANDING LITURGICAL COMMISSION

Chilton Powell, *Chairman*
John W. Ashton
Dupuy Bateman, Jr.
James D. Dunning
Robert W. Estill
William C. Frey
Charles M. Guilbert, *Secretary*
Mrs. Richard Harbour
Joseph M. Harte
Louis B. Keiter
H. Boone Porter, Jr.
Charles P. Price
Massey H. Shepherd, Jr., *Vice Chairman*
Jonathan G. Sherman
Charles W. F. Smith
Bonnell Spencer, O.H.C.
Albert R. Stuart
Leo Malania, *Co-ordinator*

Introduction

The Standing Liturgical Commission presents for the Church's consideration two versions of the Daily Office, one in contemporary English, the other in the language of the Prayer Book and the Revised Standard Version of the Bible. Each version is a single form intended for both the morning and the evening Office. In addition, new services are provided for use at noonday and at the close of the day, and short forms for use by families or individuals praying alone.

The Background

There has been little fundamental change in the structure of the Offices since Mattins and Evensong appeared in the Book of Common Prayer of 1549. The early history of daily worship which culminated in the monastic system is obscure, but the story of the development of the seven-fold medieval system is too well-known to need repetition.[1] Of the dual system developed by Cranmer and his colleagues, *Prayer Book Studies VI* (hereafter PBS VI)[2] said in 1957:

> "The genius of our Common Prayer is in no instance more clearly exemplified than in the Daily Offices of Morning and Evening Prayer. Out of the elaborate, complicated Canonical Hours of the medieval Breviary the sixteenth century Reformers produced a pattern of daily praise and prayer that was loyal to tradition, solidly Scriptural in content, simple and convenient in execution, balanced and artful in design. The older Latin Offices had been a primary duty of the clergy, the monks and friars, upon whom their recitation was imposed by canonical law. But the Reformers intended their simpler, vernacular forms to be a means of corporate worship and of edification in the knowledge of God's Word for all the laity no less than the clergy. In this purpose their labors have borne abundant fruit. To no other part of the Prayer Book have the lay people shown greater attachment and responsiveness."

---

1. The history is briefly summarized in Massey H. Shepherd, Jr.: *The Oxford American Prayer Book Commentary*, pages 1-32. For a fuller account see P. Salmon: *The Breviary Through the Centuries*, Collegeville, Minnesota, 1962. (English translation of *L'Office Divin*, 1959. A clear and persuasive rationale may be found in the opening essay, "The Daily Office" in *The Daily Offices* by the Joint Liturgical Group, edited by the Rev. Canon R.C.D. Jasper, S.P.C.K., 1968. The essay was written by a Baptist, the Rev. S. F. Winard, for the Group, which included also Anglicans, Methodists, Presbyterians, Congregationalists, members of the Church of Christ, and Roman Catholic observers. The proposals of the Church of England Liturgical Commission will be found in *Common Prayer 1970*, S.P.C.K., where a good deal of abbreviation is suggested, drawing on the work of the Joint Group.

2. *Morning and Evening Prayer* (*Prayer Book Studies VI*), Standing Liturgical Commission of the Episcopal Church, New York: Church Pension Fund, 1957, Vol. 2, p. 44.

While the central structure remained, at successive stages accretions developed at the beginning and the end. Opening sentences were added (and subsequently seasonal sentences corresponding to the old antiphons on the Psalms), an exhortation and penitential introduction, and, at the end, stated intercessions and a thanksgiving. In practice, the Sunday custom of reading the Office and the Litany before the Holy Communion, or the Ante-Communion, became burdensome, and those who stayed to the end became fewer. As a consequence there developed the practice, still largely followed, of adding Sermon, Offertory, and Blessing to the fuller form of the Office as a service of the Word of God apart from the Eucharist. In England the practice of having Holy Communion following "Matins and Sermon" is still widely observed, with but minimal attendance at the Communion.

The American revisions made no basic changes, but were designed to allow for modification on certain occasions by omission and by combination with other services. The persistence of tradition is indicated by the fact that after three revisions, the marks of the English situation — the Church established by law in close functioning with the State — are still apparent in the order in which prayers are arranged and in the content of those adapted for use in intercessions for the President, the Congress and the Courts.

Since the last revision of the Prayer Book was completed in 1928, the need for adaptation and flexibility has become increasingly acute, suddenly accelerating since the Study of 1957, so that even monastic communities are finding their modes of prayer in a state of flux. The permission given by the General Convention of 1967 in Canon 20 to use a variety of English versions of the Scriptures, extended to the lections of the Eucharist, reflects the modern advance in textual studies and the new understanding of Biblical language and forms. It has not yet been applied to the large Scriptural content of the rites themselves, and the modern critical results of Biblical exegesis have made themselves but little felt.

A new evaluation of the relation of the Church to its environment, ecological and human, urban, social and political, and its growing sense of responsibility in these areas have shown how closely the Prayer Book reflects a state of society which no longer exists. This in itself creates a proper demand for adaptability and for freedom to respond to the situation. Aspects of this rapid process of change and the Church's response, perhaps properly conservative in liturgical matters, are the steadily increasing sense of a common ministry of all God's people, a resultant demand for greater congregational participation in the rites and for modern modes of expression which reflect something of the immediacy and forthrightness of modern speech. The complete loss of the use of the second person singular as a means of address, and the need for a new language of prayer, are not met by a mere change of pronouns.

A further factor which must be taken into account, especially since the Second Vatican Council of 1962-65, is the ecumenical mood and opportunity of the times. Every Church with which we have contact is revising its liturgical forms and, the Roman Communion more urgently than others, its language. This provides an unprecedented opportunity, perhaps unlikely to be repeated, for consultation in the search for a modern liturgical style suitable to the worship of Almighty God. In particular it has produced the effort, now in progress, to arrive at common texts in contemporary English for the most widely used liturgical forms.

The Proposals of *Prayer Book Studies VI*

It is apparent that many new factors must be given weight which were not evident in 1957. The forms then proposed did not have the benefit of trial use. What has been learned from the trial use of *Prayer Book Studies XVII* must be applied in the revision of other services. In 1957 it was still possible to assume a situation in which Evening Prayer would be widely used in churches where Morning Prayer was also in use and thus provide forms for two separate Offices. Morning and Evening Prayer differed chiefly in the Sentences, appointed Canticles, Versicles and Responses, and the fixed Collects. Other proposals for both offices reflected the fact that many congregations seldom used Evening Prayer and allowed in that case for the use of the evening Canticles in the morning. This and other proposals have been taken up into this report and carried further.

The Present Situation

With the trial use of the *Liturgy of the Lord's Supper*,[3] it was hoped that there would be a growing use of "The Ministry of the Word" when the whole Liturgy was not to be used. It may be that wide enough experience of this must await a new liturgical Lectionary which will provide a more adequate coverage of the Scriptures, with more of the flexibility and availability for preaching which has characterized the Sunday lections for Morning Prayer.

Before proceeding to modify the present form or the revision proposed in 1957, the Standing Liturgical Commission had to face the question, For what use or uses should the Daily Offices be designed and on what basis should they be constructed? It decided that the Office should be so designed as to be adaptable to as many uses as possible.

The time is past when by canon or rubric the clergy could be required to read the two Offices daily, though the 1969 English Canons still require it. There are many clergymen who do read the Offices daily because of a sense of obligation or because they find the practice valuable: there are also lay-people who follow the practice, even if in modified form. They should be encouraged by the structure of the office itself. There are cathedrals and parish churches where the Daily Office is read publicly in the name of the Christian Community, no matter how

---

3. *The Liturgy of the Lord's Supper* (*Prayer Book Studies XVII*), New York: Church Pension Fund, 1966 (This study appears in Volume 4 of this edition.)

few come to share in it.[4] There are theological seminaries and colleges where the Office is used daily; and monastic communities, of course, continue the practice, though they are experimenting with new combinations.

There are small groups who read the Office together at least once a day — for example, team ministry groups, parish clergymen with their staffs, office groups, families which share housing units. There are short-term conferences where those assembled read the Offices together. If the Prayer Book Office is sufficiently adaptable, they may all be able to use it rather than construct their own services. There is a considerable number of parishes where Morning Prayer augmented by hymns, sermon, offertory, and blessing, is found to be the most effective act of worship on two or three Sundays a month.[5] The Office here proposed is in adaptability and possibility of expansion, capable of meeting the needs of these parishes and, as provided in the rubrics, may be readily combined with the Holy Communion without repeating the Ministry of the Word.

It has further to be borne in mind, as the Pusey Report on Theological Education[6] noted that over a third of the parishes and missions report fewer than 100 communicants and the median is 170. Parochial reports indicate that the typical morning congregation averages fifty people or less. Professional musicians, even a choir and adequate musical leadership for a demanding form of service, are not to be expected. The service must therefore be usable without a choir, without much expectation of congregational training, and often without the leadership of an ordained minister.

These considerations seem to demand a form which is basically simple and manageable, but readily adaptable and capable of sufficient elaboration. A splendid recent rationale for the continued use of the Offices is referred to in Note 1.

The Basic Rationale

It is accepted as fundamental that the core of the Office is the regular, systematic use of the Psalter and the rest of the Bible. This has been the genius of the Anglican tradition for over four hundred years. The ordered use of Psalms and Scriptures, distributed throughout the monastic day and night, was channeled into two daily Offices. This revision therefore has been constructed from the core outwards. In the process of the Drafting Committee's work, everything before the Psalter and the Word of God was first treated as preliminary, with a separate

---

4. There are cases of groups formed to deal with specialized needs, e.g., Alcoholics Anonymous, which meet daily in the church to read the Offices.

5. An informal survey conducted in 1969 by the Standing Liturgical Commission through the Chairmen of Diocesan Liturgical Commissions and Committees, revealed that in the two-thirds of the Dioceses of the Church which reported, this is the basis of the main Sunday Service on at least two Sundays in each month in approximately 50 percent of the parishes and missions.

6. Pusey, N. M. and Taylor, C. L.: *Ministry for Tomorrow*, New York: The Seabury Press, 1967, page 56.

"Introduction" consisting of the Opening Sentences, and another containing the Confession of Sin. Comments of consultants, however, persuaded the Committee that the service should be presented, rather, as a unit. It was also decided, in view of the relatively less frequent use of Evening Prayer and the minimal differences between the two Offices (once the Canticles have been freed for general use), that a single basic rite would suffice. In places where both Morning and Evening Prayer are used daily, it would probably become customary to use certain variables at one service rather than the other, with special types of intercession and thanksgiving. It should be the privilege of those places to arrive at such distinctions on their own, rather than to have them imposed.

The Core—Psalter and Readings from Scripture

The Psalter

The basic core of the Office is the recitation of Psalms along with the reading and hearing of passages from the Scriptures in a regular order. The section of the Office, except for the initial Sentences, named "The Psalter" includes the ancient opening versicles and the *Gloria Patri*, an invitatory Psalm, one or more Psalms, and a concluding *Gloria Patri*. When the Confession of Sin is omitted, this will conform to the traditional beginning of the Office. Any solemn opening recalling God's presence was unnecessary when, in the ordered round of worship, the monastic day was informed by a constant sense of God's presence. This is hardly so when the Office is part of a busy day's work, or follows the complications experienced by a family preparing to attend church.

The Gloria Patri

This doxology is preceded by a versicle and response designed to seek God's help in offering him praise. The changes in the doxology had two effects in, mind. First, "Glory be" sounds to the modern ear like a proposal to offer praise rather than the act itself which the people's response anticipates. Eventually the text should be uniform throughout the Prayer Book for ease in memorizing. For trial use the suggested text is that accepted by the International Consultation on English Texts (hereafter ICET).* The versicle "Praise ye the Lord" and its response have been dropped, since they also gave the impression of proposing what had already been started. Instead, the original expression of praise, Alleluia, has been restored to this place. The *Gloria Patri* occurs at the beginning and end of the Psalter-section as a "common antiphon" as proposed by PBS VI (Vol. 2, p. 55). The involvement of the congregation, which has been and must be a chief concern in all phases of liturgical renewal, is here exemplified, as with the

---

* A detailed Note on ICET is appended to this Introduction.

Lord's Prayer and Creeds, by requiring that the *Gloria Patri* be said by the Minister and people together. The habit of the Minister pre-empting the ascription to God is ingrained, but can be overcome in a surprisingly brief time, depending upon the presence of a vocal core of regular participants.

The Invitatory Psalms

In 1957, the *Jubilate* was proposed as an alternate to relieve the monotony of the invariable repetition of the *Venite*, and the proposal is repeated here, and also in the Church of England's *Common Prayer 1970*. *Jubilate* is equally an invitation to praise, and may prove to be more appropriate in festal seasons. *Venite* and *Jubilate* are not likely to coincide in the reading of the Psalms in course, and when one of them occurs the other may be read for the Invitatory. The two verses from Psalm 96, added in place of the ending of Psalm 95 in 1789, have been retained only in the first of the alternate versions. In the second version of the Office, the text is that being proposed by the Standing Liturgical Commission. The words, "O that today you would hearken to his voice!" are there restored to verse 7 as in the Hebrew original. They may be thought of as a fitting introduction to what is to follow in the service, the reading of the Word of God.

The Psalms

The distribution of the Psalms throughout the year and the question of the omission of repetitions and passages difficult to assimilate to a Christian act of worship are matters for further study.

For places where the Offices are said daily a new plan of selective distribution over a period of time may be evolved, and there are several such schemes proposed for other provinces and Churches.[7] The use of the monthly course contained in the Prayer Book Psalter may satisfy those who object to excisions or rearrangement. For places where the Office is read less frequently, as perhaps for some who use it daily, a plan tied to the Lectionary may be the most reasonable.

Refrains or Antiphons

In the Appendix will be found provision for use of the Antiphons found on page 8 in the Prayer Book. PBS VI proposed their use before and after the *Venite*, but a rubric is now proposed, which allows, on occasion, for their wider employment as refrains—a practice to which the present generation is again becoming accustomed in folk music. Provision for a wider use of Scriptural refrains may allow on

---

7. *The Daily Offices* (see note 1 above). See also the ten-week scheme proposed by the Church in Wales in *Lectionary*, Church of Wales Publications, 1969. In the alterations to the English Prayer Book proposed by the Convention of 1785, Numbers 4 and 14 suggested that the *Gloria Patri* be used only at the end of the whole Psalter.

festal occasions for more difficult settings, from which the congregation, by use of the refrain, would not be entirely excluded. It is a matter which the Joint Commission on Church Music is dealing with in its new collections of music, and this might once again encourage the singing of the Psalms.

The Readings from the Scripture

Starting with the Biblical readings at the center of the Office —the part which, paradoxically, must be represented necessarily by rubrics rather than text—it was clear that the pattern of two lections, framed in Canticles (as the *Shema* and the *Torah* of the synagogue were framed in *berakoth*), must remain basic. To accommodate the variety of possible users and, circumstances, it is provided that at any time there may be only one Lesson. This could make the Office more usable by individuals or small groups. On occasion it might be preferable to read a whole narrative or discourse from one Testament rather than to abbreviate passages artificially to make time for two. There are also parishes where the time schedule on Sunday mornings would make this opportunity to shorten the service very practical. The Church has to trust the training and instinct of its clergy not to abuse such permission.

How the Readings are to be announced is dealt with in the Additional Directions printed at the end. Lay persons, seminary students, and some clergymen find difficulties here. The traditional headings of the Biblical books (in the King James Version and even in the Revised Standard Version) are no longer reliable guides. Debatable attributions, for example of Epistles, can be avoided by announcing, without authorship, the Church or person to whom the Epistle is addressed. The esoteric or "in-group" impression given by announcing a Reading from the Gospels as from "Matthew" is properly avoided by using the actual original title, "According to Matthew," which is found in the Greek text, *Kata Matthaion*; the four are all expressions of the one Gospel. In most congregations, it is perhaps not essential to announce chapter and verse. Yet there are some places, theological schools for instance, and some parishes, where the hearers follow the reading in a Bible, perhaps in the original tongue or in a different English version. In such places, the listener needs to know first the name of the book, then the chapter, and only then (if the reading does not start at the beginning of the chapter) the verse. Now that a number of versions are authorized, it will be helpful sometimes to add the name of the version read.

The Sermon or Meditation

The Offices are not designed to be, in daily use, preaching services. The proper and required place for the liturgical sermon is the Eucharist. The placing of the sermon after the lections in *The Liturgy of the Lord's Supper* has met with favorable response in both theory and practice. In places where the Office is used daily, a brief meditation would on occasion be welcomed, and there are situations where sermons are often preached, for example in seminary chapels where faculty and student sermons are customary. In parishes and missions where the Office is a major service of the congregation, the sermon has its place, though no provision has hitherto been made for it by rubric (it having been assumed that it would follow in due course with the Eucharist). In this proposal permission is given for the insertion of a sermon or meditation. The suggested place is after the Canticle which follows the second Reading from Scripture. Consultants expressed their approval of this suggestion. In the Additional Directions and Suggestions, provision is made for a sermon at other places.

There has been increasing demand for permission to use non-Biblical Christian readings. There may be occasions when this would be appropriate; however, there should be some authoritative control over passages to be read in public worship. No provision is made for non-Biblical readings, but it may be pointed out that the option of a meditation after one or two readings from Scripture affords an opportunity for the reading of patristic, contemporary, or other post-Biblical passages. Anthologies of such material might well appear for the guidance of leaders.

Silence

It has been found, particularly where there is a stable community which has undertaken to read the Offices regularly, that corporate silent meditation on the Scriptures is fruitful. It has accordingly, been provided that silence may follow any reading. The same provision has now appeared in the Church of England's *Common Prayer 1970* (see Note 1). Two things might be observed about this. It is the kind of provision that on first trial is likely to prove awkward, but this initial awkwardness, whether of planning or response, is soon overcome. The effectiveness of corporate meditation on the Word of God can only be judged by its use as a normal part of worship. It should have a salutary effect on the development of a new Lectionary, in the choice of Readings which can not only be "heard," but also be found worthy of reflection. Again, it is a further development of a greatly neglected aspect of worship among us, who so often seem to think that constant activity or vocal expression is essential. A period of silence will be found in the Office also before the Confession. Silence has likewise been provided for in *The Liturgy of the Lord's Supper*, in the Penitential Order, and also at the Fraction.

The Permitted Options

Provision has also been made for two Readings in succession, omitting a Canticle, though perhaps silence might be kept between them. Many who read the Offices alone and wish to observe the rule of two Readings find this convenient. There are also occasions, too rare perhaps in the Lectionary, when the two Lessons read in succession make each the more effective, in that one comments on the other.

These are all optional variations upon the basic structure of Old and New Testament Lections, each with its responsory act of praise. There is required always such a response at the end of the reading of Scripture, whether there be two separate Readings, two read as one or only one. A list of the possible combinations will make clear the flexibility provided:

First Reading	First Reading	First Reading
Canticle	Silence	Silence
Second Reading	Canticle	Second Reading
Canticle	Second Reading	Silence
	Silence	Canticle
	Canticle	
First Reading		One Reading
Second Reading		Silence
Canticle		Canticle

Canticles and Hymns

There have been persistent requests for permission to substitute hymns for canticles. For many congregations, hymns are easier to sing. The irregular rhythm of canticles makes necessary continual adjustments of the melodic line. Familiar canticles using familiar melodies, however, can produce a strong corporate sound in places where the same worshipers meet regularly. But it is just here that monotony may set in and the service become mechanical. The plan proposed, for a freer use and wider variety of canticles, will, it is hoped, encourage their use.

It has seemed wise, however, to provide for the substitution of a hymn in special circumstances. Where singing of canticles is impractical, the use of hymns would encourage congregational participation. On special occasions, a well-chosen hymn may more effectively express the main theme of the service. The melody itself may help people to reflect upon Scripture or respond in a profound and powerful way. What young people may choose to sing in a summer camp, for instance, may be different from what could be sung in a suburban church. A hymn in place of a canticle should ordinarily be addressed to God, celebrating his glory and his gift of life. But opportunity is provided for those hymns which may be more specific in their expression in music of an immediate concern. The principle has been well stated in the following words:

"If another hymn or psalm is substituted for one of these canticles, it should be an objective song of praise that celebrates the glory, majesty, holiness, and righteousness of God, his purposes for his creation, his mighty acts of redemption, grace and judgment."[8]

The individual canticles have not been assigned to particular places in the Offices. PBS VI suggested some sensible changes on the ground that some were pre-Incarnational and should precede rather than follow the New Testament lection. The monotony which arises from fixed places for the canticles may be overcome by giving freedom of choice. Where so often only Morning Prayer is used, it is unfortunate that those hitherto assigned to Evening Prayer should be neglected. The canticles are therefore placed in the Appendix, listed under only two headings, those more suitable for use after the Old Testament and those for use after the New Testament, but this only by way of suggestion. Those who wish to retain the traditional placing will be free to do so.

The history of the use of certain Psalms, first to displace and then to augment the New Testament canticles, was reviewed in PBS VI, Vol. 2, pp. 55, 60. With the exception of Psalm 95 (*Venite*), and 100 (*Jubilate*) it has been decided not to use Psalms as canticles, since they are used in the course of the Psalter. It is proposed to augment the number of canticles. A passage from Isaiah 12 (*Ecce, Deus*) has been introduced in place of the passage from Isaiah 60 suggested in 1957. The desire for a canticle which might be used on Fridays and in penitential seasons has been met by verses from Isaiah 55 (*Quaerite Dominum*) which is widely known from its use in Handel's Oratorio *Messiah*. PBS VI observed, "The Commission . . . would welcome suggestions of a good Christian canticle that could serve as responsory to the New Testament Lesson." This has been met by providing two hymns from Revelation (which may be sung as one), which also have appeared recently in several other revisions as *Dignus es* and *Magna et mirabilia*. In response to a number of requests, the *Gloria in excelsis* is included among the canticles, particularly since its use is not invariably required in the eucharistic liturgy. It would seem to serve better as a canticle than in its position on page 25 of the present Prayer Book where it is so seldom used.[i]

Following the suggestion of the English *Common Prayer 1970*, the Greek third-century evening hymn *Phos Hilaron* has been provided, in a new translation made by the Commission, "O Gracious Light," for use at Evening Prayer in place of the Invitatory Psalm. It was customary in ancient times to light the lamps and candles in the Church during the singing of this hymn. *Phos Hilaron* is found in *The Hymnal 1940* in two versions: "O Brightness of the immortal Father's face" (Hymn 173) and "O Gladsome Light" (Hymn 176). The Commission's

---

8. *An Order of Worship*, Consultation on Church Union: published by Forward Movement Publications, Cincinnati, Ohio, 1968, page 50.

[i] [Ed. Note: In the 1928 prayer book, the *Gloria in excelsis* was included in Evening Prayer as an alternative to the *Gloria patri* — for use at the end of the psalms. By all indications from comments here and in PBS VI, this was not a very common practice.]

translation has not been set to music as yet, and thus it is a standing invitation to composers to enrich our musical resources.

The Easter hymn "Christ our Passover" has also been included in the section on Canticles and Hymns for use as the Invitatory during the great Fifty Days.[ii]

An initial step has been taken to give English titles to the canticles, especially since the probable use of new translations will sometimes remove the *incipit* upon which the Latin title is based. The texts of the canticles to be printed, other than those supplied by the ICET, or taken from The Book of Common Prayer, have been prepared by the Commission.

In the case of the *Te Deum*, the proposal of 1957 is repeated: the versicles added to the original hymn have been used later in the service. The Commission's comment on the use of these versicles will be found on page 57 (in Volume 2) of PBS VI, and a persuasive rationale may be found in the Church of England's *Alternative Services: Second Series*.[9] The text of the *Te Deum* used is the one developed from a fresh study of the original by the ICET, as are the *Benedictus*, *Magnificat*, *Nunc Dimittis* (except for the first two lines), and *Gloria in Excelsis*. The canticles are numbered as a matter of convenience.

The Lectionary

A new Lectionary for the Daily Offices has not yet been produced. Under the Canons, it may be approved at any one Convention. It is apparent that the Office Lectionary should have some relation to the Eucharistic Lectionary and to a revised Church Year and these must first be approved. While the basic rule of reading through at least the major portion of Scripture should be retained, a rationale should be developed which takes account of the new Calendar, of modern study of the Bible, of possible interruptions from multiplied observances, which might provide Readings for the daily Eucharist on days when no other lections are provided. The Standing Liturgical Commission will prepare proposals as soon as feasible. In the meantime, the present Prayer Book Lectionary will serve.

The Rest of the Office

The Opening Sentences

The Sentences, were selected from a long list which was proposed to the Consultants, and the final selection was materially aided by their comments. Too large a list at the beginning of the service is a difficulty for people seeking to follow the service in the book. Hence only those needed for morning and evening, for thanksgiving

---

[ii] [Ed. Note: In prior prayer books, the "Christ our Passover" text was included in the section with the Collects, Epistles, and Gospels. This is the first time that it had been included specifically with the Office materials.]

9. *Alternative Services: Second Series*, S.P.C.K., 1966, pages 18-21.

and penitence, have been placed there. General sentences and those designed for specific seasons have been placed in the Appendix. It is important to note that any of the sentences may be used at any time. The seasonal designations have been adapted to the proposed revision of the Calendar. The Lenten sentences have been made less penitential and more suitable for a season that leads into the Passion.

The Sentences are arranged so that they may be used, if desired, as a dialogue between Minister and People. The Minister may use either member of the pair alone. The responsive use is obviously difficult in the case of the sentences in the Appendix where, however, the same rule applies. The responsive arrangement has been indicated, and on special occasions may be reproduced in a printed service. In this way there can be sufficient variety.

The Confession of Sin

The Confession of Sin differs in the alternative forms of the Office. The Confession in contemporary English is the one preferred by a large majority of the Commission's Consultants from the three contemporary forms originally suggested. In the alternate service the form provided is a revision of the Prayer Book Confession proposed in PBS VI. A rubric makes possible a choice between them. The form provided in the first alternative service is based upon one which appears in the *Daily Offices*.[10]

The prayer for forgiveness is intended to be used by the person conducting the service, but provision is made by rubric for the use of a declaration of Absolution when a bishop or priest is present. In the invitation, the opening address, "Dear Friends in Christ," replaces "Dearly Beloved" here and elsewhere in the trial services. The customary form conveys an exaggerated impression to the modern ear.

The Creed

At the completion of the section designated "The Word of God," provision is made for saying the Apostles' Creed on Sundays and festivals. While the Creed may be said at any time, it should be possible for one saying the Office alone, or for a small group, to omit it. The text is that provided by the ICET. Here, as in recent eucharistic liturgies, it is intended that the people shall say or sing all the words, including the opening words both of the Creed and of the Lord's Prayer. Until this completely corporate use is established, it may be desirable for the leader in some way to announce the Creed or Lord's Prayer without pre-empting the opening words to do so.

---

10. *The Daily Offices* (see Note 1), page 77. No source is given, though some of the wording comes from the forms on page 80 of *The Book of Common Worship*, 1963, of the Church of South India. In the first draft of the service a third form was given which permitted congregational, expression of corporate contrition for involvement in common wrongs, but this has not been included. It was felt that provision for this should be made in Occasional Prayers or Litanies since, in these days, the Prayer Book should not be without a means of expressing our corporate implication in the ills of society and the world.

The Fixed Prayers

The section designated "The Prayers" is a required part of the Office, leaving the Intercessions and Thanksgivings which follow optional and open. The Prayers consist of the *Dominus vobiscum* dialogue, followed by the Lord's Prayer with its doxology, in the form recommended by the ICET. The position of the Lord's Prayer is intended to be climactic in the sense that it is a response to the Word of God and introduces the Collects. The Kyrie is used to introduce the Lord's Prayer in the Offices for Noonday and the Close of Day.

Versicles and Responses

Two sets of versicles and responses are provided. The first is an expansion and revision of those found hitherto only in Evening Prayer, in the American Prayer Books.[iii] The second set, as indicated above, has been detached from the *Te Deum* and is perhaps more appropriate for use in the morning. The first set is made available for use at either morning or evening and would be particularly appropriate when no intercessions are to follow in the Office, in a Litany or in another service.

Some modifications of language have been made. The versicle "O Lord, save the State" has been revised. It has remained unchanged since the first American book, where it was a modified version of "O Lord, save the King."[11] The word "Nation" is here preferred to "People," since in this series of suffrages "People" refers to the people of God, the Church. The response departs from the general pattern of allusions to or quotations from the Psalms (though the existing versicle and response were not a very faithful rendering of Psalm 20:9). The words provided are, however, already familiar from the Prayer Book.

The suffrage for peace, for us alone and in our time only, has been expanded into one for peace in all the world, without which, in the modern era, peace for ourselves is scarcely a possibility.[12] The Commission proposed adding a petition

---

[iii] [Ed. Note: To clarify, this is an expansion of the versicles from Evening Prayer. Morning Prayer had only contained two versicles, the first and last ("O Lord, show thy mercy upon us..." and "O God, make clean our hearts within us...").]

11. The change from "King" to State" was not accomplished without prior discussion. In 1785 Bishop Seabury in consultation with his clergy proposed the variant, "O Lord save the Church." The same proposal can be found among those made by a convention of New England clergy (attended by William White, later Bishop of Pennsylvania) the same year. The first General Convention in 1785, with no one from New England present, agreed instead on "O Lord bless and preserve these United States." South Carolina in 1786 counselled the suffrage be omitted. The 1785 Convention also proposed to omit "chosen" from "make thy chosen people joyful," and that the versicles, "O Lord save thy people" and "Give peace in our time O Lord" with their responses be omitted.

12. In the Boston Convention, 1785, the response, "And make all nations to rejoice in thy loving-kindness, O God" was proposed. The texts referred to here and in the previous Note may be found in, e.g., McGarvey, W.: *Liturgiae Americanae*, Appendix II.

for the poor, a need with universal proportions and Christian implications, and it has been provided by an adaptation of the parallelism in Psalm 9:18.

A proposal that there should be a daily stated prayer for the mission of the Church proved in experimental use to encounter difficulties. Any single collect seemed both monotonous and inadequate to represent the multiple concept of mission which now obtains. Accordingly, a further versicle and response have been added in the words of Psalm 67:2, familiar from use in the *Deus misereatur*.

To fix too closely the objects of intercession by the introduction of fixed collects would repeat the confusion which occurs when the rubric on pages 17 and 31 of the 1928 Book is ignored and the stated intercessions are invariably used, regardless of what will follow.[iv] It would preclude the open choice and adaptation to local circumstances at any given time which the rubric in this service intends. The place for fixed objects of intercession, assuring that the basic causes shall always be covered, is when the people of God are gathered about the altar in the Eucharist.

The versicles and responses give an opportunity to cover the basic needs without providing set collects. The order of the set here prepared has been rearranged to accommodate the additions and also to amend the previous order, which reflected an Established Church.[13] It brings it also into conformity with the order proposed in the revised occasional prayers. The final suffrage was modified in PBS VI by the substitution of the conclusion of Psalm 51:10 as the response. It is proposed that the second half of verse 12 would be even more suitable and would better lead into the prayers which follow.

The Collect of the Day

The placement of the Collect has been discussed by the Commission in connection with the development of the Eucharistic Prayers. When the Collect gathers up the theme of the season or day, as well as the aspirations of the gathered congregation, it would seem to belong properly to the entrance rite. Here there is no entrance rite as such. The sentences serve more effectively than many of the present Collects to set the theme. It was therefore decided to keep the Collect in

---

[iv] [Ed. Note: The rubrics referred to state: "The following prayers shall be omitted here when the Litany is said, and may be omitted when the Holy Communion is to follow" and also "The Minister may here end the Morning/Evening Prayer with such general intercessions taken out of this Book, as he shall think fit or with the Grace."]

13. The versicles for the clergy and the people in the Sarum use came before that for the monarch, but the order King, Clergy, is found in the Litany in Halsey's Primer of 1539. See Blunt, J. H.: *The Annotated Book of Common Prayer*, 1889, page 198 *ff*. The restoration of the order Church, State, is found in the 1949 book of the Church of Ireland (though the English order is retained in the suffrages) and the same is true of the 1959 Canadian book, the South African 1959, and the Church of Scotland 1929. The C.I.P.B.C. book omitted the State. The Church of England Alternative Services of 1965 maintains the State, Church, order as does *Common Prayer 1970*.

its accustomed place in the Office, after the Word Of God. It serves as the first of the fixed Collects. The direction to read the Collect of the Day is intended to fit into the proposed revised Church Year and the proposals for other rites. It is intended that only one variable Collect should be used and that, for instance, the Sunday Collect is not to be repeated after the Collect for any other day or occasion. Only when no other Collect is provided or used would that for the previous Sunday be used. A rubric makes possible the recognition of the special themes of Fridays and Saturdays by providing that on those days the revised Collects for Good Friday and Holy Saturday may be substituted.[v] When there is a Collect provided for a holy day or an observance from *Lesser Feasts and Fasts*,[14] or a Collect proper to a rite or special occasion, that Collect alone would be read.

The Morning and Evening Collects

For both Morning and Evening Prayer a choice is offered instead of the same two invariable Collects. Those hitherto provided, in particular the Collects for Peace from the ancient sacramentaries, have seemed to place an undue emphasis on security for ourselves. The first new alternate at Morning Prayer is taken from the Canadian Prayer Book[15] and has met with a general welcome. The second is a further revision and condensation of the Collect for Grace, begun in 1957, in conformity with an attempt generally to lighten the stress on "commandments" in favor of a more general and central commitment to the fulfilling of God's will.

In the evening the Collect for Aid against Perils seems less urgent in an age accustomed to electricity and yet has an urgent appeal in days of disturbed city streets. It has been included in the suggested Close of the Day Office (from which, it originally came), where it is, of course, available for use when desired. It is also provided as an option in the alternate Service. The fixed Collect supplied is a revision of the Collect for Peace. The opening phrases have so entered into Anglican devotion that they ought not to be lost, and the close has been changed to avoid the narrowing of response to obeying the law. It prays for deliverance

---

[v] [Ed. note: The "revised collects" refer to the Good Friday and Holy Saturday collects from *Prayer Book Studies* 19. The first is: "Almighty God, we pray you to graciously behold this your family, for whom our Lord Jesus Christ was content to be betrayed, and given up into the hands of sinful men, and to suffer death upon the Cross: who now lives and reigns with you and the Holy Spirit, one God, for ever and ever. Amen."

The second is: "Most Gracious God, as we have been baptized into the death of your Son our Savior Jesus Christ, so in your mercy may we be dead to sin and buried with him: that from the grave and gate of death, we may be raised up with him to newness of life; through Jesus Christ our Lord. Amen."]

14. *The Calendar and the Collects, Epistles, and Gospels for the Lesser Feasts and Fasts and for Special Occasions.* Prepared by The Standing Liturgical Commission of the Protestant Episcopal Church in the United States of America, New York: The Church Pension Fund, 1963.

15. The Book of Common Prayer, Anglican Church of Canada, 1959, page 731, under the title "For Remembrance of God's Presence."

from the fear of enemies rather than from any particular foes.[16] The words "and quietness" were retained as having in the new context a meaning beyond mere passivity. The morning Collect for Peace with its magnificent exordium will be retained in the Occasional Prayers.

The failure of the experiment with the fixed Collect for Mission left a felt need for an invariable Collect which would concern the vocation of the Church in the world and fill out the prayers before the Hymn or Anthem. It is here proposed that this need would be met by the use of what has been in the Prayer Book the second Collect for Good Friday, which now appears as the first of the Solemn Prayers of the proposed Good Friday rite. Its reference to the vocation of all Christians is an appropriate daily prayer, and its reference to offered prayers makes a fitting transition when intercessions are included in the Office.

The Hymn or Anthem

The optional Hymn or Anthem after the Collects previously found in the American Book only in Evening Prayer, provides a break in what is often a long string of prayers and provides an opportunity for the Minister to move to a more effective place for leading the Intercessions and Thanksgivings. He might, as is often done to real advantage, go down among the people. This is also one of the alternate points designated in the Additional Directions and Suggestions at which the Sermon or an Offering may, when desirable, be introduced.

Intercessions and Thanksgivings

The permission to use freely chosen but authorized prayers is intended to cover prayers and litanies to be provided elsewhere in the future Book of Common Prayer, and also to allow freedom under a general rule for the authorization by proper authority — General Convention or Diocesan Bishop — of other material suitable for occasions, regions, places, and times. Some such leeway is necessary to restore a semblance of order to the prayers used and to relieve the Prayer Book of the impossible task of providing prayers in Occasional Prayers and Thanksgivings for every conceivable object. The day has passed when we can prescribe every word uttered in public worship and not allow for variation and for openness to congregational participation. The Church must trust the clergy's discretion. The people, of course, need to be protected from too much virtuosity, and the rubric is intended to do both.

On occasion, as the Reverend Dr. John W. Suter, Jr., used to advocate, the General Thanksgiving may provide a fitting close and congregational commitment at the end of the service. Alternatively, the Prayer of St. Chrysostom may

---

16. Subsequent to the omission of "our" before "enemies" the chairman found in Blunt's *Annotated Book of Common Prayer*, page 214, the phrase "and the drede of enemyes putt awei," quoted in a version from a fourteenth-century Prymer.

stress the unity of God's people in their prayers and their common experience in the presence of Christ. Hence, both are printed in the Office and arranged for congregational use.

The General Thanksgiving was punctuated for corporate use in PBS VI. It has been slightly revised and the groupings reduced to more manageable length. The term "incomparable" has been put in place of "inestimable," "awareness" for "due sense," "truly" for "unfeignedly," reinforcing rather than diminishing the effect of its deservedly beloved expressions.

The question of the translation of the Prayer of St. Chrysostom by Archbishop Cranmer, with his alleged confusion of meaning in translating *convenire* and in conflating verses 18 and 19 of Matthew 18, was reviewed in PBS VI. It could be argued that Cranmer's version was done in full awareness of both problems. The 1957 suggestion that the Person of the Godhead addressed in the prayer could be made more clear has been followed. In this new translation and arrangement, punctuated and set for corporate use the double emphasis found in St. Matthew on agreement in prayer and on the presence of Christ has been provided for. The fact that Christ promised to be present where his people gathered and to respond when they agreed in their requests presents two of the closely related facets of the Biblical theology of prayer for which we have tried (as we believe Cranmer intended) to make allowance.[17] "Come together" and "common petitions" convey the sense of "agree together" in Matthew 18:19. Verse 20 is clearly represented by what follows. The prayer then rests on both these conditions. The term "expedient," as was observed in 1957, has acquired a meaning opposed to its original sense and intent. For the earlier suggestion of "as may be most befitting for them," it seems more euphonious and more direct to say "as may be best for us."

The Concluding Sentences

In addition to the "Grace" from 2 Corinthians 13:14, two other verses from the New Testament have been added, chosen from a large variety proposed. The alternatives may find a use at different seasons and in connection with the variation of the theme of the Office as it moves through the year with its variable Psalms, Readings, Canticles and Hymns. In experimental daily use this provision has been welcomed and frequently used.

---

17. The presence of the Shekinah with two and with three is stressed in the Tractate *Berakoth* of the Mishnah (I.1.6a). The Shekinah is present "when two occupy themselves with *Torah*" and "when three sit and judge." Its presence is connected with prayer when a minimum number for a synagogue is present, "when ten assemble for prayer." The Presence when the judgments of the assembly are handed down does not have the relevance for the Church that it had for the Synagogue (though *cf.* Matthew 18:17, 18 preceding the verses alluded to in the prayer). The "two" joined in study of the *Torah* may appropriately be applied to the hearing of God's Word in the Office, while "two or three" suggests the effectiveness of even a small group gathered for the primary purpose of the Church, its corporate prayer.

Other Offices and Devotions

It is a question whether the basic plan of two Offices for the Church at large should, in the Book of Common Prayer, be augmented by lesser Offices. For a period of trial use such supplementary services may meet certain needs. A decision can eventually be made whether they should appear in the Prayer Book or in *The Book of Offices*. It is assumed that Morning and Evening Prayer will be the basic daily service of the Church (whether apart from the Eucharist or in place of the Ministry of the Word), and that no other Offices will normally be used except when Morning and Evening Prayer have already been said. There is however, a double need to which attention ought to be given. Occasions arise when special groups meet or are together for a conference or retreat of one or more days at which a pause at noonday for intercessions, in particular for the mission of the Church, has become a tradition. There are similar situations when a brief service before retiring is desired. For these cases a noonday Office and one for the close of the day have been provided for trial use.

Secondly, it was hard to decide whether daily devotions for families and individuals should be provided separately or in connection with the Occasional Prayers and Thanksgivings. A position paper presented by the Reverend Dr. Shepherd suggested to the Commission that daily devotions of this kind should be readily accessible in the Prayer Book and should be of so simple a form that they could be easily memorized. Three such forms have been supplied. They intentionally provide echoes of the major Offices.

An Order of Prayer for Noonday

Some recent breviaries have combined the lesser offices of Terce, Sext and None into a single Office for use in the course of the day. The form provided here, at its fullest, with Hymn, Psalm and Scripture reading, might well serve individually or in conferences. In its simpler form it is designed more particularly for the many conferences whose programs include "noonday Intercessions." These, with the best of intentions, have frequently been random. It might prove a great help, especially where such conferences meet in churches or have chapels available, to be able to turn to a suitable form in the Prayer Book. The Order of Prayer for Noonday, is, however, so planned that it can be used when the Leader alone has a book. The parts requiring participation are so familiar that most groups of church people could respond by reflex.

The structure is simple and recalls the basic form of the Daily Office. It may be introduced by a sentence of Scripture or with a well-known versicle and response, leading into the *Gloria Patri*. The Hymn or Psalm is optional. Where brevity requires, or no Bible is available, a choice may be made from three brief Readings (traditionally called "Chapters"). They are self-explanatory: the first is a doxology, the second an expression of the new creation with its ministry of reconciliation in Christ, and the third a statement of the universal glory of the Lord. They are chosen as suitable statements to match the sense of world-wide mission which so often informs gatherings where noonday intercessions are the custom. The third passage will also be found as the Reading in the Family Devotion for noon-day.

Where it is desirable, a meditation may be included. Indeed, in cases where a meditation is the main object of the gathering, this Order may provide a fitting framework for it. The common salutation and the Kyrie (found in most Anglican Daily Offices) here lead to the Lord's Prayer and are familiar enough to evoke response without the need for books.

The fixed prayers, of which one or more may be chosen, are in the first two cases well-known prayers used at the hours when Christ hung on the Cross. The third prayer, for the unity of the Church, is retrieved from page 49 of the Prayer Book. It was in many medieval Missals. The third prayer will be found also in the Devotions for Midday.

In many noonday gatherings extended intercessions are bidden and offered. Provision is made for this by rubric, after which the Order closes with a customary act of praise.

It will be noted that this Order and that for the Close of Day make use of the term "Leader" instead of "Minister." This is intended to avoid the confusion the word "Minister" can occasion by being used properly to include ordained and non-ordained officiants in the liturgy. It makes it clear that it is entirely appropriate for these two Orders to be conducted by a lay member of the group, even if a clergyman is present.

An Order of Prayer for the Close of Day

The instinct of the framers of a succession of Prayer Books was not to provide an office of Compline, though it has been added to many modern Anglican books. For the ordinary parish or clergyman, Morning and Evening Prayer, was intended to suffice. Moreover it could be, and often has been, contended that the usual form of Compline exhibits some of the defects which the Preface to the first Prayer Book called attention to—repetition, consequent lack of progression, failure to provide for sustained reading of Scripture. Furthermore, the traditional Office has an overemphasis on concern for the security of the group using the Office.

There are, however, many situations in modern church experience where a quiet Office at the end of the day is desirable. At conferences, particularly those lasting for several days, at summer camps for young people, a service in the late afternoon or early evening is often not practicable. It is a time usually of strenuous activity, of climactic business, of dinners and meetings and very often of dispersal. It is, nonetheless, desirable, where possible, to have Evening Prayer. But late in the evening, in informal settings, out of doors or in dormitories, it is often more practicable to be able to use a more flexible Order with a different "atmosphere" suited to the setting, mood, and attention span of the participants.

The Commission considered the inclusion of a form which would provide for great informality of structure, of music, and of reading. It seemed unlikely that this could be put into the kind of "Order" that would find a place in the Prayer Book or would, if produced, provide anything that could not be done better on the spot to suit the conditions, the personnel and the resources.

The Order suggested is, therefore, a recognizable revision and modification of Compline with a sufficient number of reminiscent and beloved features. Many modern forms follow the accustomed order, and attention has been given to the separation and progression of parts—introduction, penitence, Scripture framed in acts of praise, common prayer, an intercession, an evening Collect, and the Nunc Dimittis with antiphons. Some of the reiteration, especially that which seemed overly self-concerned, has been removed. An intercession for people who work at night was suggested by the Commission as an appropriate special intention at the service.

Three passages from the Psalter are printed in the text to obviate the need of turning to the Prayer Book if the form is printed separately, but other Psalms are suggested so that with regular use monotony may be avoided. The parts that require a book may be omitted. On such occasions, obviously, familiar versions of the Lord's Prayer and the Nunc Dimittis would be substituted until such time as the new translations become known.

Like all liturgical forms, such an Office can be judged only by use and it is commended for trial in the hope that it may be welcomed where occasion arises and where other existing forms of Compline do not fill the need.

The Daily Devotions

These consist of a page of general directions which are intended to give guidance about resources. The Devotions might give a framework for the many families which use the *Forward and Response*[18] manuals daily, or need help in finding an alternative plan for systematic reading of the Bible together. The Devotions themselves are however, kept brief and in clear outline, so that each could, for example, be printed on a card to be slipped into the pocket, or another book, or could be committed to memory for use by an individual away from home. At noonday a brief invariable Reading has been supplied with this in mind.

As was said above, each Devotion has some contact with the corresponding Office: the Creed and one of the Collects from Morning Prayer in the morning;

---

18. *Forward Day by Day*, and *Response*, published by Forward Movement Publications, Cincinnati, Ohio.

the Reading and the Prayer for Unity at noon; in the evening, the Nunc Dimittis and the Evening Collect.

It is hoped that if these Devotions are put in an easily accessible place in the Prayer Book they may find a wide use when participation in the Daily Offices is not possible. As part of the Prayer Book they might, because of their brevity and simplicity, find a great deal of use It is recognized that the Prayer Book is a Book of *Common* Prayer, intended for corporate use, but for most people of the Church it serves as their only book of devotions, public and private. If these Devotions were in the Prayer Book they would be of great help to patients in hospitals and "shut-ins." The forms provided are intended to relate private prayer to the daily public prayer offered by the Church, to afford a means of contact with it and to lead to further participation in corporate worship.

Conclusion

Our physical, emotional, and social systems follow a twenty-four hour cycle. This cycle normally provides an alternation of fatigue and rest, hunger and eating, work and leisure, which becomes basic to our consciousness of ourselves and our world. Man must relate himself to the day and accept the discipline of it We must begin every day with the will to make it a meaningful and useful day; but we must also be content to accept the close of the day in spite of the awareness that we may have accomplished little. We must be able to sleep with reasonable confidence that we will not be attacked by enemies, beasts, dreams, or demons—yet we must be wise enough to take reasonable precautions for ourselves and others. Finally, we must not be surprised that a day will come when we do not awake. A balanced and fully human life thus demands that we accept the discipline of living day by day, while not forgetting the necessity of long-range planning in many particular matters. We must have the faith that the day is good, and thankfully receive the daily bread our heavenly Father gives.

Trial use of the forms presented in this Study for both public and private prayer should be evaluated against the background of the Jewish and Christian tradition which takes seriously this daily cycle of life, and embodies it in a daily cycle of prayer.

Appendix
A Note on the ICET Texts

When the Roman Catholic Church decided at the Second Vatican Council to translate its liturgy into contemporary vernaculars, it seemed to many an opportune time for an ecumenical endeavor to develop common texts for those liturgical formularies which all English-speaking Christians use in their corporate worship. The initiative for such an endeavor was taken by members of the

Lutheran Church—Missouri Synod, who called an informal meeting of representatives of the liturgical commissions of the Lutheran, Roman Catholic, Episcopal, and Presbyterian Churches in the United States.

Out of this meeting was formed a group known as the Consultation on Common Texts. During the years 1967-69, the group held several meetings in Chicago and Washington, and produced new versions in contemporary English of the Lord's Prayer, the Nicene and Apostles' Creeds, the *Gloria in excelsis*, and the *Sanctus*. Though the group itself was an informal and unofficial one, it was, nonetheless, made up of official representatives from the Inter-Lutheran Commission on Worship, the Bishops' Committee on Liturgy of the Roman Catholic Church in America, and the Commission on Worship of the Consultation on Church Union (including two members of the Standing Liturgical Commission of the Episcopal Church).

The texts of this group were sent to the liturgical commissions of the various Churches for their comments and suggestions; and early drafts of these texts were included in *An Order of Worship for the Proclamation of the Word of God and the Celebration of the Lord's Supper* (Cincinnati: Forward Movement Publications, 1968), prepared by the Consultation on Church Union.

Meanwhile the International Committee on English in the Liturgy (ICEL) — an official body of the Roman Catholic Church charged with producing vernacular versions of the revised Roman liturgy for use in all English-speaking countries — invited members of the American group and scholars from the several Churches of the British Isles to meet in London in the spring of 1969. This new body, the International Consultation on English Texts (ICET), met again in London in the fall of 1969 and in the spring of 1970.

The International Consultation on English Texts consists of members drawn from the official liturgical or worship commissions of the following Churches: 1) The Roman Catholic Church—members of the Advisory Committee of its International Committee on English in the Liturgy, including representatives from England, Ireland, the United States, Canada, and Australia; 2) The Anglican Churches—representatives of the liturgical commissions of the Church of England, the Episcopal Church of Scotland, the Church of Ireland, the Church in Wales, and the Episcopal Church in the United States; 3) The Inter-Lutheran Commission on Worship, which comprises members of the Lutheran Church of America, the American Lutheran Church, and the Lutheran Church—Missouri Synod; and 4) The (Presbyterian) Church of Scotland; and the English Methodist, Presbyterian, Congregational, and Baptist Churches.

The proposals of ICET have now been published in a booklet, *Prayers We Have in Common* (London: Geoffrey Chapman, 1970; Philadelphia: Fortress Press, 1970); and the several Churches of the English-speaking world are invited to use these texts on an experimental basis in the new liturgies which many of them are preparing. The International Consultation itself neither has, nor claims to have, the authority to put any of these texts into use. It fully recognizes that this is the responsibility of the official agencies which the Churches have for providing or recommending new liturgies for their own constituencies.

The texts in *Prayers We Have in Common* are grouped in two categories. Category A consists of those texts which have gone through several stages, having been revised in the light of criticisms and suggestions from individuals and members of worship commissions in all parts of the world. Further revision of texts in this category will not be considered until after a two- or three-year period of experimental use. These are the texts of the Lord's Prayer, the two Creeds, the *Gloria in excelsis*, the *Sanctus* and *Benedictus*, and the *Gloria Patri*. The texts in Category B are those now being reviewed for possible further revision. These include the *Sursum Corda*, the *Agnus Dei*, and the Canticles of the Daily Office.

The texts of Category A have been accepted for use by the Roman Catholic Committee (except for the Lord's Prayer and the Apostles' Creed). The Inter-Lutheran Commission on Worship has accepted them for their new rite which is soon to be published; and the United Presbyterian Church, U.S.A., has them under consideration in their work of revising *The Book of Common Worship*. Among Anglicans, the Liturgical Commissions of the Church of England and of the Episcopal Church in the United States have acted to include them in their proposed services in contemporary English; and other Anglican provinces will be considering them in the near future. In those Protestant Churches which require no official or synodical action to authorize texts, a number of pastors have already introduced these new versions to their congregations. Within a few years we should know whether the new texts have "caught on" and whether they are serving the ecumenical purpose for which they are intended.

The Standing Liturgical Commission of the Episcopal Church has decided to put the new ICET texts in all proposed services that use contemporary English. But the new version of the Nicene Creed will be printed in all services, whether in traditional or contemporary style. The *filioque* clause ("and the Son"), however, has been omitted, as in the *Liturgy of the Lord's Supper*, since it is not part of the original Greek text. The International Consultation was unanimous in its opinion that the *filioque* clause should be optional, and that the several Churches might include it or exclude it without any question regarding their orthodoxy.

Morning and Evening Prayer

Concerning the Service

In the Offices of Morning and Evening Prayer, the term "Minister" is used to denote the person, whether a clergyman or a lay person, leading the service.

Proper Antiphons which may be used as refrains with the Invitatory Psalm will be found on pages 144-145.

Antiphons in the words of the opening Sentences given in the Offices, or other words of Scripture, may be used with the Psalms and with the Gospel Canticles.

The Apostles' Creed is normally recited at both Morning and Evening Prayer on Sundays and other major Feasts (except when the Eucharist with its own Creed is to follow). It is desirable that the Creed be recited in at least one of the Offices on other days.

At celebrations of the Holy Eucharist, the Order for Morning or Evening Prayer may be used in place of all that precedes the Offertory, provided that a Lesson from the Gospel is always included and that the Intercession conforms to the directions on page 128.

Additional Directions and Suggestions are on pages 127-128.

Morning and Evening Prayer
First Order

The Minister begins the service with one or more of these Sentences of Scripture, or of those on pages 145-146.

The Sentences in italics may be used as responses, by the people or as separate Sentences.

Grace to you and peace from God our Father and the Lord Jesus Christ. [Romans 1:7]

Thanks be to God who gives us the victory through our Lord Jesus Christ. [1 Corinthians 15:57]

Lord, I love the habitation of thy house, and the place where thy glory dwells. [Psalm 26:8]

Let my prayer be counted as incense before thee, and the lifting up of my hands as an, evening sacrifice. [Psalm 141:2]

OCCASIONS OF THANKSGIVING

O give thanks to the Lord, call on his name, make known his deeds among the people.
Sing to him, sing praises to him, tell of all his wonderful works. [Psalm 105:1, 2]

PENITENTIAL

Seek the Lord while he may be found, call upon him while he is near; let the wicked forsake his way, and the unrighteous man his thoughts.
Let him return to the Lord that he may have mercy upon him, and to our God, for he will abundantly pardon. [Isaiah 55:6, 7]

The following Confession of Sin, or the form on page 130, may then be said; or the office may continue at once with "Lord, open thou our lips" all still standing.

Confession of Sin

Minister

Let us humbly confess our sins unto Almighty God.

SILENCE may be kept

Minister and People together, all kneeling

Almighty and most merciful Father, We have erred and strayed from thy ways like lost sheep. We have followed too much the devices and desires of our own hearts. We have offended against thy holy laws. We have left undone those things which we ought to have done; And we have done those things which we ought not to have done. But thou, O Lord, have mercy upon us; Spare thou those who confess their faults; Restore thou those who are penitent; According to thy promises declared unto mankind in Christ Jesus our Lord; And grant that hereafter we may live a godly, righteous and sober life, To the glory of thy holy Name. Amen.

The Minister says this prayer.

Almighty God have mercy on us, forgive us all our sins, through our Lord Jesus Christ; strengthen us in all goodness, and by the power of the Holy Spirit, keep us in eternal life. *Amen.*

If a Bishop or Priest is present, he may substitute an absolution.

The Psalter

All stand

Minister	O Lord, open thou our lips,
People	And our mouth shall show forth thy praise.
Minister and People	

    Glory be to the Father, and to the Son, and to the Holy Spirit; as it was in the beginning, is now and ever shall be, world without end. Amen.

    Except in Lent Alleluia.

In the morning shall be and in the evening may be sung or said

VENITE (Psalm 95:1-7; 96:9, 13)

O come let us sing unto the Lord;
    let us heartily rejoice in the strength of our salvation.
Let us come before his presence with thanksgiving;
    and show ourselves glad in him with psalms.

For the Lord is a great God;
    and a great King above all gods.
In his hand are all the corners of the earth;
    and the strength of the hills is his also.
The sea is his and he made it
    and his hands prepared the dry land.

O come let us worship and fall down
    and kneel before the Lord our Maker.
For he is the Lord our God;
    and we are the people of his pasture,
    and the sheep of his hand.

O worship the Lord in the beauty of holiness;
    let the whole earth stand in awe of him.
For he cometh, for he cometh to judge the earth;
    and with righteousness to judge the world,
    and the peoples with his truth.

JUBILATE (Psalm 100)

O be joyful in the Lord all ye lands:
    serve the Lord with gladness,
    and come before his presence with a song.

Be ye sure that the Lord he is God;
it is he that hath made us and not we ourselves;
    we are his people and the sheep of his pasture.

O go your way into his gates with thanksgiving,
and into his courts with praise;
    be thankful unto him and speak good of his Name.

For the Lord is gracious, his mercy is everlasting;
    and his truth endureth from generation to generation.

In the evening, for the Invitatory, the Hymn "O Gracious Light" may be used. And during Easter Season, the Easter Canticle may be used for the Invitatory both in the morning and in the evening.

Then follows THE PSALM OR PSALMS APPOINTED

And at the end of the Psalter the Minister and People sing or say together

Glory be to the Father, and to the Son, and to the Holy Spirit; as it was in the beginning, is now and ever shall be world without end. Amen.

The Word of God

Then is read a selection from the Old Testament and a selection from the New Testament.

And NOTE:
1. *Silence may be kept after each reading;*
2. *One of the readings may be omitted;*
3. *A Canticle from those provided on pages 146-159 may be sung or said after each reading; but there shall be one at the conclusion of the Scripture.*

Here, or in one of the other places appointed,

a SERMON *or* MEDITATION *may follow.*

THE APOSTLES' CREED

Minister and People together, all standing

I believe in God, the Father almighty,
    creator of heaven and earth.
I believe in Jesus Christ, his only Son, our Lord.
    He was conceived by the power of the Holy Spirit
        and born of the Virgin Mary.
    He suffered under Pontius Pilate,
        was crucified, died, and was buried.
    He descended to the dead.
    On the third day he rose again.
    He ascended into heaven,
        and is seated at the right hand of the Father.
    He will come again to judge the living and the dead.
I believe in the Holy Spirit,
    the holy catholic Church,
    the communion of saints,
    the forgiveness of sins,

the resurrection of the body,
and the life everlasting.

Instead of the above, the text of the Creed in the Book of Common Prayer may be used.

The Prayers

The prayers follow, the People standing or kneeling.

Minister	The Lord be with you.
People	And also with you.
Minister	Let us pray.

In place of the following the form of the the Lord's Prayer in the Second Order may be used.

Minister and People

Our Father, who art in heaven,
    hallowed be thy Name,
    thy Kingdom come,
    thy will be done,
        on earth as it is in heaven.
Give us this day our daily bread.

And forgive us our trespasses,
as we forgive those who trespass against us.

And lead us not into temptation,
but deliver us from evil.

For thine is the kingdom, and the power,
and the glory, for ever and ever. Amen.

Then follows

Minister	Show us thy mercy, O Lord:
People	And grant us thy salvation.
Minister	Clothe thy ministers with righteousness:
People	Let thy people sing with joy.
Minister	Give peace, O Lord, in all the world:
People	For only in thee can we live in safety.
Minister	Lord, keep this Nation under thy care:
People	And guide us in the way of justice and truth.
Minister	Let thy way be known upon earth:
People	Thy saving health among all nations.

Minister	Let not the needy, O Lord, be forgotten:
People	Nor the hope of the poor be taken away.
Minister	Create in us clean hearts, O God:
People	And sustain us with thy Holy Spirit.

Or this:

Minister	Save thy people, Lord, and bless thine inheritance:
People	Govern and uphold them, now and always.
Minister	Day by day we bless thee.
People	We praise thy Name for ever.
Minister	Lord, keep us from all sin today.
People	Have mercy on us, Lord, have mercy.
Minister	Lord, show us thy love and mercy;
People	For we put our trust in thee.
Minister	In thee, Lord, is our hope:
People	May we never be confounded.

The Minister then says

THE COLLECT OF THE DAY

On Fridays and Saturdays, not Holy Days, the Collect for Good Friday and Holy Saturday[i] *may be substituted for the above.*

In the morning there follows

O heavenly Father, in whom we live and move and have our being: We humbly pray thee so to guide and govern us by thy Holy Spirit, that in all the cares and occupations of life, we may never forget thee, but remember that we are ever walking in thy sight; through Jesus Christ our Lord. *Amen.*

Or this

---

[i] [Ed. note: The section in the introduction clarifies that these are the "revised collects" and thus the Good Friday and Holy Saturday collects from *Prayer Book Studies* 19. The first is: "Almighty God, we beseech thee graciously to behold this thy family, for which our Lord Jesus Christ was content to be betrayed, and given up into the hands of sinful men, and to suffer death upon the Cross: who now liveth and reigneth with thee and the Holy Spirit, one God, for ever and ever. Amen."

The second is: "Most Gracious God, who hast baptized us into the death of your Son our Savior Jesus Christ: Grant in thy mercy that we, being dead to sin, may be buried with him; that through the grave and gate of death, we may be raised up with him unto newness of life; through Jesus Christ our Lord. Amen."]

O Lord, our heavenly Father, Almighty and Everlasting God, who hast safely brought us to the beginning of this day; Defend us in the same with thy mighty power; and grant that this day we fall into no sin, neither run into any kind of danger; but that we, being ordered by thy governance, may always do what is righteous in thy sight; through Jesus Christ our Lord. *Amen.*

In the evening is said

O God, from whom all holy desires, all good counsels, and all just works do proceed: Give unto thy servants that peace which the world cannot give; that our hearts may be set to obey thy commandments, and also that by thee, we, being defended from the fear of enemies, may pass our time in rest and quietness, through the merits of Jesus Christ our Savior.
Amen.

or this:

Lighten our darkness, we beseech thee, O Lord; and by thy great mercy defend us from all perils and dangers of this night; for the love of thy only Son, our Savior, Jesus Christ.
Amen.

The following Collect is always added:

Almighty and everlasting God, by whose Spirit the whole body of the Church is governed and sanctified: Receive our supplications and prayers, which we offer before thee for all members of thy holy Church, that every member of the same, in his vocation and ministry, may truly and godly serve thee; through our Lord and Savior Jesus Christ. *Amen.*

Here may follow a Hymn or Anthem.

Authorized Intercessions and Thanksgivings may follow.

Before the close of the Office one or both of the following may be used:

A GENERAL THANKSGIVING

Minister and People

Almighty God, Father of all mercies,
we thine unworthy servants;
do give thee most humble and hearty thanks
for all thy goodness and loving-kindness to us,
and to all men.

We bless thee for our creation, preservation,
and all the blessings of this life;
but above all for thine inestimable love
in the redemption of the world by our Lord Jesus Christ;
for the means of grace, and for the hope of glory.

And, we beseech thee, give us that due sense
of all thy mercies,
that our hearts may be unfeignedly thankful;
And that we show forth thy praise,
not only with our lips, but in our lives,
by giving up our selves to thy service,
and by walking before thee
in holiness and righteousness
all our days;
through Jesus Christ our Lord,
to whom, with thee and the Holy Spirit,
be all honor and glory, world without end.
Amen.

A PRAYER OF ST. CHRYSOSTOM

Minister and People

Almighty God,
who hast given us grace at this time
with one accord to make our common supplications unto thee;
and dost promise, through thy well-beloved Son,
that when two or three shall agree in his Name
thou wilt grant their requests:
Fulfill now, O Lord, the desires and petitions of thy servants,
as may be best for them;
Granting us in this world knowledge of thy truth,
and in the world to come life everlasting;
Through the same thy Son, Jesus Christ our Lord.
Amen.

The Minister then concludes the Office with one of the following:

> The grace of our Lord Jesus Christ, and the love of God, and the fellowship of the Holy Spirit, be with us all evermore. *Amen.* [2 Corinthians 13:4]
> May the God of hope fill us with all joy and peace in believing through the power of the Holy Spirit. *Amen.* [Romans 15:13]

Glory to God whose power, working in us, can do infinitely more than we can ask or imagine: Glory to him from generation to generation, in the Church, and in Christ Jesus, for ever and ever. *Amen.*
[Ephesians 3:20, 21]

Additional Directions and Suggestions for First Order and Second Order[ii]

Additional Directions and Suggestions

The Psalm or Psalms to be used in the Office are those appointed in the Lectionary or the daily course in the Psalter of the Book of Common Prayer; or chosen from some other approved scheme, or from a Selection of Psalms for Special Occasions.

The Readings from Scripture are to be taken from an authorized Lectionary, and if the Office is read only once in the day may be taken from either the morning or evening course. On Sundays and Holy Days, the Readings may be taken from the Proper for the Eucharist; and, when desired, there may be three Readings.

Any of the Readings may be lengthened at the discretion of the Minister. Note that the Old Testament Reading may be from the Apocrypha.

Readings are announced in one of the following forms (the titles are given by way of illustration):

Old Testament:	The [First] Reading is from . . .
	. . . the Book of Genesis
	. . . the first Book of Kings
	. . . the Book of the prophet Amos
New Testament:	The [Second] Reading is from . . .
	. . . The Gospel according to Matthew
	. . . The Acts of the Apostles
	. . . The Epistle of Paul to the Romans
	. . . The Epistle to the Hebrews
	. . . The first Epistle of Peter
	. . . The Revelation of John

Or, Hear the Word of God from . . .

At the end of each Reading may be said: Here ends the Reading.

In special circumstances, in place of a Canticle, a Hymn may be sung.

[ii] [Ed. note: The placement of this section here is likely a mistake: the Table of Contents has it placed after the Second Order, and it would more logically follow after both rather than between the two orders.]

One or two versions of each of the Canticles are printed with the Orders of Service. Other translations may be used when they are associated with particular musical settings.

The Sermon or Meditation is optional. One place for it is indicated in the text. Other appropriate places are

> After the Hymn or Anthem after The Prayers (the Lord's Prayer and Collects)
> After the Intercessions and Thanksgivings (see pages 123 and 133)
> After the Office

The Meditation may, on occasion, take the form of readings from non-Biblical Christian literature.

When Morning or Evening Prayer is used as the Ministry of the Word at the Eucharist, the Nicene Creed may take the place of the Apostles' Creed; and the Intercessions shall include prayer for

> The Universal Church and all its members
> The Nation and all in authority
> The welfare of the world
> The concerns of the local community
> Those who suffer and those in any trouble
> The departed (with commemoration of a saint when appropriate).

The forms of the Intercession given in *Prayer Book Studies 21* are recommended.

When Communion is not to follow, an Offering may be received and presented at the time of the Hymn or Anthem which precedes the Intercessions and Thanksgivings; or immediately before the devotions which conclude the Office (see pages 125 and 135).

In the Intercessions and Thanksgivings, opportunity may be given for the members of the congregation to express intentions or objects of prayer and thanksgiving, either at the bidding, or in the course of the prayer; and opportunity may be given for silent prayer.

Concerning the Service

In the Offices of Morning and Evening Prayer, the term "Minister" is used to denote the person, whether a clergyman or a lay person, leading the service.

Proper Antiphons which may be used as refrains with the Invitatory Psalm will be found on pages 144-145.

Antiphons in the words of the opening Sentences given in the Offices, or other words of Scripture, may be used with the Psalms and with the Gospel Canticles.

The Apostles' Creed is normally recited at both Morning and Evening Prayer on Sundays and other major Feasts (except when the Eucharist with its own Creed is to follow). It is desirable that the Creed be recited in at least one of the Offices on other days.

At celebrations of the Holy Eucharist, the Order for Morning or Evening Prayer may be used in place of all that precedes the Offertory, provided that a Lesson from the Gospel is always included and that the Intercession conforms to the directions on page 128.

Additional Directions and Suggestions are on pages 127-128.

Morning and Evening Prayer
Second Order

The Minister begins the service with one or more of these Sentences of Scripture, or of those on pages 145-146.

The Sentences in italics may be used as responses by the people or as separate Sentences.

Grace to you and peace from God our Father and the Lord Jesus Christ. [Romans 1:7]

Thanks be to God who gives us the victory through our Lord Jesus Christ. [1 Corinthians 15:57]

Lord, I love the splendor of your house, the place where your glory dwells. [Psalm 26:8]

Let my prayer rise up before you like incense, the lifting of my hands as an evening offering. [Psalm 141:2]

OCCASIONS OF THANKSGIVING

Give thanks to the Lord, call on his Name, make his deeds known among the peoples.
Sing to him, sing praises to him, tell of all his wonderful works. [Psalm 105: 1, 2]

PENITENTIAL

Seek the Lord while he may be found, call upon him while he is near; let the wicked forsake his way, and the unrighteous man his thoughts.
Let him return to the Lord and he will have mercy on him, and to our God, for he will abundantly pardon. [Isaiah 55:6, 7]

The following Confession of Sin, or the form on page 120, may then. be said; or the office may continue at once with "Lord, open our lips," all still standing.

Confession of Sin

    Minister

Dear friends in Christ, here in the presence of Almighty God, let us kneel in silence, and with humble and obedient hearts confess our sins, so that we may obtain forgiveness by his infinite goodness and mercy.

    SILENCE may be kept

    Minister and People together, all kneeling

Most merciful God,
we confess that we have sinned against you
in thought, word and deed:
we have not loved you with our whole heart;
we have not loved our neighbors as ourselves.
We pray you of your mercy
        forgive what we have been,
        amend what we are,
        direct what we shall be;
that we may delight in your will,
and walk in your ways,
through Jesus Christ our Lord. Amen.

    The Minister says this prayer

Almighty God have mercy on us, forgive us all our sins, through our Lord Jesus Christ; strengthen us in all goodness, and by the power of the Holy Spirit, keep us in eternal life. *Amen.*

    If a Bishop or Priest is present, he may substitute an absolution.

The Psalter

    All stand

    Minister   Lord, open our lips.
    People   And our mouth shall proclaim your praise.
    Minister and People
        Glory to the Father, and to the Son, and to the Holy Spirit:
        as in the beginning, so now and for ever. Amen.
        Except in Lent Alleluia.

In the morning shall be, and in the evening may be, sung or said

VENITE (Psalm 95:1-7)

Come, let us sing to the LORD;
let us shout for joy to the Rock of our salvation.
Let us come before his presence with thanksgiving; and raise a loud shout to him with psalms.

For the LORD is a great God;
    and a great King above all gods.
In his hand are the caverns of the earth;
    and the heights of the hills are his also.
The sea is his, for he made it;
    and his hands have molded the dry land.

Come, let us bow down, and bend the knee,
    and kneel before the LORD, our Maker.
For he is our God;
and we are the people of his pasture, and the sheep of his hand.
O that today you would hearken to his voice!

JUBILATE (Psalm 100)

Be joyful in the LORD, all you lands;
    serve the LORD with gladness,
    and come before his presence with a song.
Know this: The LORD himself is God;
    he himself has made us, and we are his;
    we are his people and the sheep of his pasture.
Enter his gates with thanksgiving;
go into his courts with praise;
    give thanks to him, and call upon his Name.
For the LORD is good;
his mercy is everlasting;
    and his faithfulness endures from age to age.

In the evening, for the Invitatory, the Hymn "O Gracious Light" may be used. And during Easter Season, the Easter Canticle may be used for the Invitatory both in the morning and in the evening.

Then follows: THE PSALM OR PSALMS APPOINTED

And at the end of the Psalter the Minister and People sing or say together

Glory to the Father, and to the Son, and to the Holy Spirit:
    as in the beginning, so now, and for ever. Amen.

The Word of God

Then is read a selection from the Old Testament and a selection from the New Testament.

And NOTE:
1. *Silence may be kept after each reading;*
2. *One of the readings may be omitted;*
3. *A Canticle from those provided on pages 146–159 may be sung or said after each reading; but there shall be one at the conclusion of the Scripture.*

Here, or in one of the other places appointed,

a SERMON or MEDITATION may follow.

THE APOSTLES' CREED

Minister and People together, all standing

I believe in God, the Father almighty,
 creator of heaven and earth.
I believe in Jesus Christ, his only Son, our Lord.
 He was conceived by the power of the Holy Spirit
  and born of the Virgin Mary.
 He suffered under Pontius Pilate,
  was crucified, died, and was buried.
 He descended to the dead.
 On the third day he rose again.
 He ascended into heaven,
  and is seated at the right hand of the Father.
 He will come again to judge the living and the dead.
I believe in the Holy Spirit,
 the holy catholic Church,
 the communion of saints,
 the forgiveness of sins,
 the resurrection of the body,
 and the life everlasting.

The Prayers

The prayers follow, the People standing or kneeling.

Minister	The Lord be with you.
People	And also with you.
Minister	Let us pray.

Minister and People

Our Father in heaven,
    holy be your Name,
    your kingdom come,
    your will be done,
        on earth as in heaven.
Give us today our daily bread.
Forgive us our sins,
    as we forgive those who trespass against us.
Do not bring us to the test
    but deliver us from evil.
For the kingdom, the power, and the glory, are yours
    now and for ever. Amen.

Then follows

Minister	Show us your mercy, O Lord:
People	And grant us your salvation.
Minister	Clothe your ministers with righteousness:
People	Let your people sing with joy.
Minister	Give peace, O Lord, in all the world:
People	For only in you can we live in safety.
Minister	Lord, keep this Nation under your care:
People	And guide us in the way of justice and truth.
Minister	Let your way be known upon earth:
People	Your saving health among all nations.
Minister	Let not the needy, O Lord, be forgotten:
People	Nor the hope of the poor be taken away.
Minister	Create in us clean hearts, O God:
People	And sustain us with your Holy Spirit.

Or this:

Minister	Save your people, Lord, and bless your inheritance:
People	Govern and uphold them, now and always.
Minister	Day by day we bless you.
People	We praise your Name for ever.
Minister	Lord, keep us from all sin today.

People	Have mercy on us, Lord, have mercy.
Minister	Lord, show us your love and mercy;
People	For we put our trust in you.
Minister	In you, Lord, is our hope:
People	May we never be confounded.

The Minister then says

THE COLLECT OF THE DAY

On Fridays and Saturdays, not Holy Days, the Collect for Good Friday and Holy Saturday[iii] may be substituted for the above.

In the morning there follows

Heavenly Father, in you we live and move and have our being: We humbly pray you so to guide and govern us by your Holy Spirit, that in all the cares and occupations of our life we may not forget you, but remember that we are ever walking in your sight; through Jesus Christ our Lord. *Amen.*

Or this

Lord God, almighty and everlasting Father, you have brought us in safety to this new day: Preserve us with your mighty power, that we may not fall into sin, nor be overcome in adversity; and in all we do, direct us to the fulfilling of your purpose; through Jesus Christ our Lord. *Amen.*

In the evening is said

Most holy God, the source of all good desires, all right judgements, and all just works: Give to us, your servants, that peace which the world cannot give, that our minds may be fixed on the doing of your will, and that we, being delivered from

---

[iii] [Ed. note: The section in the introduction clarifies that these are the "revised collects" and thus the Good Friday and Holy Saturday collects from *Prayer Book Studies* 19. The first is: "Almighty God, we pray you to graciously behold this your family, for whom our Lord Jesus Christ was content to be betrayed, and given up into the hands of sinful men, and to suffer death upon the Cross: who now lives and reigns with you and the Holy Spirit, one God, for ever and ever. Amen."

The second is: "Most Gracious God, as we have been baptized into the death of your Son our Savior Jesus Christ, so in your mercy may we be dead to sin and buried with him: that from the grave and gate of death, we may be raised up with him to newness of life; through Jesus Christ our Lord. Amen."]

the fear of enemies, may live in peace and quietness, through the mercies of Jesus Christ our Savior.
Amen.

The following Collect is always added:

Almighty and everlasting God, by whose Spirit the whole company of your faithful people is governed and sanctified: Receive our prayers which we now offer before you for all members of your holy Church, that in their vocation and ministry they may truly and devoutly serve you, to the glory of your Name; through our Lord and Savior Jesus Christ. *Amen.*

Here may follow a Hymn or Anthem.

Authorized Intercessions and Thanksgivings may follow.

Before the close of the Office one or both of the following may be used:

A GENERAL THANKSGIVING

Minister and People

Almighty God, Father of all mercies,
we your unworthy servants give you humble thanks
for all your goodness and loving-kindness to us,
and to all men.

We bless you for our creation, preservation,
and all the blessings of this life;
but above all for your incomparable love
in the redemption of the world by our Lord Jesus Christ;
for the means of grace, and for the hope of glory.

And, we pray, give us such an awareness of your mercies,
that with truly thankful hearts
we may make known your praise,
not only with our lips, but in our lives,
by giving up our selves to your service,
and by walking before you in holiness and righteousness
all our days;
through Jesus Christ our Lord,
to whom, with you and the Holy Spirit,
be all honor and glory throughout all ages.
Amen.

A PRAYER OF ST. CHRYSOSTOM

Minister and People

Almighty God,
by your grace we have come together at this time
to offer you our common petitions;
and you have promised by your Son Jesus Christ
that when two or three are gathered in his Name
he will be in the midst of them.
Fulfill now, O Lord, our desires and petitions,
as may be best for us;
Granting us in this world knowledge of your truth,
and in the world to come life everlasting;
Through your Son, Jesus Christ our Lord.
Amen.

The Minister then concludes the Office with one of the following:

The grace of our Lord Jesus Christ, and the love of God, and the fellowship of the Holy Spirit, be with us all evermore. *Amen.* [2 Corinthians 13:4]

May the God of hope fill us with all joy and peace in believing through the power of the Holy Spirit. *Amen.* [Romans 15:13]

Glory to God whose power, working in us, can do infinitely more than we can ask or imagine: Glory to him from generation to generation, in the Church, and in Christ Jesus, for ever and ever. *Amen.* [Ephesians 3:20, 21]

[Music for Preces and Suffrages]

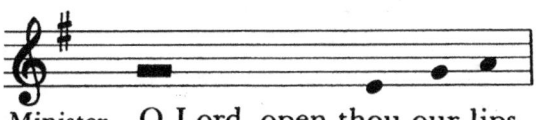

Minister O Lord, open thou our lips,

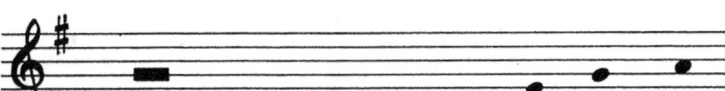

People And our mouth shall show forth thy praise.

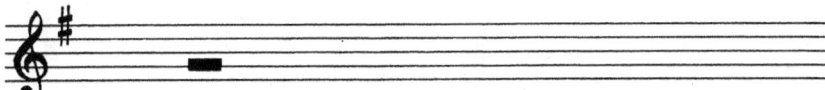

All together Glory be to the Father, and to the Son, and to

the Ho - ly Spir - it; as it was in the beginning, is

now and ever shall be, world without end. A - men.

Except in Lent Al - le - lu - ia.

Second Order
Opening Preces

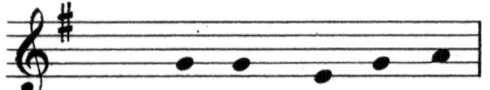
Minister Lord, open our lips.

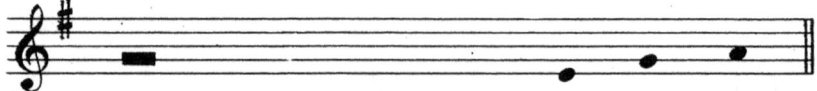
People And our mouth shall proclaim your praise.

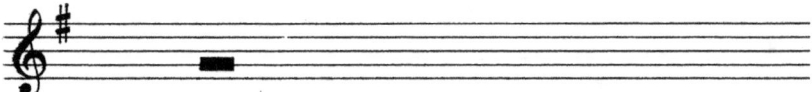
All together Glory to the Father, and to the Son, and

to the Holy Spirit; as in the beginning,

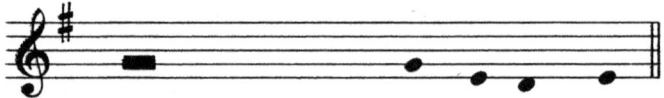
so now, and for ever. Amen.

Except in Lent Alleluia.

Both Orders of Service

The Suffrages

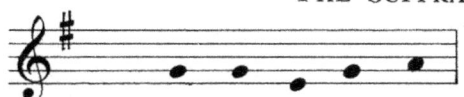

Minister The Lord be with you.

Answer And al - so with you.   Minister Let us pray.

Minister and People together

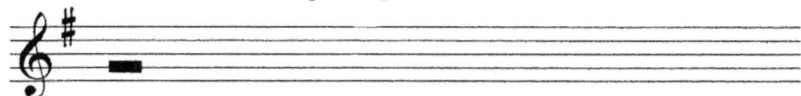

Our Father who art in heaven . . .

OR Our Father in heaven,
    holy be your Name,
    your kingdom come,
    your will be done,
        on earth as in heaven.
    Give us today our daily bread.
    Forgive us our sins
        as we forgive those who sin against us.
    Do not bring us to the test
        but deliver us from evil.
    For the kingdom, the power, and the glory are yours

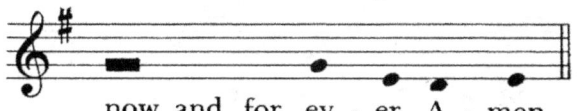

now and for ev - er. A - men.
for ever and ev - er. A - men.

The Versicles may be sung by the Minister or a Cantor, the Choir and Congregation joining in the Responses.

The Daily Office 141

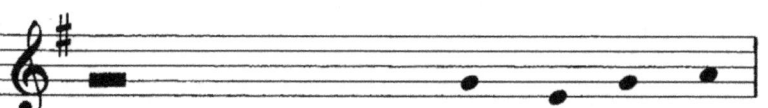
V. Lord, keep this Nation un - der your care:
                                                          thy

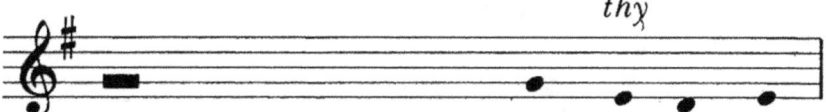
R. And guide us in the way of jus - tice and truth.

V. Let your way be known up - on earth:
            thy

R. Your saving health a - mong all na - tions.
            Thy

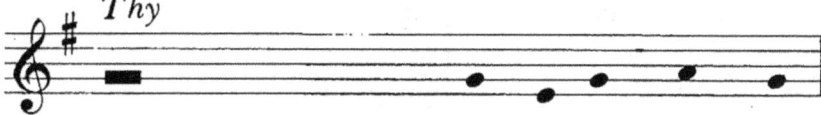
V. Let not the needy, O Lord, be for - got - ten:

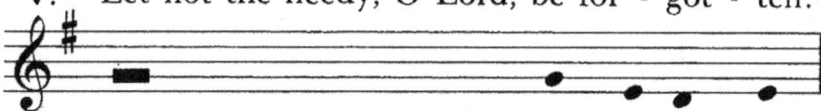
R. Nor the hope of the poor be ta - ken a - way.

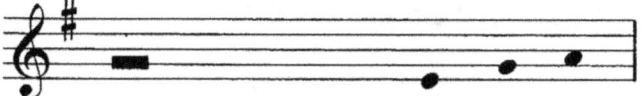
V. Create in us clean hearts, O God:

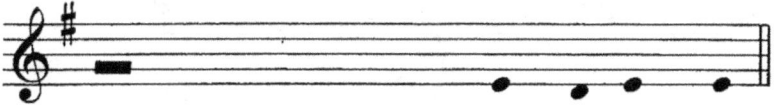
R. And sustain us with your Ho - ly Spir - it.
                              thy

Or else these Versicles and Responses

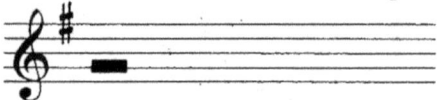

V. Save your people, Lord,
thy

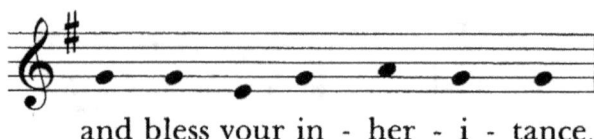

and bless your in - her - i - tance.
thine

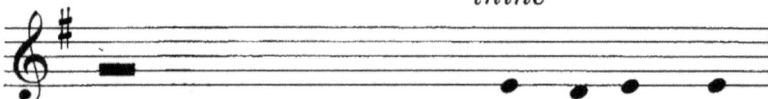

R. Govern and uphold them, now and al - ways.

V. Day by day we bless you.
thee

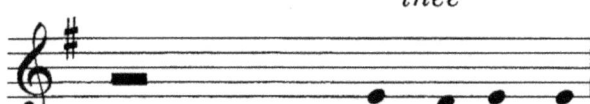

R. We praise your Name for ev - er.
thy

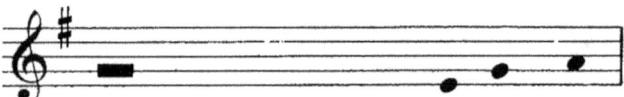

V. Lord, keep us from all sin to - day.

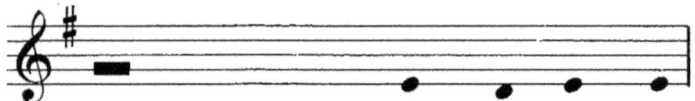

R. Have mercy on us, Lord, have mer - cy.

The Daily Office 143

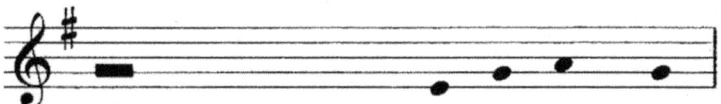

V. Lord, show us your love and mer - cy;
      thy

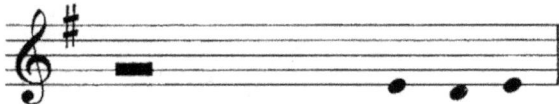

R. For we put our trust in you.
      thee

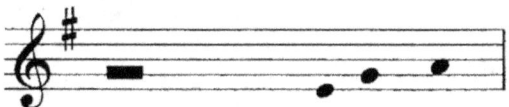

V. In you, Lord, is our hope:
      thee

R. May we never be con - foun - ded.

At the conclusion of the sung Collects, all respond

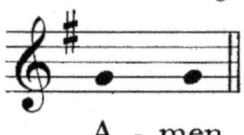

A - men.

The Invitatory Antiphons

In the seasons and on the days named the following may be sung or said with the Invitatory Psalms which begin the Psalter.

IN ADVENT

Our King and Savior now draws near: Come let us adore him. Alleluia.

IN CHRISTMAS SEASON

Unto us a child is born: Come let us adore him. Alleluia.

IN THE EPIPHANY SEASON AND ON TRANSFIGURATION

The Lord has shown forth his glory: Come let us adore him. Alleluia.

IN EASTER SEASON

Alleluia. The Lord is risen indeed: Come let us adore him. Alleluia.

ON ASCENSION DAY

Alleluia. Christ the Lord is ascended to heaven: Come let us adore him. Alleluia.

ON THE DAY OF PENTECOST

Alleluia. The Spirit of the Lord renews the face of the earth: Come let us adore him. Alleluia.

ON TRINITY SUNDAY

Father, Son, and Holy Spirit, one God: holy is his Name: Come let us adore him. Alleluia.

In Lent, the Alleluias in the following antiphons are omitted:

ON FEASTS OF THE INCARNATION

The Word was made flesh and dwelt among us: Come let us adore him. (Alleluia.)

ON OTHER FESTIVALS

The Lord is glorious in his saints: Come let us adore him. (Alleluia.)

In Easter Season, the following forms are used instead:

ON FEASTS OF THE INCARNATION

Alleluia. The Word was made flesh and dwelt among us: Come let us adore him. Alleluia.

ON OTHER FESTIVALS

Alleluia. The Lord is glorious in his saints: Come let us adore him. Alleluia.

Sentences for Seasons and Other Occasions

For use at any time at the discretion of the Minister

The Lord is in his holy temple:
Let all the earth keep silence before him. [Habakkuk 2:20]
Worship the Lord in the beauty of holiness;
Let the whole earth tremble before him. [Psalm 96:9]
God is spirit, and those who worship him must worship in spirit and truth. [John 4:24]
Let the words of my mouth and the meditation of my heart be acceptable in your sight,
O Lord, my strength and my redeemer. [Psalm 19:14]

ADVENT SEASON

In the wilderness prepare the way of the Lord:
make straight in the desert a highway for our God.
The glory of the Lord shall be revealed,
and all flesh shall see it together. [Isaiah 40:3, 5]
Rejoice: the Lord is at hand [Philippians 4:5]
Amen, Come, Lord Jesus. [Revelation 22:20]

CHRISTMAS SEASON

Behold, I bring good news of great joy which will come to all the people: for to you is born in the city of David a Savior, who is Christ the Lord. [Luke 2:10, 11]
Glory to God in the highest and on earth peace among men. [Luke 2:14]
Behold the dwelling of God is with men. He will dwell with them and they shall be his people:
God himself shall be with them, and be their God. [Revelation 21:3]

EPIPHANY SEASON

I will give you as a light to the nations, that my salvation may reach to the end of the earth. [Isaiah 49:6]
Nations shall come to your light, and kings to the brightness of your rising. [Isaiah 60:3]
If we walk in the light, as he is in the light, we have fellowship with one another:
And the blood of Jesus his Son cleanses us from all sin. [1 John 1:7]

LENT AND HOLY WEEK

Jesus said, If any man would come after me, let him deny himself and take up his cross and follow me.
For whoever would save his life will lose it; and whoever loses his life for my sake and the gospel's will save it. [Mark 8:34, 35]

All we like sheep have gone astray; we have turned every one to his own way;
And the LORD has laid on him the iniquity of us all. [Isaiah 53:6]

EASTER SEASON INCLUDING ASCENSION DAY AND THE DAY OF PENTECOST

Alleluia. He has risen. [Mark 16:6]
The Lord has risen indeed. Alleluia. [Luke 24:34]
Worthy is the Lamb who was slain, to receive power and wealth and wisdom and might and honor and glory and blessing
To him who sits on the throne and to the Lamb be blessing and honor and glory and might for ever and ever. [Revelation 5:1 2, 1 3]
God's love has been poured into our hearts.
Through the Holy Spirit who has been given to us. [Romans 5:5]

ALL SAINTS AND OTHER FESTIVALS

Since we are surrounded by so great a cloud of witnesses, let us lay aside every weight, and sin which clings so closely,
And let us run with perseverance the race which is set before us, looking to Jesus, the pioneer and perfecter of our faith. [Hebrews 12:1-2]

NATIONAL OBSERVANCES

Let the nations be glad and sing for joy.
For God judges the peoples with equity,
and guides all the nations upon earth. [Psalm 67:4]

Canticles for use after the Reading of the Scriptures

After any of the Canticles (except Benedictus es, Benedicite, Te Deum laudamus, Gloria in excelsis, and Phos hilaron) the following may be sung or said:

Glory to the Father, and to the Son, and to the Holy Spirit:
 as in the beginning, so now and for ever. Amen.
In musical settings, the following form may be used instead:

Glory to the Father, and the Son, and the Holy Spirit:
>as in the beginning, so now and for ever. Amen.

The designated places for the Canticles are suggestions only. They may be used after any reading at the discretion of the Minister.

A. After Readings from the Old Testament and Apocrypha

1. THE SONG OF ZECHARIAH (*Benedictus*)
(Luke 1:69-79)

Blessed be the Lord God of Israel;
>for he hath visited and redeemed his people;

And hath raised up a mighty salvation for us,
>in the house of his servant David;

As he spake by the mouth of his holy Prophets,
>which have been since the world began;

That we should be saved from our enemies,
>and from the hand of all that hate us.

To perform the mercy promised to our forefathers,
>and to remember his holy covenant;

To perform the oath which he sware to our forefather Abraham,
>that he would give us;

That we being delivered out of the hand of our enemies
>might serve him without fear;

In holiness and righteousness before him,
>all the days of our life.

And thou, child, shalt be called the prophet of the Highest:
>for thou shalt go before the face of the Lord to prepare his ways

To give knowledge of salvation unto his people
>for the remission of their sins,

Through the tender mercy of our God;
>whereby the day-spring from on high hath visited us;

To give light to them that sit in darkness,
and in the shadow of death,
>and to guide our feet into the way of peace.

2. THE SONG OF ZECHARIAH (*Benedictus*)
(Luke 1:69-79)

Blessed be the Lord, the God of Israel;
>he has come to his people and set them free.

He has raised up for us a mighty savior,
>born of the house of his servant David.

Through his holy prophets he promised of old,
that he would save us from our enemies,
    from the hands of all who hate us.
He promised to show mercy to our fathers
    and to remember his holy covenant.
This was the oath he swore to our father Abraham,
    to set us free from our enemies' hand,
free to worship him without fear,
    holy and righteous in his sight,
    all the days of our life.

And you my child, shall be called the prophet of the Most High,
    for you will go before the Lord to prepare his way,
to give his people knowledge of salvation
    by forgiveness of their sins.
In the tender compassion of our God
    the dawn from on high shall break upon us,
to shine on those who dwell in darkness and the shadow of death,
    and to guide our feet on the road to peace.

3. THE SONG OF THE THREE YOUNG MEN
(*Benedictus es, Domine*)
(*verses 29-34*)

Blessed art thou, O Lord God of our fathers:
    praised and exalted above all for ever.
Blessed art thou for the Name of thy Majesty:
    praised and exalted above all for ever.
Blessed art thou in the temple of thy holiness:
    praised and exalted above all for ever.
Blessed art thou that beholdest the depths,
and dwellest between the Cherubim: praised and exalted above all for ever.
Blessed art thou on the glorious throne of thy kingdom:
    praised and exalted above all for ever.
Blessed art thou in the firmament of heaven:
    praised and exalted above all for ever.
Blessed art thou, O Father, Son and Holy Spirit:
    praised and exalted above all for ever.

4. THE SONG OF THE THREE YOUNG MEN
(*Benedictus es, Domine*)
(*verses 29-34*)

Lord God of our fathers, you are blest and adored,
    praised and exalted above all for ever.

For the glory of your holy Name you are blest and adored,
    praised and exalted above all for ever.
In the splendor of your Temple you are blest and adored,
    praised and exalted above all for ever.
On the throne of your majesty you are blest and adored,
    praised and exalted above all for ever.
Throned upon Cherubim, plumbing the depths, you are blest and adored,
    praised and exalted above all for ever.
In the high vault of heaven you are blest and adored,
    praised and exalted above all for ever.
Father, Son, and Holy Spirit, you are blest and adored,
    praised and exalted above all for ever.

5. A SONG OF CREATION (Benedicite, omnia opera Domini) (Song of the Three Young Men: verses 35-65)

O all ye works of the Lord, bless ye the Lord:
    praise him and magnify him for ever.
O ye angels of the Lord, bless ye the Lord:
    praise him and magnify him for ever.

O ye heavens, bless ye the Lord;
O ye waters that be above the firmament, bless ye the Lord;
O all ye powers of the Lord, bless ye the Lord:
    praise him and magnify him for ever.

O ye sun and moon, bless ye the Lord;
O ye stars of heaven, bless ye the Lord;
O ye showers and dew, bless ye the Lord:
    praise him and magnify him for ever.

O ye winds of God, bless ye the Lord;
O ye fire and heat, bless ye the Lord;
O ye winter and summer, bless ye the Lord:
    praise him and magnify him for ever.

O ye dews and frosts, bless ye the Lord;
O ye frost and cold, bless ye the Lord;
O ye ice and snow, bless ye the Lord:
    praise him and magnify him for ever.

O ye nights and days, bless ye the Lord;
O ye light and darkness, bless ye the Lord;
O ye lightnings and clouds, bless ye the Lord:
    praise him and magnify him for ever.

O let the earth bless the Lord;
O ye mountains and hills, bless ye the Lord;
O all ye green things upon the earth, bless ye the Lord;
    praise him and magnify him for ever.

O ye wells, bless ye the Lord;
O ye seas and floods, bless ye the Lord;
O ye whales and all that move in the waters, bless ye the Lord:
    praise him and magnify him for ever.

O all ye fowls of the air, bless ye the Lord;
O all ye beasts and cattle, bless ye the Lord;
O ye children of men, bless ye the Lord:
    praise him and magnify him for ever.

O ye people of God, bless ye the Lord;
O ye priests of the Lord, bless ye the Lord;
O ye servants of the Lord, bless ye the Lord:
    praise him and magnify him for ever.

O ye spirits and souls of the righteous, bless ye the Lord;
O ye holy and humble men of heart, bless ye the Lord;
Let us bless the Father, the Son, and the Holy Spirit:
    praise him and magnify him for ever.

6. A SONG OF CREATION
(*Benedicite, omnia opera Domini*)
(Song of the Three Young Men: verses 35-65)

Let all the works of the Lord celebrate the Lord,
    praise him and exalt him above all for ever.
You angels of the Lord, celebrate the Lord,
    praise him and exalt him above all for ever.

You heavens and all waters above the heavens, celebrate the Lord;
All powers—sun and moon, stars of the sky—celebrate the Lord;
    praise him and exalt him above all for ever.

Each shower of rain and fall of dew, celebrate the Lord;
All winds, and fire and heat, celebrate the Lord;
    praise him and exalt him above all for ever.

Chill and cold, drops of dew and flakes of snow, celebrate the Lord;
Frost and cold, ice and sleet, celebrate the Lord;
    praise him and exalt him above all for ever.

Nights and days, light and darkness, celebrate the Lord;
Storm clouds and thunderbolts, celebrate the Lord;
    praise him and exalt him above all for ever.

Let the earth celebrate the Lord;
Mountains and hills and all that grows upon the earth, celebrate the Lord;
    praise him and exalt him above all for ever.

O springs of water, seas and streams, celebrate the Lord;
O whales, and all that move in the waters, celebrate the Lord;
    praise him and exalt him above all for ever.

All birds of the air, celebrate the Lord;
Cattle and wild animals, and sons of men, celebrate the Lord;
    praise him and exalt him above all for ever.

Let Israel celebrate the Lord;
O priests and servants of the Lord, celebrate the Lord;
    praise him and exalt him above all for ever.

O spirits and souls of the righteous, celebrate the Lord;
    praise him and exalt him above all for ever.
O holy and humble-hearted men, celebrate the Lord;
    praise him and exalt him above all for ever.

Let us celebrate the Father and the Son and the Holy Spirit;
let us praise him and exalt him above all for ever.

In musical settings of the Benedicite, the grouping of verses and the frequency of the refrain are at the discretion of the composer or musical editor.

7. THE FIRST SONG OF ISAIAH
(*Ecce, Deus*)
(Isaiah 12:2-6)

Surely, it is God who saves me;
    I will trust in him and not be afraid.
For the Lord is my stronghold and my sure defense,
    and he will be my Savior.
Therefore you shall draw water with rejoicing
    from the springs of salvation.
And on that day you shall say,
    Give thanks to the Lord, and call upon his Name;
Make his deeds known among the peoples;
    see that they remember that his Name is exalted.

Sing the praises of the LORD, for he has done great things,
    and this is known in all the world.
Cry aloud, ring out your joy, inhabitants of Zion,
    for the great one in the midst of you is the Holy One of Israel.

8. THE SECOND SONG OF ISAIAH
(*Quaerite Dominum*)
(Isaiah 55:6-11)

The Second Song of Isaiah is suggested for use on Fridays, and in the Season of Lent.

Seek the LORD while he wills to be found;
    call upon him when he draws near.
Let the wicked forsake his way,
    and the evil man his thoughts;
And let him turn to the LORD, and he will have compassion,
    and to our God, for he will richly pardon.
For my thoughts are not your thoughts,
    nor your ways my ways, says the LORD.
For as the heavens are higher than the earth,
    so are my ways higher than your ways,
    and my thoughts than your thoughts.
For as rain and snow fall from the heavens,
    and return not again, but water the earth,
Bringing forth life, and giving growth,
    seed for sowing and bread for eating,
So is my word that goes forth from my mouth:
    it will not return to me empty;
But it will accomplish that which I have purposed,
    and prosper in that for which I sent it.

B. After Readings from the New Testament

9. THE SONG OF MARY (*Magnificat*)
(Luke 1:46-55)

My soul doth magnify the Lord,
    and my spirit hath rejoiced in God my Savior.
For he hath regarded
    the lowliness of his handmaiden
For behold from henceforth
    all generations shall call me blessed.

For he that is mighty hath magnified me;
    and holy is his Name.
And his mercy is on them that fear him
    throughout all generations.
He hath showed strength with his arm;
    he hath scattered the proud in the imagination of their hearts.
He hath put down the mighty from their seat,
    and hath exalted the humble and meek.
He hath filled the hungry with good things;
    and the rich he hath sent empty away.
He remembering his mercy hath holpen his servant Israel;
    as he promised to our forefathers,
    Abraham and his seed for ever.

10. THE SONG OF MARY (*Magnificat*)
(*Luke* 1:46-55)

My heart magnifies the Lord,
    and my spirit rejoices in God my Savior;
    for he has looked with favor on his lowly servant,
    and from this day all generations will call me blessed.
The Almighty has done great things for me:
    holy is his Name.
He has mercy on those who fear him
    in every generation.
He has shown the strength of his arm,
    he has scattered the proud in their conceit.
He has cast down the mighty from their thrones,
    and has lifted up the lowly.
He has filled the hungry with good things,
    and sent the rich away empty-handed.
He has come to the help of his servant Israel,
    for he remembered his promise of mercy,
    the promise he made to our fathers,
    to Abraham and his children for ever.

11. THE SONG OF SIMEON
(*Nunc Dimittis*)
(*Luke* 2:29-32)

Lord, now lettest thou thy servant depart in peace,
    according to thy word.
For mine eyes have seen thy salvation,
    which thou hast prepared before the face of all people;

To be a light to lighten the Gentiles,
    and to be the glory of thy people Israel.

12. THE SONG OF SIMEON
(*Nunc Dimittis*)
(*Luke* 2:29-32)

Lord, you have fulfilled your word;
    now let your servant depart in peace.
With my own eyes I have seen the salvation,
    which you have prepared in the sight of every people:
A Light to reveal you to the nations,
    and the glory of your people Israel.

13. A SONG TO THE LAMB
(*Dignus es*)
(*Revelation* 4:11; 5:9-10, 13)

Splendor and honor and kingly power
are yours by right, O Lord our God,
    for you created everything that is,
    and by your will they were created and have their being.

And yours by right, O Lamb that was slain,
for with your Blood you have redeemed for God,
    from every family, language, people, and nation,
    a kingdom of priests to serve our God.
And so, to him who sits upon the throne,
and to Christ the Lamb,
    be worship and praise, dominion and splendor,
    for ever, and for evermore.

14. THE SONG OF THE LAMB
(*Magna et mirabilia*)
(*Revelation* 15:3-4)

O ruler of the universe, Lord God,
    great deeds are they that you have done,
    surpassing human understanding.
Your ways are ways of righteousness and truth,
    O King of all the ages.
Who can fail to do you homage, Lord,
    and sing the praises of your Name?
    for you only are the holy One.

All nations will draw near, and fall down before you,
> because your just and holy works have been revealed.

Canticles 13 and 14 may be sung as one Canticle.
A metrical version of Canticle 14 will be found in The Hymnal 1940, *number 260.*[iv]

15. WE PRAISE THEE
(Te Deum laudamus)

We praise thee O God; we acknowledge thee to be the Lord.
> All the earth doth worship thee, the Father everlasting.

To thee all Angels cry aloud:
the Heavens and all the Powers therein;
> To thee Cherubim and Seraphim continually do cry,

Holy, Holy, Holy, Lord God of Sabaoth;
> Heaven and earth are full of the Majesty of thy glory.

The glorious company of the Apostles praise thee.
> The goodly fellowship of the Prophets praise thee.

The noble army of Martyrs praise thee.
> The holy Church throughout all the world doth acknowledge thee;

The Father of an infinite Majesty;
Thine adorable, true, and only Son;
> Also the Holy Ghost the Comforter.

Thou art the King of Glory, O Christ.
> Thou art the everlasting Son of the Father.

When thou tookest upon thee to deliver man,
> thou didst humble thyself to be born of a Virgin.

When thou hadst overcome the sharpness of death,
> thou didst open the Kingdom of Heaven to all believers.

Thou sittest at the right hand of God,
> in the glory of the Father.

We believe that thou shalt come to be our Judge.
> We therefore pray thee, help thy servants,
> whom thou hast redeemed with thy precious blood.

Make them to be numbered with thy Saints,
> in glory everlasting.

[iv] [Ed. Note: The hymn indicated is "How wondrous and great thy works, God of praise!" by H. U. Onderdonk.]

16. YOU ARE GOD
(*Te Deum laudamus*)

You are God: we praise you;
You are the Lord: we acclaim you;
You are the eternal Father:
All creation worships you.
To you all angels, all the powers of heaven,
Cherubim and Seraphim, sing in endless praise:
    Holy, holy, holy Lord, God of power and might,
    heaven and earth are full of your glory.
The glorious company of apostles praise you.
The noble fellowship of prophets praise you.
The white-robed army of martyrs praise you.
Throughout the world the holy Church acclaims you:
    Father, of majesty unbounded,
        your true and only Son, worthy of all worship,
        and the Holy Spirit, Advocate and Guide.
You, Christ, are the king of glory,
eternal Son of the Father.
When you became man to set us free
you did not disdain the Virgin's womb.
You overcame the sting of death
and opened the Kingdom of heaven to all believers.
You are seated at God's right hand in glory.
We believe that you will come and be our judge.
    Come then, Lord, sustain your people,
    bought with the price of your own blood,
    and bring us with your saints
    to glory everlasting.

17. GLORY BE TO GOD
(*Gloria in excelsis*)

Glory be to God on high,
    and on earth peace, good will towards men.
We praise thee, we bless thee, we worship thee,
    we glorify thee, we give thanks to thee
    for thy great glory,
O Lord God, heavenly King,
    God the Father Almighty.
O Lord, the only-begotten Son, Jesus Christ;
    O Lord God, Lamb of God, Son of the Father,

that takest away the sins of the world,
> have mercy upon us.

Thou that takest away the sins of the world,
> receive our prayer.

Thou that sittest at the right hand of God the Father,
> have mercy upon us.

For thou only art holy;
> thou only art the Lord;

thou only, O Christ, with the Holy Ghost,
> art most high in the glory of God the Father. Amen.

18. GLORY TO GOD
(*Gloria in excelsis*)

Glory to God in the highest,
> and peace to his people on earth.

Lord God, heavenly King,
almighty God and Father,
> we worship you, we give you thanks,
> we praise you for your glory.

Lord Jesus Christ, only Son of the Father,
Lord God, Lamb of God,
you take away the sin of the world:
> have mercy on us;

you are seated at the right hand of the Father:
> receive our prayer.

For you alone are the Holy One, you alone are the Lord,
you alone are the Most High,
> Jesus Christ,
> with the Holy Spirit,
> in the glory of God the Father. Amen.

C. Canticles for use in Place of the Invitatory Psalm

19. O GRACIOUS LIGHT (*Phos hilaron*)

O gracious light,
pure brightness of the everliving Father in heaven,
O Jesus Christ, holy and blessed!

Now as we come to the setting of the sun,
and our eyes behold the vesper light,
we sing your praises, O God: Father, Son, and Holy Spirit.

You are worthy at all times to be praised by happy voices,
O Son of God, O Giver of life,
and to be glorified through all the worlds.

> *Metrical versions of this Canticle will be found in* The Hymnal 1940, *numbers 173 and 176.*[v] *Other versions may also be used.*

20. CHRIST OUR PASSOVER
(1 Corinthians 5:7-8; Romans 6:9-11;
1 Corinthians 15:20-22)

Christ our Passover is sacrificed for us:
> therefore let us keep the feast,
Not with old leaven,
neither with the leaven of malice and wickedness;
> but with the unleavened bread of sincerity and truth.

Christ being raised from the dead dieth no more;
> death hath no more dominion over him.
For in that he died, he died unto sin once:
> but in that he liveth, he liveth unto God.
Likewise reckon ye also yourselves to be dead indeed unto sin,
> but alive unto God through Jesus Christ our Lord.

Christ is risen from the dead,
> and became the first fruits of them that slept.
For since by man came death,
> by man came also the resurrection of the dead.
For as in Adam all die,
> even so in Christ shall all be made alive.

21. CHRIST OUR PASSOVER
(1 Corinthians 5:7-8; Romans 6:9-11;
1 Corinthians 15:20-22)

Alleluia. Alleluia.
Christ our Passover has been sacrificed for us;
> therefore let us celebrate the feast,
Not with the old leaven, the leaven of malice and evil,
> but with the unleavened bread of sincerity and truth. Alleluia.

---

[v] [Ed. Note: The hymns indicated are "O Brightness of the immortal Father's face" by Edward Eddis and "O Gladsome light" by Robert Bridges, respectively.]

Christ being raised from the dead will never die again;
> death no longer has dominion over him.

The death that he died, he died to sin, once for all;
> but the life he lives, he lives to God.

So also consider yourselves dead to sin,
> and alive to God in Jesus Christ our Lord. Alleluia.

Christ has been raised from the dead,
> the first fruits of those who have fallen asleep.

For since by a man came death,
> by a man has come also the resurrection of the dead.

For as in Adam all die,
> so also in Christ shall all be made alive. Alleluia.

An Order of Service for Noonday or Other Times

Leader   Our help is in the Name of the Lord.

People   The maker of heaven and earth.

Leader and People

> Glory to the Father and to the Son, and to the Holy Spirit: as in the beginning, so now and for ever. Amen.
>
> *Except in Lent* Alleluia.

Then follows a Hymn or a Psalm, or both.
(Psalm 67 or a section of Psalm 119 is suggested.)

One of the following, or some other passage of Scripture, is then read:

To the king of ages, immortal, invisible, the only God, be honor and glory for ever and ever. [1 Timothy 1:17]

If anyone is in Christ he is a new creation; the old has passed away, behold, the new has come. All this is from God, who through Christ reconciled us to himself and gave us the ministry of reconciliation. [2 Corinthians 5:17-18]

From the rising of the sun to its going down, let the Name of the Lord be praised! The Lord is high above all nations, and his glory above the heavens. [Psalm 113:3-4]

People   Thanks be to God.

> *A Meditation, silent or spoken, may follow.*

The Leader then says to the People

	The Lord be with you.
People	And also with you.
Leader	Let us pray.

Lord, have mercy.
Christ, have mercy.
Lord, have mercy.

The Lord's Prayer

The Collect of the Day may then be said and one or more of the following:

Blessed Savior, at this hour you hung upon the cross, stretching out your loving arms: Grant that all the peoples of the earth may look to you and be saved; for your mercies' sake. *Amen.*

Almighty Savior, who at noonday called your servant Saint Paul to be an apostle to the Gentiles: We pray you to illumine the world with the radiance of your glory, that all nations may come and worship you who with the Father and the Holy Spirit live and reign, one God, for ever and ever. *Amen.*

Lord Jesus Christ, you said to your Apostles, "Peace I give to you; my own peace I leave with you": Regard not our sins, but the faith of your Church, and give to us the peace and unity of that heavenly city, where with the Father and the Holy Spirit you live and reign, now and for ever. *Amen.*

Free intercessions may be offered.

The Service concludes as follows:

Leader	Let us praise the Lord.
Answer	Thanks be to God.

An Order of Service for the Close of Day (Compline)

When the people are assembled the Leader says

The Lord Almighty grant us a peaceful night and a perfect end.

People Amen.

Leader	Lord, you are in the midst of us, and we are called by your Name:
People	Do not forsake us, O Lord our God.
Leader	Be pleased, O Lord, to deliver us:

The Daily Office 161

People   O Lord, make haste to help us.
Leader   Our help is in the Name of the Lord:
People   The maker of heaven and earth.

The Leader may then say
> Let us ask God's pardon for our failures and shortcomings this day.

SILENCE may be kept for a time

Leader and People
> Almighty God, our heavenly Father:
> We have sinned against you
> through our own fault,
> in thought, and word, and deed,
> and in what we have left undone.
> For your Son our Lord Jesus Christ's sake,
> forgive us all our offenses;
> and grant that we may serve you
> in newness of life,
> to the glory of your Name. Amen.

Leader   May the Almighty God grant us forgiveness of all our sins, and the grace and comfort of the Holy Spirit. Amen.

The Leader and People then say together
> Glory to the Father, and to the Son, and to the Holy Spirit: as in the beginning, so now, and for ever. Amen.
> *Except in Lent* Alleluia.

One or more of the following Psalms is then sung or said (or other suitable selections from the Psalter):

[Psalm 4][vi]

Answer me when I call, O God, defender of my right;
    you set me at liberty when I am hard-pressed;
    have pity on me and hear my petition.

[vi] [Ed. Note: Of the psalm texts given, this is the only one that does not appear in *Prayer Book Studies 23*: The Psalter. Clearly, it follows the same principles of translation, and is very close to the form that will appear in the completed prayer book; nevertheless, there are some variants from the final version.]

O man, how long will you dishonor my Glory?
>   how long will you worship dumb idols and resort to false gods?
>
> Know this, that the Lord looks with favor on him who serves him.
>   The Lord will listen when I call to him.
> Tremble, then, and do not sin;
>   ponder these things in your heart,
>   upon your bed, and be silent.
> Offer the rightful sacrifices,
>   and put your trust in the Lord.
> While many are saying, "Who will show us any favor?",
>   Lift up upon us the light of your countenance, Lord.
> You have put joy in my heart,
>   more than when one sees his grain and wine and oil increase.
> Let me lie down and sleep in peace,
>   for only you, Lord, make me dwell in safety.

[Psalm 33:1-5, 12-14, 18-22]

Rejoice in the Lord, O you righteous;
>   to sing praises is becoming to the upright.
> Praise the Lord with the harp;
>   play to him upon the psaltery and lyre.
> Sing for him a new song;
>   sound a fanfare with all your skill upon the trumpet.
> For the word of the Lord is right,
>   and all his works are sure.
> He loves righteousness and justice;
>   the loving-kindness of the Lord fills the whole earth.

Happy is the nation whose God is the Lord!
>   happy the people he has chosen to be his own!
> The Lord looks down from heaven,
>   and beholds all the children of men.
> From where he sits enthroned he turns his gaze
>   on all who dwell on the earth.
> Behold, the eye of the Lord is upon those who fear him,
>   on those who wait upon his love.
> To pluck their lives from death,
>   and to keep them in the time of famine.
> Our soul waits for the Lord;
>   he is our help and our shield.
> Indeed, our heart rejoices in him,
>   for in his holy Name we put our trust.

Let your loving-kindness, O Lord, be upon us,
>   as we have put our trust in you.

[Psalm 134]

Behold now, bless the Lord, all you servants of the Lord,
>   you that stand by night in the house of the Lord.
Lift up your hands to the holy place, and bless the Lord.
>   The Lord who made heaven and earth
>   bless you out of Zion.

The following Psalms are also suggested:
Psalms 31:1-6, 34, 77, 91

>   *After the Psalter all say together*

Glory to the Father, and to the Son, and to the Holy Spirit:
>   as in the beginning, so now, and for ever. Amen.

One of the following, or some other short passage of Scripture, is then read.

Come to me, all who labor and are heavy-laden, and I will give you rest. Take my yoke upon you, and learn from me; for I am gentle and lowly in heart, and you will find rest for your souls. For my yoke is easy, and my burden is light. [Matthew 11:28-30]

May the God of peace who brought again from the dead our Lord Jesus, the great shepherd of the sheep, by the blood of the eternal covenant, equip you with everything good that you may do his will, working in you that which is pleasing in his sight, through Jesus Christ; to whom be glory for ever and ever. [Hebrews 13:20-21]

>   *People*   Thanks be to God.

A Hymn suitable for the evening may then be sung or said.

Then follows

>   *Leader*   Into your hand, O Lord, I commend my spirit:
>   *People*   For you have redeemed me, O Lord, O God of truth.
>   *Leader*   Keep us, O Lord, as the apple of an eye:
>   *People*   Hide us under the shadow of your wings.
>   *Leader*   Lord, hear our prayer:
>   *People*   And let our cry come to you.
>   *Leader*   Let us pray.

Lord, have mercy.
Christ, have mercy.
Lord, have mercy.

Leader and People

Our Father in heaven,
> holy be your Name,
> your kingdom come,
> your will be done,
>> on earth as in heaven.

Give us today our daily bread.
Forgive us our sins,
> as we forgive those who trespass against us.

Do not bring us to the test
> but deliver us from evil.

Intercession may be offered in the following form:

Eternal God, to you, our heavenly Father, the darkness and the light are both alike, and the night is as clear as the day. We therefore pray you to be with those who watch and work throughout the night on behalf of others:

Here the Leader or members of the congregation may mention specific persons and occupations.

Grant them courage in danger, diligence in emergencies, and the presence of your Holy Spirit in the long and lonely hours. When we awake may we be thankful for their labors and take thought in turn for their needs: through Jesus Christ our ever-reigning Lord. *Amen.*

Silence may be kept; and free intercessions and thanksgivings may be offered.

One of the following Collects is then said

Lighten our darkness, Lord, we pray; and in your mercy defend us from all the dangers of the night; for the love of your only Son, Jesus Christ. *Amen.*

Be present, O merciful God, and protect us through the hours of this night, so that we who are wearied by the changes and chances of this life may rest in your eternal changelessness; through Jesus Christ our Lord. *Amen.*

Look down, O Lord, from your heavenly throne, and illumine the darkness of this night with your celestial brightness; and from the children of light banish the deeds of darkness; through Jesus Christ our Lord. *Amen.*

The Service concludes with the Song of Simeon with this Antiphon, which is sung or said by all.

Antiphon

Guide us waking, O Lord, and guard us sleeping; that awake we may watch with, Christ, and asleep we may rest in peace.

In Easter Season add

Alleluia, Alleluia, Alleluia.

Lord, you have fulfilled your word;
    now let your servant depart in peace.
With my own eyes I have seen the salvation,
    which you have prepared in the sight of every people;
A Light to reveal you to the nations, and the glory of your people Israel.

All repeat the Antiphon

Guide us waking, O Lord, and guard us sleeping; that, awake we may watch with Christ, and asleep we may rest in peace.

In Easter Season add

Alleluia, Alleluia, Alleluia.

Leader	Let us praise the Lord.
People	Thanks be to God.
Leader	The almighty and merciful Lord, Father, Son, and Holy Spirit, bless us and keep us. *Amen.*

Daily Devotions for Individuals and Families

When more than one person is present, the devotions, except for the Reading, may be said in unison. Individuals may find it helpful, when possible, to say the devotions aloud.

The Readings may be taken from:

The Psalms or Lessons for the day listed in the Prayer Book Lectionary (pages x to xli)
The Lessons or Gospels for Sundays and Holy days in the Prayer Book (pages 90 to 269)

Some other manual of devotion which provides daily selections for the Church Year.

In The Morning

AN ACT OF PRAISE [Psalm 103:1-4, 22]

Bless the Lord, O my soul;
    and all that I am, bless his holy Name.
Bless the Lord, O my soul,
    and never forget his goodness.
He forgives all my sins,
    and heals all my infirmities.
He saves my life from death,
    and crowns me with mercy and love.
Bless the Lord, all his creation,
    in every place where he rules;
Bless the Lord, O my soul.

A READING

followed, when possible, by silent meditation.
A Hymn or Canticle may follow.
The Apostles' Creed may be recited.

THE PRAYERS

Heavenly Father, in you we live and move and have our being: We humbly pray you so to guide and govern us by your Holy Spirit, that in all the cares and occupations of our life we may not forget you, but remember that we are ever walking in your sight; through Jesus Christ our Lord. *Amen.*

Remember today, O Lord, especially . . .

(Here may be mentioned names and particular concerns)

We ask this in the Name of Jesus Christ.
Amen.

THE LORD'S PRAYER

At Noon
AN ACT OF RECOLLECTION

O God, you will keep him in perfect peace,
    whose mind is steadfast in you;
For in returning and rest we shall be saved;
    in quietness and trust shall be our strength.
    [Isaiah 26:3, 30:15]

THE READING

From the rising of the sun to its going down, let the Name of the Lord be praised! The Lord is high above all nations, and his glory above the heavens. [Psalm 113:3-4]

THE PRAYERS

Either or both of the following:

Blessed Savior, at this hour you hung upon the cross, stretching out your loving arms: Grant that all the peoples of the earth may look to you and be saved; for your mercies' sake. *Amen.*

Lord Jesus Christ, you said to your Apostles, "Peace I give to you; my own peace I leave with you": Regard not our sins, but the faith of your Church, and give to us the peace and unity of that heavenly city, where with the Father and the Holy Spirit you live and reign, now and for ever. *Amen.*

Other prayers may be added.

THE LORD'S PRAYER

At the Close of Day
AN ACT OF PRAISE   [Psalm 67]

God be merciful to us, and bless us;
    show us the light of his countenance, and come to us.
Let your ways be known upon earth,
    your saving health among all nations.
Let the peoples praise you, O God; let all the peoples praise you.

A READING

*followed, when possible, by silent meditation.
The Song of Simeon may be said*

Lord, you have fulfilled your word;
> now let your servant depart in peace.
With my own eyes I have seen the salvation,
> which you have prepared in the sight of every people.
A Light to reveal you to the nations,
> and the glory of your people Israel.

THE PRAYERS

THE LORD'S PRAYER

Most holy God, the source of all good desires, all right judgments, and all just works: Give to us your servants that peace which the world cannot give, so that our minds may be fixed on the doing of your will; and that we, being delivered from the fear of enemies, may live in peace and quietness; through the mercies of Christ Jesus our Savior. *Amen.*

Other prayers may be added. Those from the Service for the Close of Day are suggested (page 164).

CONCLUSION

> Let me lie down and sleep in peace, O Lord;
> for only you, Lord, make me dwell in safety.

PRAYER BOOK STUDIES 23: THE PSALTER PART I

A Selection of the Most Frequently Appointed Psalms

1970

INTRODUCTION

The Standing Liturgical Commission offers to the Church a collection of seventy-one Psalms for trial use in the triennium 1971-1973, as one phase of the revision of the Book of Common Prayer. It is anticipated that the revision of the remaining Psalms will be completed during the triennium and published in time to be considered by the General Convention of 1973.

In accordance with the Plan of Prayer Book Revision adopted by the General Convention of 1967, responsibility for the revision of the Psalter was assigned to a Drafting Committee composed of

> The Reverend Canon Charles M. Guilbert, member of the Standing Liturgical Commission, and Chairman,
> Mr. W. H. Auden
> The Very Reverend Robert F. Capon
> Mr. Vernon Perdue Davis
> The Reverend Robert C. Dentan
> The Right Reverend Walter C. Klein*
> The Reverend Ivan T. Kaufman*
> The Reverend R. Rhys Williams

* Bishop Klein found it necessary to withdraw from the Committee in 1969 because of the press of diocesan responsibilities, and the Reverend Ivan T. Kaufman was appointed in his place.

In addition to its own members, the Committee was greatly assisted by Mr. Jack Noble White, Secretary of the Joint Commission on Church Music, who attended several meetings.

The draft versions of the Psalms, as they were completed, were thoroughly studied by the Standing Liturgical Commission, and during the consideration the Commission had the expert advice and help of two other members of the Music Commission, the Venerable Frederic P. Williams and the Reverend Norman C. Mealy.

The present collection is not a random assortment. As soon as it became apparent to the Drafting Committee that the task of revising the Psalter (amounting in bulk to one-third of the Book of Common Prayer) could not be completed in three years, a careful study was undertaken to draw up a list of the most frequently used Psalms, so that the Church would have a usable partial Psalter while revision went forward. All Psalms used as Canticles and most of those appointed for use in the several Offices of the Prayer Book, were included. The Lectionary for Morning and Evening Prayer on Sundays and Prayer Book Holy Days was largely represented. Finally, when that portion of the proposed eucharistic lectionary for the period between Advent Sunday and Pentecost became available to the Committee, it was carefully examined to ensure that, so far as possible, at least one of the Psalms suggested for the Sundays and Holy Days within that period would be available in a revised version.[i]

The Standing Liturgical Commission intends to proceed with the revision of the remaining Psalms, and at the same time to study carefully the experience of worshipers in the trial use of this first Part, should trial use be authorized by the General Convention. It is hoped that all who use this version will send comments and suggestions to the Commission. The experience of using this version of the Psalms in actual worship should greatly assist both the Commission and its Drafting Committee in carrying forward the remaining task.

It will be at once apparent that the Commission is not presenting a new version of the Psalms. This is a further revision of that Psalter which has been a part of the Book of Common Prayer (with very little change) since 1549, and which derives from the Great Bible of 1536, the work, basically, of Miles Coverdale. The decision to revise and up-date the Prayer Book Psalter was made early in the process, but was arrived at only after careful consideration of the alternatives: namely, the adoption of an existing modern-language version or the producing of an entirely new translation.[ii]

Even before the program of Prayer Book Revision got underway, the Standing Liturgical Commission explored, with the help of a panel of the Church's Old Testament scholars, the adequacy of modern versions of the Psalter. At that time, in 1965, there were four translations of the Psalms meriting serious consideration: the version included in *The Complete Bible: An American Translation*,[1] and that in *The Holy Bible: Revised Standard Version*;[2] and two versions of the Psalter

---

[i] [Ed. Note] Despite a reference in this paragraph to the "Lectionary for Morning and Evening Prayer", no such lectionary would appear publicly until the publication of PBS 27 in 1973.

[ii] [Ed. Note] A much more complete explanation of the Drafting Committee's process is found in the fascinating work *Auden, The Psalms, and Me* by J. Chester Johnson (Church Publishing, 2017) who would replace Auden on the Drafting Committee in 1971. Anyone with a further interest in the methods and intentions of Psalter revision should examine this book as well.

1. *The Complete Bible: An American Translation*. Chicago: The University of Chicago Press, 1939.

2. *The Holy Bible: Revised Standard Version* (Old Testament Section). New York: Thomas Nelson & Sons, 1952.

itself—*The Psalms: A New Translation* (the so-called "Grail Version")[3] and *The Revised Psalter of the Church of England*.[4] It was the consensus of the scholars consulted that none of these versions would serve the needs of the Church, although it was agreed that the Revised Standard Version and the English Revised Psalter ought to be carefully considered in detail in any revision undertaken. It was further agreed that the Grail version (but only when used with the Gelineau musical settings)[5] might very well be authorized for alternative use in the Church.

After the preliminary exploration, several new translations of the Psalms became available. The first was the 1966 English Version of the *Jerusalem Bible*[6] and then, in rapid succession, *Psalms* 1-50 and *Psalms* 51-100 in THE ANCHOR BIBLE,[7] *The Psalms in Modern Speech*,[8] and the *New English Bible* version.[9] The Drafting Committee on the Psalter has also had the privilege of consulting the manuscript work-in-progress of the American Bible Society, a privilege for which the Standing Liturgical Commission is grateful. None of these newer works has changed the earlier judgment that the Prayer Book Psalter, though in need of extensive revision, remains the most satisfactory version for the varied uses to which the Psalms are put in the worship of the Episcopal Church.

The very excellencies of the several modern versions militate against their suitability for the Church's purposes. With one exception (the English Revised Psalter), they are attempts, and some of them brilliantly successful attempts, to render into contemporary English speech the received Hebrew text of the Psalms, and even to press behind the received text (where it offers difficulties) to probable original readings. This is a laudable ambition in Biblical translation, and one rightly values the results of such scholarship in liturgical readings and for study. The Psalter, however, is not just another Old Testament reading; it is a thoroughly naturalized Christian literature, so that the question is not only, "What did this passage mean to the Jewish worshiper in pre-Christian Jerusalem?"; but also, "What does the passage mean to the Christian Church which continues to use it in its worship?"

---

3. *The Psalms: A New Translation*. Philadelphia: The Westminster Press, 1963. International copyright, THE GRAIL (*England*) 1963.

4. *The Revised Psalter*. London: S.P.C.K., 1966.

5. *The Psalms: Singing Version*. A new translation from the Hebrew arranged for singing to the Psalmody of Joseph Gelineau. New York: Paulist Press Deus Books, 1968.

6. *The Jerusalem Bible*. Garden City: Doubleday & Company, Inc., 1966.

7. Dahood, Mitchell, S. J., THE ANCHOR BIBLE, *Psalms* I, 1-50. Garden City: Doubleday & Company, Inc., 1966.

_____, THE ANCHOR BIBLE, *Psalms* II, 51-100. Garden City: Doubleday & Company, Inc., 1968.

8. Richard S. Hanson, *The Psalms in Modern Speech* (3 volumes). Philadelphia: Fortress Press, 1968.

9. *The New English Bible*. Oxford and Cambridge: The Oxford University Press and the Cambridge University Press, 1970.

The Prayer Book Psalter, unlike the rest of the Great Bible of 1536, was not translated "out of the original tongues". It was an English translation, with reference to contemporary German versions, from the Latin Vulgate Psalter, and that, in turn, was St. Jerome's revision of an Old Latin version, not his own translation from the Hebrew. Finally, the Old Latin was a translation from a Greek translation made in the second and first centuries before Christ (the "Septuagint"). Our Psalter, then, stands at several removes from the Hebrew original, and comes to us steeped in centuries of Jewish and Christian worship and interpretation.

Moreover, the Psalter is not primarily a body of chapters to which one listens, or which one reads in solitude. It is a hymnal intended for corporate congregational recitation. A version of the Psalms for public worship, therefore, must lend itself to congregational singing and reading. Any text, of course, can be set to music and sung by trained choirs; but the Prayer Book Psalter is demonstrably suitable, because of its flexible prose lines and its strongly rhythmical terminal patterns, both to reading and singing, not only by solo voices, but in unison, antiphonally, and responsively, by a worshiping congregation. The metrical Psalters and the modern Grail version are designed for singing, but their strong metrical pulse makes for monotony and jerkiness in reading.[10] Modern prose versions, though more satisfactory than metrical versions for reading aloud, can only be sung successfully to anthem settings, which render them unavailable to all but trained singers.

On the *continuum* which ranges from utilitarian, unstructured speech at one extreme, to strict metrical composition on the other, the Prayer Book Psalter must be characterized as prose rather than verse. Unlike the Hebrew text, there are no dominant metrical patterns. The lines are of varying length and there is great variety of rhythms. However, whether by instinct or design, the Prayer Book Psalter is marked by recurrent rhythmic patterns at the mid-verse pauses and at the ends of verses (including, but not limited to, the classical cursus[11]), which are of great assistance in reading, and which render it singable, both to plainsong and to Anglican chant, and also to new varieties of chant-forms now being developed.

---

10. Both the Grail version and Dr. Hanson's translation are attempts to reproduce in English the stress-patterns of Hebrew poetry, whether two or three or four stresses to the half-verse. The Hanson version is the more successful, on the whole, in this attempt, since it does not require the arbitrary passing over of naturally strong stresses in English speech to achieve its effect.

Aside from the insistence of the frequently recurring stress, a monotonous effect occurs in reading aloud because of the brevity of the lines. The Hebrew ear seems to have found an alternation of three- and two-stress lines solemn and elegiac. The English ear demands a longer line—four stresses, at least, and preferably five.

11. The *cursus* was a system of Latin accentual prose rhythm especially marked before strong pauses. The three main forms of the classical *cursus* were:

a. *cursus planus*—a dactyl followed by a trochee—"séat of the scórnful".

b. *cursus tardus*—two dactyls—"Gód of my ríghteousness".

c. *cursus velox*—a dactyl, followed by two trochees—"stóod in the wáy of sínners".

While classifying the form of the Prayer Book Psalm-line as prose, it is obvious that the Psalter is a body of poetry, characterized as such by its concentration, figurative language, rhythmic quality, and elevated and impassioned tone. This poetic character has been obscured in the past by printing it as if it were prose, and one of the Drafting Committee's earliest decisions was to present the Psalter in poetic lines. Set forth thus in poetic lines, it is apparent that a typographical convention to mark the middle of the verse (the colon, the diagonal slash, the asterisk) is no longer necessary—an indentation serves to indicate the change from one half-verse to the next, whether in chanting or reading.

Having decided, then, that it would revise the Prayer Book Psalter, the Standing Liturgical Commission adopted certain principles of procedure: first, the Prayer Book text is normative and will only be revised where a word or passage is deemed to be an absolute mistranslation or where, in modern usage, a word or phrase has become obsolete (not merely archaic) or positively misleading; secondly, when revision is agreed upon, the primary reference will be to the received Hebrew text, but full weight will be given to the Septuagint and to the Vulgate readings which lie behind the English text; thirdly, all pronouns and verbal forms (even when addressed to, God) will be rendered in contemporary second-person forms. The Commission also decided to follow the traditional practice of printing "Lord" in capitals when it renders the divine Name *Yahweh* (or Jehovah), and "Lord" when it translates the word *Adonai*. The Commission feels that the use of "O" as a vocative particle or as an exclamation conforms to contemporary usage, but that as a cohortative (as in "O come let us worship") it may now be regarded as obsolete.

With each Psalm, the Drafting Committee has worked from a first draft prepared by the Chairman, to which the criteria listed above were applied. The Drafting Committee's first task was to produce a translation, as accurate as possible, of the Hebrew text, drawing upon the vast store of recent scholarship of Hebrew and cognate languages and with constant reference to the best scholarly editions of the ancient Greek and Latin versions. Where substantive differences from the Prayer Book version appeared, each was considered carefully to determine whether it represented a legitimate variant translation, a translation from the Greek or Latin,

---

Scholars have pointed out that the Prayer Book Psalter contains a higher proportion of these rhythmical patterns than the King James version of the Bible and a much higher proportion than ordinary prose.

English, of course, has a very high incidence of words accented on the last syllable, and where strong pauses end on such an accent, one would not, therefore, find a classical cursus. However, Coverdale seems to have developed a native English cursus. Thus, we frequently find such terminal rhythmical patterns as the following:

a. "láw of the Lórd" (*planus*, without the last syllable).

b. "Yét have I sét my Kíng" (*velox*, without the last syllable).

c. "cáll upon the Lórd with my vóice" (*tardus*, with an extra accent).

or an obvious mis-translation. Normally, only the last were changed. The resultant English text was then minutely studied, after which it was sent out to the Commission's Consultants. Their comments, together with those of the Liturgical Commission, formed the basis for further revision. The result, it is hoped, will be found by the Church a fitting modern garb for her ancient song of praise.

The Standing Liturgical Commission

Chilton Powell, *Chairman*
John W. Ashton
Dupuy Bateman, Jr.
James D. Dunning
Robert W. Estill
William C. Frey
Charles M. Guilbert, *Secretary*
Mrs. Richard Harbour
Joseph M. Harte
Louis B. Keiter
H. Boone Porter, Jr.
Charles P. Price
Massey H. Shepherd, Jr., *Vice-Chairman*
Jonathan G. Sherman
Charles W. F. Smith
Bonnell Spencer, O.H.C.
Albert R. Stuart

Leo Malania, *Co-ordinator*

Concerning the Recitation of the Psalms

The Psalter is a body of liturgical poetry. It is designed for vocal, congregational use, whether by singing or reading. There are several traditional methods of psalmody. The exclusive use of a single method makes the recitation of the Psalter needlessly monotonous. The traditional methods, each of which can be elaborate or simple, are the following:

Direct recitation denotes the reading or chanting of a whole Psalm, or portion of a Psalm, in unison. It is particularly appropriate for the Psalm verses suggested in the eucharistic lectionary for use at the Entrance of the Ministers and between the Lessons, when the verses are recited rather than sung, and may often be found the most satisfactory method of chanting them.

Antiphonal recitation is the verse-by-verse alternation between groups of singers or readers; e.g., between choir and congregation, or between one side of the congregation and the other. The alternate recitation concludes either with the *Gloria Patri* or a refrain (called the Antiphon) recited in unison. This is probably the most satisfying method for reciting the Psalms in Morning and Evening Prayer.

Responsorial recitation is the name given to a method of psalmody in which the verses of a Psalm are sung by a solo voice, with the choir and congregation singing a refrain after each verse or group of verses. This was the traditional method of singing the *Venite*, and the restoration of Invitatory Antiphons for the *Venite* makes possible a recovery of this ancient form of sacred song in the daily Office. It was also an ancient manner of chanting the Psalms between the Lessons in the Eucharist, and it is increasingly favored by modern composers.

Responsive recitation is the method most frequently in use in Episcopal churches at the present time: the Minister alternating with the congregation, verse by verse. Despite the long tradition of this use in Anglicanism, there is increasing evidence of dissatisfaction with it on the grounds of artificiality and monotony.

The version of the Psalter which follows is printed as poetry—in lines of verse. Most Psalm verses are in two sections, which has brought it about that chants, both Anglican and plainsong, are predominantly in two sections as well: a reciting note, followed by an inflection; then a new reciting note, and a final cadence. The 1928 Prayer Book Psalter marked the division within verses by an asterisk; in this version, an indentation serves the same purpose; but the elimination of the asterisk or other sign of internal division makes possible the singing of the Psalms to the three-section or four-section chants now being composed.

The Psalter
Part I

A Selection of the Most Frequently Appointed Psalms

Suggestions concerning the recitation of the Psalms will be found on page 177.

Psalm 1

1 How blest is the man who has not walked in the counsel of the wicked,
   nor loitered in the way of sinners;
   nor sat in the seats of the scornful!
2 His delight is in the law of the Lord,
   and he meditates on his law day and night.
3 He is like a tree planted near streams of water,
   bearing its fruit in due season and with leaves that do not wither;
   and everything he does shall prosper.
4 It is not so with the wicked;
   they are like the chaff which the wind blows away.
5 Therefore the wicked shall not stand when judgment comes,
   nor the sinner when the righteous assemble.
6 For the Lord knows the way of the righteous;
   but the way of the wicked is doomed.

Psalm 2

1 Why are the nations in an uproar,
   and the peoples muttering empty threats?
2 Why do the kings of the earth rise up in revolt,
   and the princes plot together,
      against the Lord and against his anointed?
3 "Let us break their yoke," they say;
   "Let us cast off their bonds from us."
4 He whose throne is in heaven is laughing;
   our Lord has them in derision.
5 Then he speaks to them in his wrath;
   and his rage fills them with terror.
6 "I myself have set up my King upon
   my holy hill of Zion."
7 Let me recite the decree of the Lord:
   he said to me, You are my Son;
   this day have I begotten you.

8   Ask of me, and I will give you the nations for your inheritance,
     and the ends of the earth for your possession.
9   You shall crush them with an iron rod,
     and shatter them like a piece of pottery.

10 Now, therefore, you kings, be wise;
     be warned, you rulers of the earth.
11 Submit to the Lord with fear,
     and with trembling bow before him;
12 Lest he be angry and you perish;
     for his wrath is quickly kindled.

13 How blest are they all
     who take refuge in him!

Psalm 8

1   O Lord our Governor,
     how exalted is your Name in all the world!
2   Above the heavens your majesty is praised in song,
     out of the mouths of infants and children.
3   You have set up a stronghold against your adversaries,
     to quell the enemy and the avenger.

4   When I consider your heavens, the work of your fingers,
     the moon and the stars you have set in their courses,
5   What is man that you should be mindful of him?
     the sons of men that you should seek them out?
6   You have made man but little lower than the angels;
     you adorn him with glory and honor;
7   You give him mastery over the works of your hands;
     you put all things under his feet:
8   All sheep and oxen;
     even the wild beasts of the field;
9   The birds of the air, the fish of the sea,
     and whatsoever walks in the paths of the sea.
10 O Lord our Governor,
     how exalted is your Name in all the world!

Psalm 11

1   In the Lord have I taken refuge:
     how then can you say to me,
     "Fly away like a bird to the hilltop."?

2   For see how the wicked bend the bow,
    and fit their arrows to the string,
        to shoot from ambush at the true of heart.
3   When the foundations are being destroyed,
        what can the righteous do?
4   The LORD is in his holy temple;
        the LORD's throne is in heaven.
5   His eyes behold the inhabited world;
        his piercing eye weighs the worth of men.
6   The LORD weighs the righteous as well as the wicked;
        but him who delights in violence he abhors.
7   Upon the ungodly he shall rain coals of fire and burning sulphur;
        a scorching wind shall be their lot.
8   For the LORD is righteous;
    he delights in righteous deeds;
        and the upright shall see his face.

Psalm 12

1   Help me, LORD, for there is not one godly man left;
        for the faithful have vanished from the children of men.
2   Every man speaks falsely with his neighbor;
        with a smooth tongue they speak from a double heart.
3   O that the LORD would cut off all smooth tongues,
        and close the lips that utter proud boasts!
4   Those who say, "With our tongue will we prevail;
        our lips are our own;
        who is LORD over us?"

5   "Because the needy are oppressed,
    and the poor cry out in misery,
        I will up," says the LORD,
        "and will give them the help they long for."
6   The words of the LORD are pure words,
        like silver refined from ore in a furnace,
            and purified seven times over.
7   O LORD, watch over us,
        and save us from this generation for ever.
8   The wicked prowl on every side;
        and that which is worthless is highly prized by the children of men.

Psalm 15

1 Lord, who may dwell in your tabernacle?
      or who may abide upon your holy hill?
2 "He who leads a blameless life,
      and does what is right,
      and speaks the truth from his heart."
3 There is no guile upon his tongue;
   he does no evil to his friend;
      he does not heap contempt upon his neighbor.
4 In his sight the wicked is rejected,
      but he honors those who fear the Lord;
5 He has sworn to do no wrong,
      and does not go back on his word.
6 He does not give his money in hope of gain,
      nor does he take a bribe against the innocent.
7 Whoever does these things
      shall stand fast for ever.

Psalm 18

1 I love you, O Lord my strength;
      O Lord my stronghold, my crag, and my haven.
2 My God, my rock in whom I put my trust;
   My shield, the horn of my salvation, and my refuge.
      You are worthy of praise.

3 I will call upon the Lord,
      and so shall I be saved from my enemies.
4 The breakers of death rolled over me,
      and the torrents of oblivion made me afraid.
5 The cords of hell entangled me,
      and the snares of death were set for me.
6 I called upon the Lord in my anguish;
      and cried out to my God for help.
7 He heard my voice from his palace in the heavens;
      my cry came to his ears.

8 The earth reeled and rocked;
   the roots of the mountains shook;
      they reeled because of his anger.
9 Smoke rose from his nostrils,
   and a consuming fire out of his mouth;
      hot burning coals blazed out from him.

10 He parted the heavens and came down,
    a storm-cloud under his feet.
11 He mounted a cherub and flew;
    he swooped on the wings of the wind.
12 He wrapped darkness about him;
    he made dark waters and thick clouds his pavilion.
13 From the brightness of his presence, through his clouds,
    there burst hailstones and coals of fire.
14 The Lord thundered out of heaven;
    the Most High uttered his voice.
15 He loosed his arrows in showers;
    he hurled volleys of thunderbolts.
16 The beds of the seas were uncovered,
    and the foundations of the world laid bare;
        at your battle-cry, O Lord;
        at the blast of the breath of your nostrils.

17 He reached down from on high and grasped me;
    he drew me out of great waters.
18 He delivered me from my strong enemies,
    and from those who hated me;
        for they were too mighty for me.
19 They confronted me in the day of my disaster;
    but the Lord was like a shepherd's staff to me.
20 He brought me out into a place of liberty;
    he set me free, because he delighted in me.

21 The Lord rewarded me because of my righteous dealing;
    because my hands were clean, he recompensed me:
22 For I have kept the ways of the Lord,
    and have not offended against my God;
23 For all his judgments are before my eyes,
    and his decrees I have not put away from me;
24 For I have been blameless with him,
    and have kept myself from iniquity;
25 Therefore the Lord rewarded me according to my righteous dealing;
    because of the cleanness of my hands in his sight.

26 With the faithful you show yourself faithful;
    with the upright you deal forthrightly.
27 With the pure you show yourself pure;
    but with the crooked you are wily.
28 For you will save a lowly people;
    but you will humble the haughty eyes.

29 For you, O Lord, are my lamp;
    my God, you make my darkness bright.
30 For with you I will break down an enclosure
    with the help of my God I will scale any wall.
31 This God, his ways are perfect;
    the words of the Lord are tried in the fire;
    he is a shield to all who trust in him.
32 For who is God, but the Lord?
    who is the Rock, except our God?
33 It is God who girds me about with strength,
    and makes my way secure.
34 He makes me sure-footed like a deer,
    and lets me stand firm on the heights;
35 He trains my hands for battle,
    and my arms for bending even a bow of bronze.
36 You have given me your shield of victory;
    your right hand also sustains me;
    your loving care makes me great.
37 You lengthen my stride beneath me,
    and my ankles do not give way.
38 I pursue my enemies and overtake them;
    I will not turn back till I have destroyed them.
39 I strike them down and they cannot rise;
    they fall defeated at my feet.
40 You have girded me with strength for the battle;
    you have cast down my adversaries beneath me;
    you have put my enemies to flight.
41 I destroy those who hate me;
    they cry out, but there is none to help them;
    they cry to the Lord, but he does not answer.
42 I beat them small, like dust before the wind;
    I trample them like mud in the streets.
43 You deliver me from the strife of the peoples;
    you put me at the head of the nations.
44 A people I have not known shall serve me;
    no sooner shall they hear than they shall obey me;
    aliens shall cringe before me.
45 The alien people shall lose heart;
    they shall come trembling out of their strongholds.

46 The Lord lives! Blessed is my Rock!
    Exalted is the God of my help!

47 He is the God who gave me victory,
      and cast down the peoples beneath me.
48 You rescued me from the fury of my enemies;
   you exalted me above those who rose against me;
      you saved me from the man of violence.
49 Therefore will I extol you among the nations, O LORD,
      and sing praises to your Name.

50 He multiplies the victories of his king;
      he shows loving-kindness to his anointed,
      to David and his descendants for ever.

Psalm 19

1 The heavens declare the glory of God;
      and the firmament shows his handiwork.
2 One day tells its tale to another;
      and one night imparts knowledge to another.
3 There are no words, there is no language,
      in which their voices are not heard.
4 Their sound has gone out into all lands;
      and their message to the ends of the world.
5 In the deep has he set a pavilion for the sun;
      it comes forth, like a bridegroom out of his chamber;
      it rejoices, like a champion, to run its course.
6 It goes forth from the uttermost edge of the heavens,
      and runs about to the end of it again;
      and nothing is hidden from its burning heat.
7 The Law of the Lord is perfect,
         and revives the soul;
      the testimony of the Lord is sure,
         and gives wisdom to the innocent.
8 The statutes of the Lord are just,
         and rejoice the heart;
      the commandment of the Lord is dear,
         and gives light to the eyes.
9 The fear of the Lord is clean,
         and endures forever;
      the judgments of the Lord are true,
         and righteous altogether.
10 More to be desired are they than gold;
         more than much fine gold;
      sweeter far than honey,
         than honey in the comb.

11 By them also is your servant enlightened;
    and in keeping them there is a great reward.
12 Who can tell how often he offends?
    Cleanse me from my secret faults.
13 Above all, keep your servant from presumptuous sins;
    let them not get dominion over me;
        then shall I be whole and sound,
        and innocent of the great offence.
14 Let the words of my mouth and the meditation of my
            heart be acceptable in your sight,
    O Lord, my strength and my redeemer.

Psalm 20

1 The Lord answer you in the day of trouble;
    the Name of the God of Jacob defend you;
2 Send you help from his holy place,
    and strengthen you out of Zion;
3 Remember all your offerings,
    and accept your burnt-sacrifices;
4 Grant you your heart's desire,
    and prosper all your plans.
    We will shout for joy at your victory,
    and triumph in the Name of our God.
    May the Lord grant all your requests.
6 Now I know that the Lord gives victory to his anointed;
    he will answer him out of his holy heaven,
        with the victorious strength of his right hand.
7 Some put their trust in chariots,
    and some in horses;
        but we will call upon the Name of the Lord our God.
8 They collapse and fall down;
    but we will arise and stand upright.
9 O Lord, give victory to the King,
    and answer us when we call.

Psalm 22

1 My God, my God, why have you forsaken me?
    and are so far from my cry,
    and from the words of my distress?
2 O my God, I cry in the daytime, but you do not answer;
    by night also, but I find no rest.

3 Yet you are the Holy One,
    enthroned upon the praises of Israel,
4 Our fathers put their trust in you;
    they trusted, and you delivered them.
5 They cried out to you, and were delivered;
    they trusted in you, and were not put to shame.
6 But as for me, I am a worm, and no man.
    scorned by men, and despised by the people.
7 All who see me laugh me to scorn;
    they curl their lips and wag their heads, saying,
8 He trusted in the Lord; let him deliver him;
    let him rescue him, if he delights in him."
9 Yet you are he who took me out of the womb,
    and made me trustful on my mother's breast.
10 I have been cast upon you ever since I was born;
    you were my God when I was still in my mother's womb.
11 Be not far from me, for trouble is near,
    and there is none to help.

12 Many young bulls encircle me;
    strong bulls of Bashan surround me.
13 They open wide their jaws at me,
    like a ravening and a roaring lion.
14 I am poured out like water,
    and all my bones are out of joint;
        my heart within my breast is melting wax.
15 My mouth is dried out like a pot-sherd;
    my tongue sticks to the roof of my mouth;
        and you have laid me in the dust of the grave.
16 Packs of dogs close me in,
    and gangs of evil-doers circle around me;
        they pierce my hands and my feet;
        I can count all my bones.
17 They stare and gloat over me;
    they divide my garments among them;
    they cast lots for my clothing.
18 Be not far away, O Lord;
    you are my strength; hasten to help me.
19 Save me from the sword,
    my life from the power of the dog.

20 Save me from the lion's mouth,
        and from the horns of wild oxen—
        O God, you have answered me.
21 I will declare your Name to my brethern;
        in the midst of the congregation I will praise you.

22 Praise the LORD, you that fear him!
        all you of Jacob's line, give glory!
        stand in awe of him, O offspring of Israel!
23 For he does not despise nor abhor the poor in his poverty;
        neither does he hide his face from him:
        but when he cries to him he hears him.
24 My praise is of him in the great assembly;
        I will perform my vows in the presence of those who worship him.
25 The poor shall eat and be satisfied,
        and those who seek the LORD shall praise him.
        "May your heart live for ever!"
26 All the ends of the earth shall remember and turn to the LORD;
        and all the families of the nations shall bow before him.
27 For kingship is the LORD's;
        he rules over the nations.
28 To him alone all who sleep in the earth bow down in worship;
        all who go down to the dust fall before him.
29 My soul shall live for him;
    my descendants shall serve him;
        they shall be known as the LORD's for ever.
30 They shall come and make known to a people yet unborn
        the saving deeds that he has done.

Psalm 23

1 The Lord is my shepherd;
        nothing, therefore, shall I lack.
2 He makes me lie down in green pastures;
        and leads me beside still waters.
3 He revives my soul,
        and guides me along safe pathways for his Name's sake.

4 Though I walk through the valley of the shadow of death,
   I shall fear no evil;
        for you are with me;
        your rod and your staff, they comfort me,

5 You spread a table before me,
   in the presence of those who trouble me;
      you have anointed my head with oil,
      and my cup is full.
6 Surely your goodness and mercy shall follow me all the days of my life;
   and I will dwell in the house of the Lord for ever.

Psalm 24

1 The earth is the Lord's, and all that is in it;
   the world, and all who dwell therein.
2 For he it is who founded it upon the seas,
   and made it firm upon the rivers of the deep.
3 "Who can ascend the hill of the Lord?
   and who can stand in his holy place?"
4 "He who has clean hands and a pure heart;
   who has not pledged himself to falsehood,
   nor sworn by what is a fraud.
5 "He shall receive a blessing from the Lord,
   and a just reward from the God of his salvation."
6 Such is the generation of those who seek him,
   of those who seek out your face, O God of Jacob.

7 Lift up your heads, O gates,
   lift them high, O ancient doors,
      and the King of Glory shall come in.
8 "Who is this King of Glory?"
      "The Lord, strong and mighty;
      The Lord, mighty in battle."
9 Lift up your heads, O gates,
   lift them high, O ancient doors,
      and the King of Glory shall come in.
10 "Who is he, this King of Glory?"
      "The Lord of hosts,
      he is the King of Glory."

Psalm 25

1 To you, O Lord, I lift up my soul;
   my God, I put my trust in you;
      let me not be humiliated,
      nor let my enemies triumph over me.
2 Let none who look to you be put to shame;
   let them be put to shame who deal treacherously without a cause.

3   Show me your ways, O Lord,
         and teach me your paths.
4   Lead me in your truth, and teach me;
    for you are the God of my salvation;
         in you have I trusted all the day long.
5   Remember, O Lord, your compassion and love,
         for they are from everlasting.
6   Remember not the sins of my youth and my transgressions;
         remember me according to your love,
         and for the sake of your goodness, O Lord.
7   Gracious and upright is the Lord;
         therefore, he teaches sinners in his way.
8   He guides the humble in doing right,
         and teaches his way to the lowly.
9   All the paths of the Lord are love and faithfulness
         to those who keep his covenant and his testimonies.
10 For your Name's sake, O Lord,
         forgive my wickedness, for it is great.
11 Who is the man who fears the Lord?
         him will he teach the way that he should choose.
12 He shall dwell in prosperity,
         and his children shall inherit the land.
13 The Lord is a friend to those who fear him,
         and will show them his covenant.
14 My eyes are ever looking to the Lord,
         for he shall pluck my feet out of the net.
15 Turn to me and have pity on me,
         for I am left alone and in misery.
16 The sorrows of my heart have increased;
         bring me out of my troubles.
17 Look upon my adversity and misery,
         and forgive me all my sin.
18 Look upon my enemies, for they are many,
         and they bear a violent hatred against me.
19 Protect my life, and deliver me;
         let me not be put to shame,
         for I have trusted in you.
20 Let integrity and uprightness preserve me,
         for my hope has been in you.
21 Deliver Israel, O God,
         out of all his troubles.

Psalm 27

1 The LORD is my light and my salvation;
    whom then shall I fear?
        the LORD is the strength of my life;
    of whom then shall I be afraid?
2 When evildoers came upon me to eat up my flesh,
        it was they, my foes and my adversaries, who stumbled and fell.
3 Though an army should encamp against me,
    yet shall not my heart be afraid;
        and though war should rise up against me,
        yet will I put my trust in him.
4 For one thing have I asked the Lord;
    for one thing I seek:
        that I may dwell in the house of the LORD all the days of my life;
5 To behold the fair beauty of the LORD,
        and to seek him in his temple.
6 For in the day of trouble he shall keep me safe in his shelter;
        he shall hide me in the secrecy of his dwelling,
        and set me up upon a rock of stone.
7 Even now he lifts up my head
        above my enemies round about me.
8 Therefore, I will offer in his dwelling an oblation,
    with sounds of great gladness;
        I will sing and make music to the LORD.
9 Hearken to my voice, O LORD, when I call;
        have mercy on me and answer me.
10 My heart speaks for you and says, "Seek my face."
        Your face, LORD, will I seek.
11 Hide not your face from me;
        nor turn away your servant in displeasure.
12 You have been my helper;
        cast me not away; do not forsake me,
        O God of my salvation.
13 Though my father and my mother forsake me,
        the LORD will sustain me.
14 Teach me your way, O LORD;
        and lead me by the right way,
        because of my enemies.
15 Deliver me not into the will of my adversaries;
        for false witnesses have risen up against me,
        and such as speak malice.

16 What if I had not believed
       that I should see the goodness of the Lord
          in the land of the living!
17 O tarry, and await the Lord's pleasure;
       be strong, and he shall comfort your heart;
          and wait patiently for the Lord.

Psalm 28

1 O Lord, I call to you;
       my Rock, do not be deaf to me;
          lest, if you do not hear me,
          I become like those who go down to the Pit.
2 Hear the voice of my prayer when I cry out to you,
       when I lift up my hands to your holy of holies.

3 Do not snatch me away with the wicked,
   or with the evil doers,
          who speak peaceably with their neighbors,
          while strife is in their hearts.
4 Repay them according to their deeds,
       and according to the wickedness of their actions.
5 According to the work of their hands repay them,
       and give them their just deserts.
6 For they have no understanding of the Lord's doings,
   nor of the operation of his hands;
          therefore he will break them down and not
             build them up.
7 Blessed is the Lord!
       for he has heard the voice of my prayer.
8 The Lord is my strength and my shield;
   my heart trusts in him, and I have been helped;
          therefore my heart dances for joy,
          and in my song will I praise him.
9 The Lord is the strength of his people,
       a safe refuge for his anointed.
10 Save your people, and bless your inheritance;
       shepherd them, and carry them for ever.

Psalm 29

1 Ascribe to the Lord, you gods,
       ascribe to the Lord glory and strength.

2　Ascribe to the Lord the glory due his Name;
　　　worship the Lord in the beauty of holiness.
3　The voice of the Lord is upon the waters;
　　the God of Glory thunders;
　　　the Lord is upon the mighty waters.
4　The voice of the Lord is a powerful voice;
　　　the voice of the Lord is a voice of splendor.
5　The voice of the Lord breaks the cedar-trees;
　　　the Lord breaks the cedars of Lebanon;
6　He makes Lebanon skip like a bull-calf,
　　　and Mount Hermon like a young wild ox.
7　The voice of the Lord splits the flames of fire;
　　the voice of the Lord shakes the wilderness;
　　　the Lord shakes the wilderness of Kadesh.
8　The voice of the Lord makes the oak-trees writhe,
　　　and strips the forests bare.
9　And in his temple,
　　　all are crying, "Glory!"
10　The Lord sits enthroned above the flood;
　　　the Lord sits enthroned as King for evermore.
11　The Lord shall give strength to his people;
　　　the Lord shall give his people the blessing of peace.

Psalm 31

1　In you, O Lord, have I taken refuge;
　　let me never be put to shame;
　　　deliver me in your righteousness.
2　Incline your ear to me,
　　　make haste to deliver me.
3　Be my strong rock, a castle to keep me safe;
　　for you are my crag and my stronghold;
　　　for the sake of your Name, lead me and guide me.
4　Take me out of the net that they have secretly set for me;
　　　for you are my tower of strength.
5　Into your hands I commend my spirit;
　　　for you have redeemed me,
　　　O Lord, O God of truth.

6　I hate those who cling to worthless idols,
　　　and put my trust in the Lord.

7   I will rejoice and be glad because of your mercy;
　　for you have seen my affliction;
　　you know my distress.
8   You have not shut me up in the power of the enemy;
　　you have set my feet in an open place.

9   Have mercy on me, O Lord; for I am in trouble;
　　my eye is consumed with sorrow;
　　my throat, also, and my belly.
10 For my life is wasted with grief,
　and my years with sighing;
　　my strength fails me because of affliction,
　　and my bones are consumed.
11 I have become a reproach to all my enemies,
　　　　and even to my neighbors,
　and a dismay to my acquaintances;
　　when they see me in the street they avoid me.
12 I am forgotten like a dead man, out of mind;
　　I am as useless as a broken pot.
13 For I have heard the whispering of the crowd
　(terror all around!);
　　they put their heads together against me:
　　they plot to take my life.
14 But as for me, I have trusted in you, O Lord:
　　I have said, "You are my God."
15 My times are in your hand;
　rescue me from the hand of my enemies,
　　and from those who persecute me.
16 Make your face to shine upon your servant;
　　in your loving-kindness, save me.
17 Lord, let me not be ashamed for having called upon you;
　　rather, let the wicked be put to shame;
　　let them be silent in the grave.
18 Let the lying lips be dumb which insolently speak
　　　　against the righteous,
　　disdainfully, and with contempt.
19 How great is your goodness, O Lord,
　which you have laid up for those who fear you;
　　which you have done, in the sight of all men,
　　for those who put their trust in you!
20 You hide them in the covert of your presence from the slanderings of men;
　　you keep them in your shelter from the strife of tongues.

21 Blessed be the Lord!
    for he has been wonderfully kind to me in a beseiged city.
22 Yet I said, when I was alarmed,
    "I have been cut out of the sight of your eyes."
        Nevertheless, you heard the sound of my entreaty,
        when I cried out to you.
23 Love the Lord; all you who worship him;
    the Lord protects the faithful,
    but repays to the full those who act haughtily.
24 Be strong, and let your heart take courage,
    all you who wait for the Lord.

Psalm 33

1 Rejoice in the Lord, O you righteous;
    to sing praises is becoming to the upright.
2 Praise the Lord with the harp;
    play to him upon the psaltery and lyre.
3 Sing for him a new song;
    sound a fanfare with all your skill upon the trumpet.
4 For the word of the Lord is right,
    and all his works are sure.
5 He loves righteousness and justice;
    the loving-kindness of the Lord fills the whole earth.

6 By the word of the Lord were the heavens made,
    by the breath of his mouth all the heavenly hosts.
7 He gathers up the waters of the ocean as in a water-skin,
    and stores up the depths of the sea.
8 Let all the earth fear the Lord;
    let all who dwell in the world stand in awe of him.
9 For he spoke and it came to pass;
    he commanded and it stood fast.
10 The Lord brings the will of the nations to naught;
    he thwarts the designs of the peoples.
11 But the Lord's will stands fast for ever,
    and the designs of his heart from age to age.
12 Happy is the nation whose God is the Lord!
    happy the people he has chosen to be his own!
13 The Lord looks down from heaven,
    and beholds all the children of men.
14 From where he sits enthroned he turns his gaze
    on all who dwell on the earth.

15 He who fashions all the hearts of them,
   he it is who understands all their works.
16 There is no king that can be saved by a mighty army;
   a strong man is not delivered by his great strength.
17 The horse is a vain hope for deliverance;
   for all its strength it cannot save.
18 Behold, the eye of the Lord is upon those who fear him,
   on those who wait upon his love.
19 To pluck their lives from death,
   and to keep them in the time of famine.
20 Our soul waits for the Lord;
   he is our help and our shield.
21 Indeed, our heart rejoices in him,
   for in his holy Name we put our trust.
22 Let your loving-kindness, O Lord, be upon us,
   as we have put our trust in you.

Psalm 34

1 I will bless the Lord at all times;
   his praise shall ever be in my mouth.
2 I will glory in the Lord;
   let the humble hear and rejoice.
3 Magnify the Lord with me,
   and let us exalt his Name together.
4 I sought the Lord, and he answered me,
   and delivered me out of all my terror.
5 Look upon him, and be radiant,
   and let not your faces be ashamed.
6 This poor man called, and the Lord heard him,
   and saved him from all his troubles.
7 The angel of the Lord encompasses those who fear him,
   and he will deliver them.
8 Taste and see that the Lord is good;
   happy is the man who trusts in him.
9 Fear the Lord, you saints of his,
   for those who fear him lack nothing.
10 The young lions lack, and suffer hunger;
   but those who seek the Lord shall lack nothing that is good.
11 Come, children, and listen to me;
   I will teach you the fear of the Lord.

12 Who is the man who loves life;
   who desires long life to enjoy prosperity?
13 Keep your tongue from evil-speaking,
   and your lips from lying words.
14 Turn from evil, and do good;
   seek peace, and pursue it.
15 The eyes of the LORD are upon the righteous,
   and his ears are open to their cry.
16 The face of the LORD is against those who do evil,
   to root out the remembrance of them from the earth.
17 The righteous cry, and the LORD hears them,
   and delivers them from all their troubles.
18 The LORD is near to the broken-hearted,
   and will save those who spirits are crushed.
19 Many are the troubles of the righteous;
   but the LORD will deliver him from them all.
20 He will keep safe all his bones;
   not one of them shall be broken.
21 Evil shall slay the wicked,
   and those who hate the righteous will be punished.
22 The LORD ransoms the life of his servants,
   and none will be punished who trust in him.

Psalm 36

1 There is a voice of rebellion deep in the heart of the wicked;
   there is no fear of God before his eyes.
2 He flatters himself in his own eyes;
   but to find out his sin is to hate it.
3 The words of his mouth are wicked and deceitful;
   he has left off acting wisely and doing good.
4 He thinks up wickedness upon his bed,
   and has set himself in no good way;
   he does not abhor that which is evil.
5 Your love, O God, reaches the heavens,
   and your faithfulness the clouds.
6 Your righteousness is like the strong mountains,
   your justice like the great deep;
   you save both man and beast, O LORD.
7 How priceless is your love, O God!
   the sons of men take refuge under the shadow of your wings.
8 They feast upon the abundance of your house;
   you give them drink from the river of your delights.

9   For with you is the well of life,
       and in your light we see light.
10 Continue your loving-kindness to those who know you,
       and your favor to those who are true of heart.

11 Let not the foot of the proud come near me,
       nor the hand of the wicked push me aside.
12 See how they are fallen, those who work wickedness!
       they are cast down, and shall not be able to rise.

Psalm 40

1   I waited patiently upon the Lord;
       he stooped to me and heard my cry.
2   He lifted me out of the desolate pit,
   out of the muck and mire;
       he set my feet upon a high cliff,
       and made my footing sure.
3   He put a new song in my mouth,
   a song of praise to our God;
       many shall see, and stand in awe,
       and shall put their trust in the Lord.
4   Happy is the man who trusts in the Lord!
       he does not resort to evil spirits,
       or turn to false gods.

5   Great things are they that you have done, O Lord my God,
   your miracles and your plans for us!
       there is none who can be compared with you.
6   O that I could make them known and tell them!
       but they are more than I can count.
7   In sacrifice and offering you take no pleasure
       (you have given me ears to hear you);
8   Burnt-offering and sin-offering you have not required;
       and so I said, "Behold, I come."
9   In the roll of the book it is written concerning me:
       "I love to do your will, O my God;
       your law is deep in my heart."
10 I proclaimed righteousness in the great congregation;
       behold, I did not restrain my lips;
       and that, O Lord, you know.
11 Your righteousness have I not hidden in my heart;
   I have spoken of your faithfulness and your deliverance;
       I have not concealed your love and faithfulness from the great congregation.

12 You are the Lord; do not withhold your compassion from me;
>let your love and your faithfulness keep me safe for ever.
13 For innumerable troubles have crowded upon me;
>my sins have overtaken me and I cannot see;
>>they are more in number than the hairs of my head,
>>and my heart fails me.

14 Be pleased, O Lord, to deliver me;
>O Lord, make haste to help me.
15 Let them be ashamed and altogether dismayed
>who seek after my life to destroy it;
>>let them draw back and be disgraced
>>who take pleasure in my misfortune.
16 Let them be desolate, because they are ashamed,
>who say to me, "You had it coming to you."
17 Let all who seek you rejoice in you and be glad;
>let those who love your salvation continually say,
>"Great is the Lord!"
18 Though I am poor and afflicted,
>the Lord will have regard for me.
19 You are my helper and my deliverer;
>do not tarry, O my God.

Psalm 42

1 As the deer longs for the water-brooks,
>so longs my soul for you, O God,
2 My soul is athirst for God, athirst for the living God;
>when shall I come to appear before the presence of God?
3 My tears have been my food day and night,
>while all day long they say to me, "Where is now your God?"
4 I pour out my soul, when I think on these things:
>how I went with the multitude and led them into the house of God,
5 With the voice of praise and thanksgiving,
>among such as keep holy-day.

6 Why are you so full of heaviness, O my soul?
>and why are you so disquieted within me?
7 O put your trust in God;
>for I will yet give thanks to him,
>who is the help of my countenance, and my God.

8 My soul is heavy within me;
   therefore, I will remember you from the land of Jordan,
   and from the peak of Mizar among the heights of Hermon.
9 One deep calls to another in the noise of your cataracts;
   all your rapids and floods have gone over me.
10 The Lord grants his loving-kindness in the day-time;
   in the night-season his song is with me,
   a prayer to the God of my life.
11 I will say to the God of my strength, "Why have you forgotten me?
   and why do go I so heavily while the enemy oppresses me?"
12 My bones are smitten asunder;
   while my enemies mock me to my face;
13 While all day long they mock me, saying,
   "Where is now your God?"

14 Why are you so full of heaviness, O my soul?
   and why are you so disquieted within me?"
15 O put your trust in God;
   for I will yet give thanks to him,
   who is the help of my countenance, and my God.

Psalm 43

1 Give judgment for me, O God;
   and defend my cause against an ungodly people;
   deliver me from deceitful and wicked men.
2 For you are the God of my strength;
   why have you put me from you?
   and why do I go so heavily while the enemy oppresses me?
3 Send out your light and your truth, that they may lead me;
   and bring me to your holy hill,
   and to your dwelling.
4 That I may go to the altar of God,
   to the God of my joy and gladness;
   and on the harp will I give thanks to you, O God my God.
5 Why are you so full of heaviness, O my soul?
   and why are you so disquieted within me?
6 Put your trust in God;
   for I will yet give thanks to him,
   who is the help of my countenance and my God.

Psalm 46

1 God is our refuge and strength;
    a very present help in trouble.
2 Therefore we will not fear, though the earth be moved;
    and though the mountains be toppled into the depths of the sea;
3 Though its waters rage and foam;
    and though the mountains tremble at the tumult of the same.

4 There is a river, whose streams make glad the city of God,
    the holy habitation of the Most High.
5 God is in the midst of her; she shall not be overthrown;
    God shall help her, and that right early.
6 The nations make much ado, and the kingdoms are shaken;
    God has spoken, and the earth shall melt away.
7 The Lord of hosts is with us;
    the God of Jacob is our stronghold.

8 Come now and look upon the works of the Lord,
    what awesome things he has done on earth.
9 It is he who makes war to cease in all the world;
    he breaks the bow, and shatters the spear asunder,
    and burns the chariots with fire.
10 "Be still, then, and know that I am God;
    I will be exalted among the nations;
    I will be exalted in the earth."
11 The Lord of hosts is with us;
    the God of Jacob is our stronghold.

Psalm 48

1 Great is the Lord, and highly to be praised;
    in the city of the Lord is his holy hill.
2 Beautiful and lofty, the joy of all the earth,
   is the hill of Zion,
        the very center of the world,
        and the city of the great King.
3 God is in her citadels;
    he is known to be her sure refuge.
4 Behold, the kings of the earth assembled,
    and marched forward together.
5 They looked, and were astounded;
    they retreated, and fled in terror.

6 Trembling siezed them there;
  they writhed like a woman in child-birth,
    like ships of the sea when the east wind shatters them.
7 As we have heard, so have we seen,
  in the city of the Lord of hosts, in the city of our God:
    God has established her for ever.
8 We have meditated on your loving-kindness, O God,
    in the midst of your temple.
9 Your praise, like your Name, reaches to the world's end;
    your right hand is full of justice.
10 Let Mount Zion be glad;
  let the cities of Judah rejoice,
    because of your judgments.
11 Make the circuit of Zion
  walk round about her;
    count the number of her towers.
12 Consider well her bulwarks,
  examine her citadels,
    that you may tell those who come after.
13 This God is our God for ever and ever;
    he shall be our guide for evermore.

Psalm 50

1 The Lord, the God of gods, has spoken;
    he has called the earth from the rising of the sun to its setting.
2 Out of Zion, perfect in its beauty,
    God reveals himself in glory.
3 Our God shall come and shall not keep silence;
    before him there is a consuming flame,
    and round about him a raging storm.
4 He calls the heavens and the earth from above
    to witness the judgment of his people.
5 "Gather before me my loyal followers,
    those who have made a covenant with me,
    and sealed it with sacrifice."
6 Let the heavens declare the rightness of his cause;
    for God himself is judge.
7 Hear, O my people, and I will speak:
  O Israel, I will bear witness against you;
    for I am God, your God.
8 I do not accuse you because of your sacrifices;
    your offerings are always before me.

9   I will take no bull-calf from your stalls;
        nor he-goats out of your pens;
10 For all the beasts of the forest are mine,
        the cattle in their thousands upon the hills;
11 I know every bird in the sky,
        and the creatures of the fields are in my sight.
12 If I were hungry, I would not tell you;
        for the whole world is mine and all that is in it.
13 Do you think I eat bulls' flesh,
        or drink the blood of goats?
14 Offer to God a sacrifice of thanksgiving,
        and make good your vows to the Most High.
15 Call upon me in the day of trouble;
        I will deliver you and you shall honor me.

16 But to the wicked man God says,
    Why do you recite my statutes,
        and take my covenant upon your lips,
17 When you refuse discipline,
        and toss my words behind your back?
18 When you see a thief, you make him your friend,
        and you cast in your lot with adulterers.
19 You have loosed your lips for evil,
        and harnessed your tongue to a lie.
20 You are always speaking evil of your brother;
        and slandering your own mother's son.
21 These things you have done, and I kept still,
        and you thought that I am like you.
22 I have made my accusation;
        I have put my case in order before your eyes.
23 Consider this well, you who forget God,
        lest I rend you and there be none to deliver you.
24 Whoever offers me the sacrifice of thanksgiving,
            he honors me;
        but to him who keeps himself in my way will I show
            the salvation of God.

Psalm 51

1   Have mercy on me, O God, according to your loving-kindness;
        in your great compassion blot out my offences.
2   Wash me through and through from my wickedness,
        and cleanse me from my sin.

3   For I know my transgressions only too well,
       and my sin is ever before me.
4   Against you only have I sinned,
       and done what is evil in your sight.
5   And so you are justified when you speak,
       and upright in your judgment.
6   Indeed, I have been wicked from my birth,
       a sinner from my mother's womb.
7   For behold, you look for truth in the inward parts,
       and shall make me understand wisdom secretly.
8   Take away my sin, and I shall be pure;
       wash me, and I shall be cleaner than snow.
9   Make me hear of joy and gladness,
       that the body you have broken may rejoice.
10 Hide your face from my sins,
       and blot out all my iniquities.
11 Create in me a clean heart, O God,
       and renew a right spirit within me.
12 Cast me not away from your presence,
       and take not your holy Spirit from me.
13 Give me the joy of your saving help again,
       and sustain me with your bountiful spirit.
14 I shall teach your ways to the wicked,
       and sinners shall return to you.
15 Deliver me from death, O God,
       and my tongue shall sing of your righteousness,
       O God of my salvation.
16 Open my lips, O Lord,
       and my mouth shall show forth your praise.
17 Had you desired it, I would have offered sacrifice;
       but you take no delight in burnt-offerings.
18 The sacrifice of God is a troubled spirit;
       a broken and contrite heart, O God, you will not despise.
19 Be favorable and gracious to Zion,
       and build the walls of Jerusalem.
20 Then you will be pleased with the appointed sacrifices, with burnt-offerings and oblations;
       then shall they offer young bullocks upon your altar.

Psalm 65

1   You are to be praised, O God, in Zion;
       to you shall vows be performed.

2 To you that hear prayer shall all men come,
    because of their transgressions.
3 Our sins are stronger than we are;
    but you will blot them out.
4 How blest is the man you choose,
   whom you draw to your courts to dwell there!
      we shall be satisfied by the beauty of your house,
      by the holiness of your temple.
5 Awesome things will you show us in your righteousness,
   O God of our salvation,
      O Hope of all the ends of the earth,
      and of the seas that are far away.
6 You make fast the mountains by your power,
    they are girded about with might.
7 You still the roaring of the seas,
    the roaring of their waves,
    and the clamor of the peoples.
8 Those who dwell at the ends of the earth
   shall tremble at your marvelous signs;
      you make the dawn and the dusk to sing for joy.
9 You visit the earth and water it abundantly;
    you make it very plenteous:
    the river of God is full of water.
10 You prepare the grain,
    for so you provide for the earth.
11 You thoroughly drench the furrows
   and smooth out the ridges;
      with heavy rain you soften the ground;
      and bless its increase.
12 You crown the year with your goodness,
    and your paths overflow with plenty.
13 May the fields of the wilderness be rich for grazing,
    and the hills be clothed with joy.
14 May the meadows cover themselves with flocks,
   and the valleys cloak themselves with grain;
      let them shout for joy and sing.

Psalm 66

1 Be joyful in God, all you lands;
    sing the glory of his Name;
    sing the glory of his praise.

2 Say to God, "How awesome are your deeds!
> because of your great strength your enemies
>> cringe before you.
3 All the earth bows down before you,
> sings to you, sings out your Name.[i]

4 Come now, and see the works of God,
> how wonderful he is in his doing toward
>> the children of men.
5 He turned the sea into dry land,
> so that they went through the water on foot;
> there we rejoiced in him.
6 In his might he rules for ever;
> his eyes keep watch over the nations;
>> let no rebel rise up against him.
7 Bless our God, you peoples;
> make the voice of his praise to be heard.
8 Who holds our souls in life,
> and will not allow our feet to slip.
9 For you, O God, have proved us;
> you tried us just as silver is tried.
10 You brought us into the snare;
> you laid heavy burdens upon our backs.
11 You let men ride over our heads;
> we went through fire and water;
>> but you brought us out into a place of refreshment.
12 I will enter your house with burnt-offerings;
> and will pay you my vows,
>> which I promised with my lips, and spoke with my mouth,
>> when I was in trouble.
13 I will offer you sacrifices of fat beasts,
> with the smoke of rams;
>> I will give you oxen and goats.

14 Come and listen, all you who fear God,
> and I will tell you what he has done for me.
15 I called out to him with my mouth,
> and his praise was on my tongue.
16 If I had found evil in my heart
> the LORD would not have heard me;

---

[i] [Ed. Note: There is no closing quotation mark for the quote that begins in the middle of the first line of verse 2 in the *Prayer Book Studies* printing. However, in the printing of this psalm in the *Services For Trial Use* (page 181), the quote ends here with the conclusion of verse 3.]

17 But in truth God has heard me;
    he has attended to the voice of my prayer.
18 Blessed be God, who has not rejected my prayer,
    nor withheld his love from me.

Psalm 67

1 God be merciful to us, and bless us,
    show us the light of his countenance, and come to us,

2 Let your ways be known upon earth,
    your saving health among all nations.
3 Let the peoples praise you, O God;
    let all the peoples praise you.
4 Let the nations be glad and sing for joy;
    for you judge the peoples with equity,
    and guide all the nations upon earth.
5 Let the peoples praise you, O God;
    let all the peoples praise you.

6 The earth has brought forth her increase;
    may God, our own God, give us his blessing.
7 May God give us his blessing;
    and may all the ends of the earth stand in awe of him.

Psalm 70

1 Be pleased, O God, to deliver me;
    O LORD, make haste to help me.
2 Let those who seek my life be ashamed,
and altogether dismayed;
    let those who take pleasure in my misfortune
    draw back and be disgraced.
3 Let those who say to me, "You had it coming to you."
    turn back because they are ashamed.
4 Let all who seek you rejoice in you and be glad;
    let those who love your salvation continually say,
    "Great is the LORD!"
5 But as for me, I am poor and needy;
    come to me speedily, O God.
6 You are my helper and my deliverer;
    O LORD, do not tarry.

Psalm 72

1 Give the king your justice, O God,
    and your righteousness to the king's son;
2 That he may rule your people righteously,
    and the poor with justice.
3 May the mountains bring prosperity to the people,
    and the little hills bring righteousness.
4 May he defend the needy among the people;
    may he rescue the poor,
    and crush the oppressor.
5 May he live as long as the sun and the moon endure,
    from one generation to another.
6 May he come down like rain upon the mown field;
    like showers may he water the earth.
7 In his time may the righteous flourish;
    may there be abundance of peace, till the moon shall be no more.
8 May he rule from sea to sea,
    and from the River to the ends of the earth.
9 May his foes bow down before him,
    and his enemies lick the dust.
10 May the kings of Tarshish and of the isles pay tribute,
    and the kings of Arabia and Saba offer gifts.
11 May all kings bow down to him,
    and all the nations do him service.
12 For he shall deliver the poor who cries out in distress,
    and the oppressed who has no helper.
13 He shall have pity on the lowly and poor;
    he shall preserve the lives of the needy.
14 He shall redeem their lives from oppression and violence,
    and dear shall their blood be in his sight.
15 Long may he live!
    and may there be given to him of the gold of Arabia;
        may prayer be made for him continually,
        and may they bless him all the day long.
16 May there be abundance of grain on the earth,
    growing thick even on the hilltops;
        may its fruit flourish like Lebanon,
        and its grain like grass upon the earth.
17 May his name endure forever,
    and be established as long as the sun endures;
        through him may all the nations bless themselves, and
        call him blessed.

18 Blessed be the LORD God, the God of Israel,
       who alone does wondrous deeds!
19 And blessed be his glorious Name forever!
       and may all the earth be filled with his
          glory. Amen. Amen.

Psalm 80

1   Hear, O Shepherd of Israel, leading Joseph like a flock;
       shine forth, you that are enthroned upon the cherubim.
2   In the presence of Ephraim, Benjamin, and Manasseh,
       stir up your strength, and come and help us.
3   Restore us, O God of hosts;
       show the light of your countenance
       and we shall be saved.

4   O LORD God of hosts,
       how long will you be angered with
          the prayers of your people?
5   You have fed them with the bread of tears;
       you have given them bowls of tears to drink.
6   You have made us the derision of our neighbors,
       and our enemies laugh us to scorn.
7   Restore us, O God of hosts;
       show the light of your countenance
       and we shall be saved.

8   You have brought a vine out of Egypt;
       you cast out the nations, and planted it.
9   You prepared the ground for it;
       it took root and filled the land.
10 The mountains were covered by its shadow,
       and the towering cedar-trees by its boughs.
11 You stretched out its tendrils to the sea
       and its branches to the River.
12 Why have you broken down its wall,
       so that all who pass by pluck off its grapes?
13 The wild boar of the forest has ravaged it,
       and the wild beasts of the field have grazed upon it.
14 Turn now, O God of hosts,
       look down from heaven, and behold, and tend this vine;
          preserve what your right hand has planted.

15 They burn it with fire like rubbish;
    at the rebuke of your countenance let them perish.
16 Let your hand be upon the man whom you favor,
    the son of man you have made so strong for yourself.
17 And so we will never turn away from you;
    give us life, that we may call upon your Name.
18 Restore us, O Lord God of hosts;
    show the light of your countenance and we shall be saved.

Psalm 84

1 How dear to me is your dwelling, O Lord of hosts!
    My soul has a desire and longing for the courts of the Lord;
    my heart and my flesh rejoice in the living God.
2 The sparrow has found her a house,
    and the swallow a nest, where she may lay her young;
        upon your altars, O Lord of hosts,
        my King and my God.
3 How blest are they who dwell in your house!
    they will always be praising you.
4 How blest are the men whose strength is in you!
    whose hearts are set on the pilgrims' way.
5 They who go through the desolate valley
    will find it a place of springs;
        for the early rains have covered it with pools of water,
6 They will climb from height to height;
    the God of Gods will reveal himself in Zion.

7 Lord God of hosts, hear my prayer;
    hearken, O God of Jacob.
8 Behold our defender, O God;
    and look upon the face of your anointed.
9 For one day in your courts
    is better than a thousand in my own room;
        and to stand at the threshold of the house of my God
        than to dwell in the tents of the wicked.
10 For the Lord God is a sun and a shield;
    he will give grace and glory;
        and no good thing will the Lord withhold
        from those who walk with integrity.
11 Lord God of hosts,
    how blest is the man who puts his trust in you!

Psalm 85

1 You have been gracious to your land, O Lord;
    you have restored the good fortune of Jacob.
2 You have forgiven the iniquity of your people,
    and blotted out all their sins.
3 You have withdrawn all your fury;
    and turned yourself from your wrathful indignation.
4 Restore us, then, O God our Savior;
    let your anger depart from us.
5 Will you be displeased with us forever?
    will you prolong your anger from age to age?
6 Will you not give us life again,
    so that your people may rejoice in you?
7 Show us your mercy, O Lord,
    and grant us your salvation.

8 I will hearken to what the Lord God is saying;
    for he is speaking peace to his faithful people,
    and to those who turn their hearts to him.
9 Truly, his salvation is very near to those who fear him,
    so that his glory may dwell in our land.
10 Mercy and truth have met together;
    righteousness and peace have kissed each other.
11 Truth shall spring up from the earth,
    and righteousness shall look down from heaven.
12 The Lord will grant prosperity indeed,
    and our land shall yield her increase.
13 Righteousness shall go before him,
    and peace shall be a pathway for his feet.

Psalm 86

1 Bow down your ear, O Lord,
    and answer me, for I am poor and in misery.
2 Keep watch over my life, for I am faithful;
    save your servant who puts his trust in you.
3 You are my God;
  be merciful to me,
    for I call upon you all the day long.
4 Gladden the soul of your servant,
    for to you, O Lord, I lift up my soul.

5 For you, O Lord, are good and forgiving,
    and great is your love toward all who call upon you.
6 Give ear, O Lord, to my prayers,
    and attend to the voice of my supplication.
7 In the time of my trouble I will call upon you,
    for you will answer me.
8 Among the gods there is none like you, O Lord,
    nor anything like your works.
9 All nations you have made will come and
        worship you, O Lord,
    and glorify your Name.
10 For you are great;
  you do marvelous things;
    you alone are God.
11 Teach me your way, O Lord,
  and I will walk in your truth;
    knit my heart to you, that I may fear your Name.
12 I will thank you, O Lord my God, with all my heart,
    and glorify your Name for evermore.
13 For great is your love toward me;
    you have delivered me from the nethermost Pit.
14 The arrogant rise up against me, O God,
  and a band of violent men seeks my life;
    they have not set you before their eyes.
15 But you, O Lord, are compassionate and gracious,
    slow to anger, and full of kindness and truth.
16 Turn to me, and have mercy upon me;
    give your strength to your servant,
    and save the son of your handmaid.
17 Show me a sign of your favor,
  so that those who hate me may see it and be ashamed;
    because you, O Lord, have helped me and comforted me.

Psalm 90

1 Lord, you have been our refuge
    from one generation to another.
2 Before the mountains were brought forth,
  or the land and the earth were born,
    from age to age you are God.
3 You turn man back to the dust,
    and say, "Go back, O mortal man."

4 For a thousand years in your sight are like yesterday
        when it is past,
    and like a watch in the night.
5 You sweep men away like a dream;
    they fade away suddenly like the grass.
6 In the morning it is green and flourishes;
    in the evening it is dried up and withered.
7 For we consume away in your displeasure;
    we are afraid at your wrathful indignation.
8 You have set our iniquities before you;
    and our secret sins in the light of your countenance.
9 When you are angry, all our days are gone;
    we bring our years to an end like a sigh.
10 The span of our life is seventy years;
perhaps by strength even eighty;
    yet the sum of them is but labor and sorrow,
    for they pass away quickly and we are gone.
11 Who regards the power of your wrath?
    who rightly fears your indignation?
12 So teach us to number our days,
    that we may apply our hearts to wisdom.
13 Return, O Lord; how long will you tarry?
    Be gracious to your servants.
14 Satisfy us by your loving-kindness in the morning;
    so shall we rejoice and be glad all the days of our life.
15 Make us glad by the measure of the days that you afflicted us,
    and the years in which we suffered adversity.
16 Show your servants your works,
    and your splendor to their children.
17 May the graciousness of the Lord our God be upon us;
    prosper the work of our hands;
    prosper our handiwork.

Psalm 91

1 He who dwells in the shelter of the Most High,
    abides under the shadow of the Almighty.
2 He shall say to the Lord,
    "You are my refuge and my stronghold,
    my God in whom I put my trust."

3 He shall deliver you from the snare of the hunter,
    and from the deadly pestilence.

4   He shall cover you with his pinions,
        and you shall find refuge under his wings;
            his faithfulness shall be a shield and buckler.
5   You shall not be afraid of any terror by night,
        nor of the arrow that flies by day;
6   Of the plague that stalks in the darkness,
        nor of the sickness that lays waste at mid-day.
7   A thousand shall fall at your side,
        and ten thousand at your right hand;
            but it shall not come near you.
8   Your eyes have only to behold,
        to see the reward of the wicked.
9   Because you have made the Lord your refuge,
        and the Most High your habitation,
            there shall no evil happen to you,
            neither shall any plague come near your dwelling.
10 For he shall give his angels charge over you,
        to keep you in all your ways.
11 They shall bear you in their hands,
        lest you dash your foot against a stone.
12 You shall tread upon the lion and adder;
        you shall trample the young lion and the serpent
            under your feet.

13 Because he is bound to me in love,
            therefore will I deliver him;
        I will protect him, because he knows my Name.
14 He shall call upon me, and I will answer him;
        I am with him in trouble;
        I will rescue him and bring him to honor.
15 With long life will I satisfy him,
        and show him my salvation.

Psalm 92

1   It is a good thing to give thanks to the Lord;
        and to sing praises to your Name, O Most High;
2   To tell of your loving-kindness early in the morning,
        and of your faithfulness in the night season;
3   On the psaltery and on the lyre,
        and to the melody of the harp.
4   For you have made me glad by your acts, O Lord;
        and I shout for joy because of the works of your hands.

5 Lord, how great are your works!
   your thoughts are very deep.
6 The dullard does not know,
   nor does the fool understand,
      that though the ungodly grow like weeds,
      and all the workers of wickedness flourish,
7 They flourish only to be destroyed for ever;
      but you, O Lord, are exalted for evermore.
8 For lo, your enemies, O Lord,
   lo, your enemies shall perish,
      and all the workers of wickedness shall be scattered.
9 But my horn you have exalted like the horns of wild oxen;
   I am anointed with fresh oil.
10 My eyes also gloat over my enemies;
   and my ears have heard the last of the wicked
      who rise up against me.

11 The righteous shall flourish like a palm-tree;
      and shall spread abroad like a cedar of Lebanon.
12 Such as are planted in the house of the Lord
      shall flourish in the courts of our God;
13 They shall still bear fruit in old age;
      they shall be green and succulent;
14 That they may show how upright the Lord is,
      my Rock, in whom there is no fault.

Psalm 93

1 The Lord is King;
   he has put on splendid apparel;
      the Lord has put on his apparel,
      and girded himself with strength.
2 He has made the whole world so sure,
      that it cannot be moved.
3 Ever since the world began, your throne has been established;
      you are from everlasting.
4 The waters have lifted up, O Lord,
   the waters have lifted up their voice;
      the waters have lifted up their pounding waves.
5 Mightier than the sound of many waters,
   mightier than the breakers of the sea,
      mightier is the Lord who dwells on high.

6 Your testimonies are very sure,
    and holiness adorns your house, O Lord,
    for ever and for ever.

Psalm 95

1 Come, let us sing to the Lord;
    let us shout for joy to the Rock of our salvation.
2 Let us come before his presence with thanksgiving;
    and raise a loud shout to him with psalms.
3 For the Lord is a great God;
    and a great King above all gods.
4 In his hand are the caverns of the earth;
    and the heights of the hills are his also.
5 The sea is his, for he made it;
    and his hands have molded the dry land.
6 Come, let us bow down, and bend the knee,
    and kneel before the Lord our Maker.
7 For he is our God;
  and we are the people of his pasture,
    and the sheep of his hand.
    O that today you would hearken to his voice!

8 Harden not your hearts,
  as your fathers did in the wilderness,
    at Meribah, and on that day at Massah,
    when they tempted me:
9 They put me to the test,
    though they had seen my works.
10 Forty years long I detested that generation, and said,
    "This people waver in their hearts,
    for they do not know my ways."
11 So I swore in my wrath,
    "They shall not enter into my rest."

Psalm 96

1 Sing to the Lord a new song;
    sing to the Lord, all the whole earth.
2 Sing to the Lord, and bless his Name;
    proclaim the good news of his salvation from day to day.
3 Declare his glory among the nations;
    and his wonders among all peoples.

4 For great is the Lord, and greatly to be praised;
   he is more to be feared than all gods.
5 As for all the gods of the nations, they are but idols;
   but it is the Lord who made the heavens.
6 O the majesty and magnificence of his presence!
   O the power and the splendor of his sanctuary!
7 Ascribe to the Lord, you families of the peoples;
   ascribe to the Lord honor and power.
8 Ascribe to the Lord the honor proper to his Name;
   bring offerings, and come into his courts.
9 Worship the Lord in the beauty of holiness;
   let the whole earth tremble before him.
10 Tell it out among the nations: "The Lord is King!"
   the world, also, has he made so firm
       that it cannot be moved;
   and he will judge the peoples with equity.
11 Let the heavens rejoice, and let the earth be glad;
   let the sea make a noise, and all that is in it;
   let the field be joyful and all that therein is.
12 Then shall all the trees of the wood shout for joy
       before the Lord when he comes,
   when he comes to judge the earth.
13 He will judge the world with righteousness
   and the peoples with his truth.

Psalm 97

1 The Lord is King;
   let the earth rejoice;
       let the multitude of the isles be glad.
2 Clouds and darkness are round about him;
   righteousness and justice are the foundation of his throne.
3 A fire goes before him,
   and burns up his enemies on every side.
4 His lightnings light up the world;
   the earth sees it and is afraid.
5 The mountains melt like wax at the presence of the Lord,
   at the presence of the Lord of the whole earth.
6 The heavens declare his righteousness,
   and all the peoples see his glory.
7 Confounded be all who worship carved images,
   and delight in false gods!
       Bow down before him, all you gods.

8 Zion hears and is glad,
    and the cities of Judah rejoice;
        because of your judgments, O Lord.
9 For you are the Lord,
    most high over all the earth;
        you are exalted far above all gods.

10 The Lord loves those who hate evil;
    he preserves the lives of his saints,
    and delivers them from the hand of the wicked.
11 Light has sprung up for the righteous,
    and joyful gladness for such as are true-hearted.
12 Rejoice in the Lord, O you righteous,
    and give thanks to his holy Name.

Psalm 98

1 Sing to the Lord a new song;
    for he has done marvelous things.
2 With his right hand and his holy arm
    has he got for himself the victory.
3 The Lord has made known his victory;
    his righteousness has he openly showed
        in the sight of the nations.
4 He remembers his mercy and faithfulness
        to the house of Israel;
    and all the ends of the earth have seen
        the victory of our God.

5 Shout with joy to the Lord, all you lands;
    lift up your voice, rejoice, and sing.
6 Sing to the Lord with the harp;
    with the harp and the voice of song.
7 With trumpets and the sound of the horn,
    shout with joy before the King, the Lord.
8 Let the sea make a noise, and all that is in it;
    the lands, and those who dwell therein.
9 Let the rivers clap their hands;
    and let the hills ring out with joy before the Lord,
    when he comes to judge the earth.
10 In righteousness shall he judge the world,
    and the peoples with equity.

Psalm 99

1 The LORD is King,
   let the people tremble;
      he is enthroned upon the cherubim,
      let the earth shake.
2 The LORD is great in Zion;
   he is high above all peoples.
3 Let them confess his Name,
   which is great and awesome;
      he is the Holy One.
4 "O mighty King, Lover of justice,
   you have established equity;
      you have executed justice and righteousness in Jacob."
5 Magnify the LORD our God,
   and fall down before his footstool;
      he is the Holy One.
6 Moses and Aaron among his priests,
   and Samuel among those who call upon his Name;
      they called upon the LORD, and he answered them.
7 He spoke to them out of the pillar of cloud;
      they kept his testimonies,
      and the decree that he gave them.
8 O LORD our God, you answered them indeed;
      you were a God who forgave them,
      yet punished them for their evil deeds.

9 Magnify the LORD our God,
   and worship him upon his holy hill;
      for the LORD our God is the Holy One.

Psalm 100

1 Be joyful in the LORD, all you lands;
      serve the LORD with gladness,
      and come before his presence with a song.
2 Know this: The LORD himself is God;
      he himself has made us, and we are his;
      we are his people and the sheep of his pasture.
3 Enter his gates with thanksgiving;
      go into his courts with praise;
         give thanks to him and call upon his Name.

4   For the Lord is good;
      his mercy is everlasting;
        and his faithfulness endures from age to age.

Psalm 102

1   Lord, hear my prayer,
      and let my cry come before you;
        hide not your face from me,
        in the day of my trouble.
2   Incline your ear to me;
      when I call, make haste to answer me.
3   For my days drift away like smoke,
      and my bones are hot as burning coals.
4   My heart is smitten like grass and withered,
      so that I forget to eat my bread.
5   Because of the voice of my groaning,
      I am but skin and bones.
6   I have become like a vulture in the wilderness,
      like an owl among the ruins.
7   I lie awake and groan;
      I am like a sparrow, lonely on a house-top.
8   My enemies revile me all day long;
      and those who conspire against me are satisfied.
9   For I have eaten ashes for bread,
      and mingled my drink with weeping,
        because of your indignation and wrath;
        for you have lifted me up and thrown me away.
10 My days pass away like a shadow;
      and I wither like the grass.
11 But you, O Lord, endure for ever,
      and your Name from age to age.

12 You shall arise and have compassion on Zion;
      for it is time to have mercy upon her;
        indeed, the appointed time has come.
13 For your servants love her very rubble,
      and are moved to pity even for her dust.
14 The nations shall fear your Name, O Lord,
      and all the kings of the earth your glory.

15 For the Lord will build up Zion,
      and his glory will appear.

16 He will look with favor on the prayer of the homeless;
    he will not despise their plea.
17 Let this be written for a future generation,
    so that a people yet unborn may praise the Lord.
18 For the Lord looked down from his holy place on high;
    from the heavens he beheld the earth;
19 That he might hear the groan of the captive,
    and set free those condemned to die;
20 That men may declare in Zion the Name of the Lord,
    and his praise in Jerusalem;
21 When the peoples are gathered together,
    and the kingdoms also, to serve the Lord.

22 He has brought down my strength before my time
    he has shortened the number of my days;
23 And I said, O my God,
    do not take me away in the midst of my days;
    your years endure throughout all generations.
24 In the beginning, O Lord, you laid the foundations of the earth,
    and the heavens are the work of your hands;
25 They shall perish, but you will endure;
    they all shall wear out like a garment;
    like clothing you will change them,
        and they shall be changed;
26 But you are always the same;
    and your years will never end.
27 The children of your servants shall continue;
    and their offspring shall stand fast in your sight.

Psalm 103

1 Bless the Lord, O my soul;
    and all that is within me, bless his holy Name.
2 Bless the Lord, O my soul;
    and forget not all his benefits.

3 He forgives all my sins,
    and heals all my infirmities;
4 He redeems my life from the grave,
    and crowns me with mercy and loving-kindness;
5 He satisfies me with good things,
    and my youth is renewed like an eagle's.

6 The Lord executes righteousness,
    and judgment for all who are oppressed.
7 He made his ways known to Moses;
    and his works to the children of Israel.
8 The Lord is full of compassion and mercy,
    slow to anger and of great kindness.
9 He will not always accuse us,
    nor will he keep his anger forever.
10 He has not dealt with us according to our sins,
    nor rewarded us according to our wickedness.
11 For as the heavens are high over the earth,
    so is his mercy great over those who fear him.
12 Far as the east is from the west,
    so far has he removed our sins from us.
13 As a father cares for his children,
    so does the Lord care for those who fear him.
14 For he himself knows whereof we are made;
    he remembers that we are but dust.
15 The days of man are like the grass:
    he flourishes like a flower of the field;
16 When the wind goes over it, it is gone;
    and its place shall know it no more.
17 But the merciful goodness of the Lord endures for ever
    on those who fear him,
    and his righteousness on children's children;
18 On those who keep his covenant;
    and remember his commandments and do them.
19 The Lord has set his throne in heaven;
    and his kingship has dominion over all.

20 Bless the Lord, you angels of his,
    you mighty ones who do his bidding.
    and hearken to the voice of his word.
21 Bless the Lord, all you his hosts,
    you ministers of his who do his will.
22 Bless the Lord, all you works of his
    in all places of his dominion.
    Bless the Lord, O my soul.

Psalm 104

1 Bless the Lord, O my soul.
    O Lord my God, how excellent is your greatness!
    you are clothed with majesty and splendor.

2 You wrap yourself with light as with a cloak,
   and spread out the heavens like a curtain.
3 You lay the beams of your chambers in the waters above;
   youmake the clouds your chariot;
   you ride on the wings of the wind.
4 You make the winds your messengers,
   and flames of fire your servants.
5 You have set the earth upon its foundations,
   so that it never shall move at any time
6 You covered it with the Deep as with a mantle;
   the waters stood higher than the mountains.
7 At your rebuke they fled;
   at the voice of your thunder they hastened away.
8 They went up into the hills,
   and down to the valleys beneath,
   to the places you had appointed for them.
9 You set the limits that they should not pass;
   they shall not again cover the earth.

10 You send the springs into the valleys;
   they flow between the mountains.
11 All the beasts of the field drink their fill of them,
   and the wild asses quench their thirst.
12 Beside them the birds of the air make their nests,
   and sing among the branches.
13 You water the mountains from your dwelling on high;
   the earth is satisfied by the fruit of your works.
14 You make the grass grow for the cattle,
   and plants for the use of men;
15 That they may bring forth food from the earth,
   and wine to make glad the heart of man;
16 Oil to give man a cheerful countenance,
   and bread to strengthen his heart.

17 The trees of the LORD are full of sap,
   the cedars of Lebanon which he planted;
18 In which the birds build their nests,
   and in whose tops the stork makes his dwelling.
19 The high hills are a refuge for the mountain-goats,
   and the stony cliffs for the badgers.

20 You appointed the moon to mark the seasons,
   and the sun knows the time of its setting.

21 You make darkness that it may be night, *
   in which all the beasts of the forest prowl about.
22 The lions roar after their prey; *
   they seek their food from God.
23 The sun rises and they slip away, *
   and lay themselves down in their dens.
24 Man goes forth to his work, *
   and to his labor, until the evening.

25 O Lord, how manifold are your works! *
   in wisdom you have made them all;
   the earth is full of your creatures.
26 Yonder is the great and wide sea,
   with its living things too many to number, *
   creatures both small and great.
27 There move the ships,
   and there is that leviathan, *
   which you have made for the sport of it.
28 All of them look to you, *
   to give them their food in due season.
29 You give it to them, they gather it; *
   you open your hand,
   and they are filled with good things.
30 You hide your face, and they are terrified; *
   you take away their breath, and they die,
   and return to their dust.
31 You send forth your breath, and they are created; *
   and so you renew the face of the earth.

32 May the glory of the Lord endure for ever; *
   may the Lord rejoice in all his works.
33 He looks at the earth, and it trembles; *
   he touches the mountains, and they smoke.
34 I will sing to the Lord as long as I live; *
   I will praise my God while I have my being.
35 May these words of mine please him; *
   I will rejoice in the Lord.
36 Let sinners be consumed out of the earth, *
   and the wicked be no more.
37 Bless the Lord, O my soul; *
   Hallelujah!

Psalm 108

1 My heart is fixed, O God;
   my heart is fixed;
      I will sing and make melody.
2 Wake up, my spirit;
   awake, lute and harp;
      I myself will waken the morning.
3 I will confess you among the peoples, O Lord;
      I will sing praises to you among the nations.
4 For your loving-kindness is greater than the heavens,
      and your faithfulness reaches to the clouds.
5 Exalt yourself above the heavens, O God,
      and your glory over all the earth.
6 Deliver those who are dear to you;
      save with your right hand, and answer me.

7 God spoke from his holy place, and said:
   I will exult, and parcel out Shechem;
      I will divide up the valley of Succoth.
8 Gilead is mine, and Manasseh is mine;
      Ephraim is my helmet, and Judah my scepter.
9 As for Moab, she is my wash-basin;
   on Edom I throw down my sandal,
      and over Philistia will I shout in triumph.

10 Who will lead me into the strong city?
      who will bring me to Edom?
11 Have you not cast us off, O God?
      you no longer go out with our armies.
12 Grant us your help against the enemy,
      for vain is the help of man.
13 With God we will do valiant deeds,
      and he shall tread our enemies under foot.

Psalm 110

1 The Lord said to my Lord:
   "Sit at my right hand,
      until I make your enemies your footstool."
2 The Lord will send the scepter of your power out of Zion,
      saying, "Rule over your enemies round about you."

3 In the day of battle, your people will offer themselves freely
    upon the holy mountain;
  Your young men will come to you
    like dew from the womb of the morning.
4 The LORD has sworn, and he will not retract:
  "You are a Priest for ever,
  after the order of Melchizedek."
5 The Lord who is at your right hand
  will smite kings in the day of his wrath.

6 So the king will judge among the nations;
  he will heap high the corpses;
    he will smash heads over the wide earth.
7 He will drink from the brook beside the road;
  therefore, he will lift high his head.

Psalm 111

1 Hallelujah!
  I will give thanks to the LORD with my whole heart,
    in the assembly of the upright, in the congregation.
2 Great are the works of the LORD!
  they are studied by all who delight in them.
3 His work is full of majesty and splendor,
  and his righteousness endures for ever.
4 He makes his marvelous works to be remembered;
  the LORD is gracious and compassionate.
5 He gives food to those who fear him;
  he is ever mindful of his covenant.
6 He has shown his people the power of his works,
  in giving them the lands of the nations.
7 The works of his hands are faithfulness and justice;
  all his commandments are sure.
8 They stand fast for ever and ever,
  because they are done in truth and equity.
9 He sent redemption to his people;
  he commanded his covenant for ever;
    holy and awesome is his Name.
10 The fear of the LORD is the beginning of wisdom;
  those who act accordingly have a good understanding;
    his praise endures for ever.

Psalm 112

1 Hallelujah!
How blest is the man who fears the Lord,
    and has great delight in his commandments!
2 His descendants will be mighty in the land;
    the generation of the upright shall be blest.
3 Wealth and riches shall be in his house,
    and his righteousness shall last for ever.
4 Light shines in the darkness for the upright;
    the righteous man is merciful and compassionate.

5 It is good for a man to be generous in lending,
    and to manage his affairs with justice.
6 For he will never be shaken;
    the righteous shall be kept in everlasting remembrance.
7 He shall not be afraid of any evil rumors;
    his heart is right;
    he puts his trust in the Lord.
8 His heart is established, and will not shrink,
    until he sees his desire upon his enemies.
9 He has given freely to the poor;
    his righteousness stands fast for ever;
    he will hold up his head with honor.
10 The wicked shall see it, and be angry;
he shall gnash his teeth, and pine away;
    the desires of the wicked shall perish.

Psalm 113

1 Hallelujah!
Give praise, you servants of the Lord;
    praise the Name of the Lord.
2 Let the Name of the Lord be blest,
    from this time forth for evermore.
3 From the rising of the sun to its going down,
    let the Name of the Lord be praised.
4 The Lord is high above all nations,
    and his glory above the heavens.
5 Who is like the Lord our God,
    who sits enthroned on high,
        but stoops to behold the heavens and the earth?

6 He takes up the weak out of the dust,
    and lifts up the poor out of the ashes.
7 He sets him with the princes,
    with the princes of his people.
8 He makes the woman of a childless house
    to be a joyful mother of children.
    Hallelujah!

Psalm 114

1 When Israel came out of Egypt,
    the house of Jacob from among a people of strange speech,
2 Judah became the sanctuary of the Lord,
    and Israel his dominion.
3 The sea beheld it, and fled;
    and Jordan turned and went back.
4 The mountains skipped like rams,
    and the little hills like young sheep.
5 What ails you, O sea, that you fled?
    O Jordan, that you turned back?
6 You mountains, that you skipped like rams?
    You little hills, like young sheep?
7 Tremble, O earth, at the presence of the Lord;
    at the presence of the God of Jacob,
8 Who turned the hard rock into a pool of water,
    and the flint-stone into a flowing spring.

Psalm 116

1 I love the Lord, because he has heard
the voice of my entreaty;
    because he has inclined his ear to me
    whenever I called upon him.
2 The cords of death entangled me,
the grip of the grave took hold of me;
    I came to grief and sorrow.
3 Then I called upon the Name of the Lord:
    "O Lord, I pray you, save my life."

4 Gracious is the Lord, and righteous;
    our God is full of compassion.
5 The Lord watches over the innocent:
    I was brought very low, and he helped me.

6 Turn again to your rest, O my soul;
   for the Lord has treated you well.
7 For you have rescued my life from death,
   my eyes from tears, and my feet from stumbling.
8 I will walk in the presence of the Lord
   in the land of the living.
9 I believed, even when I said,
  "I have been brought very low."
   In my distress I said, "All men are liars."
10 How shall I repay the Lord
   for all the good things he has done for me?
11 I will lift up the cup of salvation,
   and call upon the Name of the Lord,
12 I will fulfill my vows to the Lord in the presence of all his people.
13 Precious in the sight of the Lord
   is the death of his servants.

14 O Lord, I am your servant;
   I am your servant, and the son of your handmaiden;
   you have freed me from my bonds.
15 I will offer you the sacrifice of thanksgiving,
   and call upon the Name of the Lord.
16 I will fulfill my vows to the Lord
   in the presence of all his people,
   in the courts of the Lord's house,
   in the midst of you, O Jerusalem. Hallelujah!

Psalm 117

1 Praise the Lord, all you nations;
   praise him, all you peoples.
2 For his loving-kindness toward us is great;
   and the faithfulness of the Lord endures for ever.
   Hallelujah!

Psalm 118

1 Give thanks to the Lord, for he is good;
   for his love endures for ever.
2 Let Israel now proclaim,
   "His love endures for ever."
3 Let the house of Aaron now proclaim,
   "His love endures for ever."

4   Let those who fear the Lord now proclaim,
        "His love endures for ever."
5   I called to the Lord in my distress;
        he answered by setting me free.
6   The Lord is on my side;
    therefore I will not fear;
        what can man do to me?
7   The Lord is on my side to help me;
        I will triumph over those who hate me.
8   It is better to rely on the Lord
        than to put any trust in man.
9   It is better to rely on the Lord
        than to put any trust in princes.
10 All nations compass me round about;
        in the Name of the Lord I will repel them.
11 They compass me, they compass me round about;
        inthe Name of the Lord I will repel them.
12 They swarm about me like bees;
    they blaze like a fire of thorns;
        in the Name of the Lord I will repel them.
13 I was pressed so hard that I almost fell;
        but the Lord came to my help.

14 The Lord is my strength and my song,
        and he has become my salvation.
15 There is a sound of exultation and victory
        in the tents of the righteous:
16 The right hand of the Lord has triumphed!
        the right hand of the Lord is exalted!
        the right hand of the Lord has triumphed!"
17 I shall not die, but live,
        and declare the works of the Lord.
18 The Lord has punished me sorely;
        but he did not hand me over to death.

19 Open for me the gates of righteousness;
        I will enter them;
        I will offer thanks to the Lord.
20 "This is the gate of the Lord,
        he who is righteous may enter."
21 I will give thanks to you, for you answered me,
        and have become my salvation.
22 The same stone which the builders rejected
        has become the chief corner-stone.

23 This is the Lord's doing,
    and it is marvelous in our eyes.
24 On this day the Lord has acted;
    we will rejoice and be glad in it.
25 Save us, Lord, we pray you;
    O Lord, grant us deliverance.

26 Blessed is he who comes in the Name of the Lord;
    we bless you from the house of the Lord.
27 God is the Lord; he has shined upon us;
    form a procession with branches
    up to the horns of the altar.
28 "You are my God, and I will thank you;
    you are my God, and I will exalt you."
29 Give thanks to the Lord, for he is good;
    for his love endures for ever,

Psalm 121

1 I will lift up my eyes to the hills.
    "Where is my help to come from?"
2 My help comes from the Lord,
    the Maker of heaven and earth.
3 He will not let your foot be moved,
    and he who watches over you will not fall asleep.
4 Behold, he who keeps watch over Israel
  shall neither slumber nor sleep:
    he who watches over you is the Lord.
5 The Lord is your shade at your right hand,
    so that the sun shall not strike you by day,
    nor the moon by night.
6 The Lord shall preserve you from all evil;
    it is he who shall keep you safe.
7 The Lord shall watch over your going out
      and your coming in,
  from this time forth for evermore.

Psalm 122

1 I was glad when they said to me,
    "Let us go to the house of the Lord."
2 Now our feet are standing,
    Jerusalem, within your gates.

3   Jerusalem is built as a city
        that is at unity with itself;
4   To which the tribes go up, the tribes of the Lord,
    the assembly of Israel,
        to praise the Name of the Lord.
5   For there are the thrones of judgment,
        the thrones of the house of David.
6   Pray for the peace of Jerusalem:
        May they prosper who love you.
7   Peace be within your walls;
        and quietness within your towers.
8   For my brethren and companions' sake,
        I pray for your prosperity.
9   Because of the house of the Lord our God,
        I will seek to do you good.

Psalm 124

1   If the Lord had not been on our side,
        now may Israel say;
2   If the Lord had not been on our side,
        when men rose up against us;
3   Then would they have swallowed us up alive,
        in their fierce anger toward us;
4   Then would the waters have overwhelmed us,
        and the torrent gone over us;
5   Then would the raging waters
        have gone right over us.
6   Blessed be the Lord! he has not given us over
        to be a prey for their teeth.
7   We have escaped, like a bird from the snare of the fowler;
        the snare is broken, and we have escaped.
8   Our help is in the Name of the Lord,
        the maker of heaven and earth.

Psalm 126

1   When the Lord restored the fortunes of Zion,
        then were we like men who dream.
2   Then was our mouth filled with laughter,
        and our tongue with joy.
3   Then they said among the nations,
        "The Lord has done great things for them."

4   The LORD has done great things for us,
        and we are glad indeed.
5   Restore our fortunes, O LORD,
        like the water-courses of the Negev.
6   Those who sowed with tears,
        will reap with songs of joy.
7   He who goes out weeping, carrying the seed,
        will come again with joy, shouldering his sheaves.

Psalm 130

1   Out of the depths have I called to you, O Lord;
    Lord, hear my voice;
        let your ears consider well the voice of my supplication.
2   If you, LORD, were to note what is done amiss,
    O LORD, who could survive?
        but there is forgiveness with you;
        therefore you shall be feared.
3   I wait for the LORD; my soul waits for him;
        in his word is my hope.
4   My soul waits for the LORD,
    more than watchmen for the morning,
        more than watchmen for the morning.
5   O Israel, wait for the LORD;
        for with the LORD there is mercy;
6   With him there is plenteous redemption;
        and he shall redeem Israel from all his sins.

Psalm 133

1   O, how good and pleasant it is,
        when brothers live together in unity!
2   It is like fine oil upon the head,
        that runs down upon the beard,
3   Upon the beard of Aaron,
        and runs down upon the collar of his robe.
4   It is like the dew of Hermon,
        that falls upon the hills of Zion.
5   For there the LORD has ordained the blessing,
        even life for evermore.

Psalm 134

1   Behold now, bless the Lord, all you servants of the Lord,
         you that stand by night in the house of the Lord.
2   Lift up your hands to the holy place, and bless the Lord.
         The Lord who made heaven and earth
              bless you out of Zion.

Psalm 139

1   Lord, you have searched me out, and known me;
         you know my sitting down, and my rising up again;
              you discern my thoughts from afar.
2   You trace my journeys, and my resting-places,
         and are acquainted with all my ways.
3   Indeed, there is not a word on my lips,
         but you, O Lord, know it altogether.
4   You press upon me behind and before,
         and lay your hand upon me.
5   Such knowledge is too wonderful for me;
         it is so high that I cannot attain to it.

6   Where can I go then from your Spirit?
         and where can I flee from your presence?
7   If I climb up to heaven, you are there;
         if I make the grave my bed, you are there also.
8   If I take the wings of the morning,
         and dwell in the uttermost parts of the sea,
9   Even there your hand will lead me,
         and your right hand hold me fast.
10 If I say, "Surely the darkness will cover me,
         and the light around me turn to night",
11 Darkness is not dark to you;
       the night is as bright as the day
         darkness and light to you are both alike.
12 For you yourself created my inmost parts;
         you knit me together in my mother's womb.
13 I will thank you because I am marvelously made;
         your works are wonderful, and I know it well
14 My body was not hidden from you,
       while I was being made in secret,
         and woven in the depths of the earth.

15 Your eyes beheld my limbs, yet unfinished in the womb;
all of them were written in your book;
they were fashioned day by day,
when as yet there was none of them.

16 How deep I find your thoughts, O God!
how great is the sum of them!
17 If I were to count them, they would be more in number than the sand;
to count them all, my life-span
would need to be like yours.
18 O that you would slay the wicked, O God!
You men of blood, depart from me.
19 They speak despitefully against you;
your enemies take your Name in vain.
20 Do I not hate them, O Lord, who hate you?
and do I not loathe them who rise up against you?
21 I hate them with a perfect hatred;
they have become my own enemies.
22 Search me out, O God, and know my heart;
try me, and know my restless thoughts.
23 Look well whether there be any wickedness in me,
and lead me in the way that is everlasting.

Psalm 142

1 I cry to the Lord with my voice;
to the Lord I make loud supplication.
2 I pour out my complaint before him,
and tell him all my trouble.

3 When my spirit languishes within me,
you know my path;
in the way wherein I walk they have hidden a trap for me.
4 I look to my right hand, and find no one who knows me;
I have no place to flee to, and no one cares for me.
5 I cry out to you, O Lord;
I say, "You are my refuge,
my portion in the land of the living."
6 Listen to my cry for help, for I am very low;
save me from those who pursue me,
for they are too strong for me.
7 Bring me out of prison, that I may give thanks to your Name;
when you have dealt bountifully with me,
the righteous will gather around me.

Psalm 145

1 I will exalt you, O God my King,
    and bless your Name for ever and ever.
2 Every day will I bless you,
    and praise your Name for ever and ever.
3 Great is the Lord, and greatly to be praised;
    there is no end to his greatness.
4 One generation shall praise your works to another,
    and shall declare your power.
5 I will ponder the glorious splendor of your majesty,
    and all your marvelous works.
6 Men shall speak of the might of your wondrous acts;
    and I will tell of your greatness.
7 They shall publish the remembrance of your great goodness;
    they shall sing of your righteous deeds.
8 The Lord is gracious and compassionate,
    slow to anger, and of great kindness.
9 The Lord is loving to every man;
    and his compassion is over all his works.
10 All your works praise you, O Lord:
    and your faithful servants bless you
11 They make known the glory of your kingdom,
    and speak of your power;
12 That men may know of your power,
    and the glorious splendor of your kingdom.
13 Your kingdom is an everlasting kingdom;
    your dominion endures throughout all ages.
14 The Lord is faithful in all his words,
    and merciful in all his deeds.
15 The Lord upholds all those who fall;
    he lifts up those who are bowed down.
16 The eyes of all wait upon you, O Lord:
    and you give them their food in due season.
17 You open wide your hand,
    and satisfy the needs of every living creature.
18 The Lord is righteous in all his ways,
    and loving in all his works.
19 The Lord is near to all who call upon him,
    to all who call upon him faithfully.
20 He fulfills the desire of those who fear him;
    he hears their cry, and helps them.

21 The Lord preserves all those who love him;
    but he destroys all the wicked.
22 My mouth shall speak the praise of the Lord;
    let all flesh bless his holy Name,
    for ever and ever.

Psalm 147

1 Hallelujah!
  How good it is to sing praises to our God!
    how pleasant it is to honor him with praise!
2 The Lord rebuilds Jerusalem;
    he gathers the exiles of Israel.
3 He heals the broken-hearted,
    and binds up their wounds.
4 He counts the number of the stars,
    and calls them all by their names.
5 Great is our Lord, and mighty in power;
    thereis no limit to his wisdom.
6 The Lord gives relief to the lowly,
    but casts the wicked to the ground.
7 Sing to the Lord with thanksgiving;
    make music to our God upon the harp.
8 He covers the heavens with clouds,
  and prepares rain for the earth;
    he makes grass to grow upon the mountains,
    and green plants for the use of men.
9 He provides food for the cattle,
    and for the young ravens when they cry.
10 He is not impressed by the might of a horse;
    he has no pleasure in the strength of a man.
11 But the Lord has pleasure in those who fear him,
    in those who await his gracious favor.
12 Worship the Lord, O Jerusalem;
    praise your God, O Zion.
13 For he has strengthened the bars of your gates;
    he has blessed your children within you.
14 He has established peace on your borders;
    he satisfies you with the finest wheat.
15 He sends out his command to the earth,
    and his word runs very swiftly.
16 He gives snow like wool;
    he scatters hoar-frost like ashes.

17   He scatters his ice like bread-crumbs;
         who can stand against his cold?
18   He sends forth his word, and melts them;
         he blows with his wind, and the waters flow.
19   He declares his word to Jacob,
         his statutes and his judgments to Israel.
20   He has not done so to any other nation;
         to them he has not revealed his judgments.
     Hallelujah!

Psalm 148

1   Hallelujah!
     Praise the Lord from the heavens;
         praise him in the heights.
2   Praise him all you angels of his;
         praise him, all his host.
3   Praise him, sun and moon;
         praise him, all you shining stars.
4   Praise him, heavens of heavens,
         and you waters above the heavens.
5   Let them praise the Name of the Lord;
         for he commanded, and they were created.
6   He made them fast for ever and ever;
         he gave them a law which shall not pass away.
7   Praise the Lord from the earth,
         you sea-monsters and all deeps;
8   Fire and hail, snow and fog,
         tempestuous wind, doing his will;
9   Mountains and all hills,
         fruit-trees and all cedars;
10   Wild beasts and all cattle,
         creeping things and winged birds;
11   Kings of the earth and all peoples,
         princes and all rulers of the world;
12   Young men and maidens,
         old and young together;
13   Let them praise the Name of the Lord;
         for his Name only is exalted,
         his splendor is over earth and heaven.
14   He has raised up strength for his people,
     and praise for all his loyal servants,
         the children of Israel, a people that is near him.
     Hallelujah!

Psalm 150

1 Hallelujah!
   Praise God in his holy temple;
      praise him in the firmament of his power.
2 Praise him for his mighty acts;
      praise him for his excellent greatness.
3 Praise him with the blast of a horn;
      praise him with lyre and harp.
4 Praise him with timbrel and dance;
      praise him with strings and pipe.
5 Praise him with resounding cymbals;
      praise him with loud-clanging cymbals.
6 Let everything that breathes
      praise the Lord.
      Hallelujah!

PRAYER BOOK STUDIES 24: PASTORAL OFFICES

1970

The readings from the Scriptures quoted in *The Order for the Burial of the Dead* (Second Service) are from *The New English Bible with the Apocrypha*. © The Delegates of the Oxford University Press and The Syndics of the Cambridge University Press, 1961, 1970. Reprinted by permission.

The three poems quoted in *The Order for the Burial of the Dead* (Second Service) are from *Your Word is Near* by Huub Oosterhuis. Copyright © 1968 by The Missionary Society of St. Paul the Apostle in the State of New York. Reprinted by permission.

PREFACE

The several services and forms presented in this Study are the work of three Drafting Committees set up by the Standing Liturgical Commission under the terms of the Plan for the Revision of the Book of Common Prayer, adopted by the General Convention in 1967.

Under this Plan, the Commission set up fourteen Drafting Committees and assigned to each the initial task of revising a section of the Book of Common Prayer. Each Committee worked under the chairmanship of a member of the Commission, in order to ensure the fullest possible liaison and co-ordination between the Commission and the Committee. The work of each Drafting Committee was circulated, at each stage of its development, to the Consultants appointed under the Revision Plan. Their comments and suggestions were taken fully into account by the Drafting Committees concerned, and were brought to the attention of the Commission itself. Each successive draft was studied by the Commission, debated, revised, returned to the Drafting Committee and, when finally approved, was referred by the Commission to its Editorial Committee for final editing and publication.[1]

Since each of the rites and forms included in this Study is too brief for separate printing as a Prayer Book Study, the Commission decided, for reasons both of convenience and economy, to group them together under the heading of Pastoral Offices.

Each of the offices has to do with an aspect of personal relationship between the Church member and the Church. Each is, generally speaking, concerned with the sanctification of an important part of a Christian's personal life. In a larger sense, all rites of the Church have to do with the personal relationship between the individual worshiper and the Church, and all are channels of divine grace to the individual worshiper. Nonetheless, it is generally true that in the great rites

---

1. The Editorial Committee consists of four members of the Commission: The Rev. Robert W. Estill, Chairman; the Rev. Canon Charles M. Guilbert; the Rev. H. Boone Porter, Jr.; and the Rev. Massey H. Shepherd, Jr. The Rev. Donald L. Garfield, one of the Commission's Consultants and a member of its Drafting Committee on the Church Year, was appointed as full member of the Editorial Committee. The Committee also had the assistance, as members *ex officio*, of the Rev. Leo Malania, Co-ordinator for Prayer Book Revision, and Captain Howard E. Galley, C.A. of the Co-ordinator's staff. Although other responsibilities prevented the Rev. Dr. Shepherd from attending all but a few meetings of the Editorial Committee, he was frequently consulted by mail and telephone.

of Baptism, the Laying-on-of-Hands, and the Holy Eucharist, as well as in the Ordination of Bishops, Priests and Deacons, in the Daily Offices of Morning and Evening Prayer, and in the celebration of the Church Year, the primary emphasis is on the life of the Church as an organic community, and on the building up of the people of God as the Body of Christ and the instrument of God's purpose and mission to the world.

In the Pastoral Offices, the main emphasis is on the personal life of the individual, and on his personal relationship to the larger life of the Church.

"The Celebration and Blessing of a Marriage" and "A Thanksgiving for the Birth of a Child" are the work of a Drafting Committee constituted as follows:

> The Rev. Louis B. Keiter, member of the Standing Liturgical Commission and Chairman of the Drafting Committee
> The Rev. Robert H. Cochrane
> The Rev. Canon Nicholas Kouletsis
> Mr. and Mrs. L. Dale Pederson
> Mrs. Harold Sorg
> The Rev. George F. Tittmann

"The Ministration to the Sick and Suffering," "The Reconciliation of a Penitent," "The Anointing of the Sick," and "The Order for Private Communions" were prepared by a Drafting Committee consisting of the following:

> Dr. John W. Ashton, member of the Standing Liturgical Commission and Chairman of the Drafting Committee
> The Rev. Don H. Gross, member of the Joint Commission on Religion and Health
> The Rev. Kenneth W. Mann
> Dr. John E. Sweeney[2]
> The Rev. Thomas Talley

"The Order for the Burial of the Dead" was prepared by a Drafting Committee constituted as follows:

> Mr. James D. Dunning, member of the Standing Liturgical Commission and Chairman of the Drafting Committee
> The Right Reverend Charles F. Boynton
> The Rev. Francis F. E. Blake
> The Rev. R. F. Hipwell

---

2. Dr. Sweeney died on 15 November, 1969.

The Right Reverend Albert R. Stuart[3]
The Rev. Lloyd E. Teter, Jr.

"A Form of Commitment to Christian Service" was prepared, pursuant to a formal request of the Standing Liturgical Commission, by the Chairman of the Drafting Committee on Christian Initiation, the Reverend Bonnell Spencer, O.H.C. This Form is a response to the suggestions made by the Commission's Consultants, Chairmen of Diocesan Liturgical Commissions and Committees, and others, in the course of discussions of the proposal in *Prayer Book Studies* 18 to reunite Baptism and Confirmation within the context of a celebration of the Eucharist.

The Commission wishes to place on record its sincere thanks to all who have contributed to the preparation of the offices and rites presented here, whether as members of the Drafting Committees, or as Consultants and other interested members of the Church. In particular, the Commission expresses its appreciation to the Dean and Faculty of the Church Divinity School of the Pacific, Berkeley, California, for their hospitality to the Drafting Committee on Marriage; to Mr. James D. Dunning and the other Officers of the New York Life Insurance Company for their hospitality to the Drafting Committee on the Burial of the Dead; and to the President and Faculty of the University of Indiana for their hospitality both to the Commission itself and to the Drafting Committee headed by Dr. Ashton. The Commission is grateful to the Delegates of the Oxford University Press and the Syndics of the Cambridge University Press for permission to reprint passages from The *New English Bible with the Apocrypha*, and to the Missionary Society of St. Paul the Apostle in the State of New York for permission to reprint several passages from *Your Word is Near* by Huub Oosterhuis.

A basic principle of the 1967 Plan of Prayer Book Revision is to involve as many as possible in the process of drafting the new rites and forms of service and in evaluating their effectiveness. In commending the Pastoral Offices for trial use by the whole Church, the Commission invites all who may read this Study to send their comments, criticisms, and suggestions to the Standing Liturgical Commission, 815 Second Avenue, New York, N.Y., 10017.

All communications will be gratefully acknowledged and will be taken into account in any further work of Prayer Book Revision.
THE STANDING LITURGICAL COMMISSION

Chilton Powell, *Chairman*
John W. Ashton
Dupuy Bateman, Jr.

---

[3]. Because of the pressure of other duties, Bishop Stuart found it necessary to resign from the Drafting Committee.

James D. Dunning
Robert W. Estill
William C. Frey
Charles M. Guilbert, *Secretary*
Mrs. Richard Harbour
Joseph M. Harte
Louis B. Keiter
H. Boone Porter, Jr.
Charles P. Price
Massey H. Shepherd, Jr., *Vice Chairman*
Jonathan G. Sherman
Charles W. F. Smith
Bonnell Spencer, O.H.C.
Albert R. Stuart
Leo Malania, Co-ordinator

Introduction

The Standing Liturgical Commission offers for the consideration of the whole Church two complete services, The Celebration and Blessing of a Marriage and The Order for the Burial of the Dead, together with shorter forms and orders for A Thanksgiving for the Birth of a Child, The Ministration to the Sick and Suffering, The Anointing of the Sick, a Form for the Reconciliation of a Penitent, a Form of Commitment to Christian Service, and The Order for Private Communions. These have been grouped together under the title of Pastoral Offices, since the main concern of these various services is the relationship between the individual and God through the Church.

While the services are published together in one volume at this stage of the work of Prayer Book Revision, it is the Commission's intention, should they be approved for trial use, to arrange for the separate publication of at least two of them: The Celebration and Blessing of a Marriage and The Order for the Burial of the Dead.

The various offices in this Study reflect the distinctive tradition of the Episcopal Church. They are clearly rooted in the Book of Common Prayer. Two of the services in the present Prayer Book, "The Solemnization of Matrimony" and "The Burial of the Dead," have been widely used by other churches. They have been, in a sense, the contribution of the Episcopal Church to the ecumenical life of the Christian community before the present expansion of ecumenical contacts.

For its part the Episcopal Church has been deeply engaged in contemporary ecumenical exchanges. A member of the Liturgical Commission has attended meetings of the Consilium of the Roman Catholic Church at the Vatican,[1] and the Commission's Study on "The Church Year"[2] is greatly indebted to the scholars and officials of the Roman Catholic Church for the work they have accomplished since Vatican Council II. Two members of the Commission have represented the Episcopal Church on the Committee on Worship of the Consultation on Church Union.[3]

---

1. The Reverend Massey H. Shepherd, Jr., is one of two representatives appointed by the Archbishop of Canterbury to represent the Anglican Communion as Observers at meetings of the *Consilium*. The other is the Rev. Canon R.C.D. Jasper of the Liturgical Commission of the Church of England.

2. *The Church Year* (*Prayer Book Studies* 19), prepared by the Standing Liturgical Commission, New York, The Church Hymnal Corporation, 1970.

3. The Reverend Massey H. Shepherd, Jr., and the Reverend Charles W. F. Smith. Following Dr. Shepherd's resignation from the COCU's Committee on Worship, early in 1970, he was replaced by the Reverend H. Boone Porter, Jr. The COCU's *An Order of Worship* (Cincinnati, Forward Movement Publications, 1969) incorporates many of the features of *The Liturgy of the Lord's Supper* (*Prayer Book Studies* XVII, 1966), and the Ordinal prepared by COCU has borrowed some features from *The Ordination of Bishops, Priests, and Deacons* (*Prayer Book Studies* 20) prepared by the Standing Liturgical Commission and published by The Church Hymnal Corporation in 1970.

Mention should also be made of the International Consultation on English Texts (ICET), a body formed in 1969 for the purpose of preparing agreed English versions of prayers common to most Christian Churches.[4] The Standing Liturgical Commission has decided to use several of these texts in the contemporary-language versions of revised rites and services prepared under the 1967 Plan for the Revision of the Book of Common Prayer.

In an age of rapidly expanding ecumenical contacts and far-reaching revisions by all Churches of their time-honored formularies of worship, it is the Liturgical Commission's hope that the revised services presented here may be found useful by other Christian bodies and congregations, and that they also will subject these services to critical study and trial use, and communicate to the Commission the evaluation of their experience together with their criticisms and suggestions.

The Celebration and Blessing of a Marriage

Marriage is a solemn contract between a man and a woman, concluded and ratified in public because it concerns the entire community. The qualifications for marriage are today primarily a matter for the civil authorities although the Church maintains its own additional criteria for marriage in the Canon Law. Yet the role of the clergyman as a civil magistrate continues to be recognized. To be properly registered as a valid legal document, the license issued by the civil authority must be duly signed by a magistrate or the officiating clergyman and returned within a specified period after its issuance. Thus, a juridical element continues to be a part of the marriage rite.

In the eyes of the Church, even more than in the eyes of the civil authority, marriage can never be merely a private contract. It is a solemn act, the creation of a new family within the larger family of mankind, of which the Christian

---

4. The ICET consists of members drawn from the official liturgical or worship commissions of the following Churches:

1) The Roman Catholic Church—members of the Advisory Committee of its International Committee on English in the Liturgy, including representatives from England, Ireland, the United States, Canada and Australia;

2) The Anglican Churches—representatives of the liturgical commissions of the Church of England, the Episcopal Church of Scotland, the Church of Ireland, the Church in Wales, and the Episcopal Church in the United States;

3) The Inter-Lutheran Commission on Worship, which comprises members of the Lutheran Church of America, the American Lutheran Church, and the Lutheran Church of the Missouri Synod; and

4) The (Presbyterian) Church of Scotland; and the English Methodist, Presbyterian, Congregational, and Baptist Churches.

The Episcopal Church has been represented on the ICET by the Reverend Massey H. Shepherd, Jr., and the Reverend Charles W. F. Smith. The ICET has published its versions of certain formularies in "Prayers We Have in Common" (London, Geoffrey Chapman, 1970; Philadelphia, Fortress Press, 1970).

community is a part. It is the highest expression of love between a man and a woman, and the Church has always recognized in all legitimate expressions of love a sacramental sign of the love of God for man, and more specifically, of Christ's love for the Church. Marriage is a solemn commitment by two persons to follow a new way of life, and therefore, marriage between two Christians is a renewed commitment by them to ground their new life together in the life of Christ. Considered as a formal bond between two persons, marriage is their life-long undertaking to love one another in all the circumstances and vicissitudes of human life and to remain faithful to one another; as the creation of a new family, marriage is a commitment to show forth the meaning of love to the larger community in which the new family makes its home, and to bring up a new generation of Christians in the knowledge and love of God.

An undertaking of such far-reaching consequences needs for its fulfillment all the strength and support the Church can give it. It needs grace, the power of the love of Christ, not only at the beginning, but throughout the life of the marriage. There is considerable evidence in pastoral experience that among the young especially, for whom marriage is often the first major act of their maturity, there is a growing desire to relate their commitment to one another to a larger life of transcendent dimensions.

In preparing this revision, the Standing Liturgical Commission has sought to give expression to these various elements, while preserving a clearly recognizable continuity with the traditional service. But the proposed rite is not a mere translation of an older rite into more contemporary terms. The Commission hopes that the new rite will be recognized as an expression of the fundamental realities of life in a contemporary form, and without loss of the dignity, solemnity and eloquence which have been distinctive marks of the Anglican tradition.

The new note is set by the title "The Celebration and Blessing of a Marriage." It reflects contemporary attitudes more accurately than the older "Solemnization of Matrimony."

The Service consists of three parts: an opening section, the Marriage proper, and the Blessing of the Marriage. The Service may end immediately after the Blessing which follows the proclamation of the Marriage, or, more logically, conclude with the celebration of a nuptial Eucharist.

In the opening section, the meaning and importance of marriage are briefly stated: mutual joy, mutual help and comfort, and, when it is God's will, "the procreation of children and their nurture in the knowledge and love of the Lord."

The possibility of developing any of these themes is permitted in the provision for a sermon or homily, but this is optional. The "cautions" are preserved, though the specific mention of the "dreadful day of judgment" is eliminated, and the legalistic note is toned down, since the question whether or not a marriage is lawful is a matter primarily for the civil authority.

The role of society, which is often crucial in sustaining or breaking a marriage, is recognized in the question to the wedding party and the congregation and in their pledge to do all in their power "to support and uphold this marriage in the years ahead."

The readings are a new feature of this American revision. The readings provided offer a wide choice. They include the account from Genesis of the creation of the first man and woman and the institution of the unbreakable bond between them; St. Paul's admonition from Colossians to love and forgive; the passage from Ephesians provided in the Prayer Book for the nuptial Eucharist (pages 267-268); the great hymn of love in the thirteenth Chapter of First Corinthians; and a passage on the love of God from the First Epistle of John.

The readings from the Gospel consist of our Lord's restatement, from the Gospel according to Mark, of the bond of union between man and woman at Creation; Matthew's account of our Lord's parable of the house built on the rock and the house built on sand, included here because the grounding of a marriage in the life of Christ is, in fact, building it on the Rock; the admonition from the Sermon on the Mount that one's light should not be hidden under a bucket, thus suggesting the mission of the new Christian family in the world; and our Lord's command to his disciples from the Gospel of St. John, to love one another.

In addition to enriching the Marriage Service itself with a biblical frame of reference, the introductory section of the rite constitutes a full Ministry of the Word for the celebration of the nuptial Eucharist.

The "giving away of the bride" has been retained, but made optional. Although the significance of this survival from the days when women were property has been rationalized as no longer a "transfer of obedience" but that of loving care,[5] it is nevertheless an anomaly, which no doubt could be rationalized still further as the severing of parental bonds preliminary to the establishing of new family bonds.

The second section is entitled "The Marriage," and here the man and woman exchange their vows in the traditional words beloved of many generations. These have been slightly revised to eliminate archaisms. The distinction between the man's "plighting his troth" and the woman merely giving it—presumably because she has nothing to "pledge"—has disappeared. In place of these words each concludes with the declaration, "This is my solemn vow."

A blessing of two rings has been provided, in recognition of a growing custom. The sentence accompanying the exchange of the rings carries an echo of two clauses from the original English form, "With my body I thee worship," eliminated in The Proposed Book of 1786, and "With all my worldly goods I thee endow," dropped in the revision of 1928. The sentence now concludes, "With all that I am, and all that I have, I honor you, in the name of God." The Trinitarian formula has been replaced here by the simpler form, in recognition of the increase in the number of marriages between Episcopalians and persons of other faiths,

---

5. Massey H. Shepherd, Jr., "The Oxford American Prayer Book Commentary", pages 301-302.

for whom the necessity of their verbalizing the Trinitarian formula may be an imposition. But it has been retained in the Declaration of the Marriage and in the solemn nuptial Blessing.

The declaration of the marriage follows in the traditional wording, and the injunction "Those whom God has joined together let not man put asunder" is added immediately afterwards, without any intervening prayers. To this injunction the congregation responds *Amen*.

The Blessing of the Marriage begins with the Lord's Prayer (printed here in the ICET version).[6] Of the prayers which follow, the first, said over the newly-married couple, and the last are required. The others are optional. The traditional nuptial Blessing of the couple is followed by the exchange of the Peace, after which, the wedding party may leave the Church.

In all the Pastoral Offices, the Commission has had it in mind that Holy Communion should be the climactic action, or the context within which the service is placed. Nor should Communion be limited to those directly concerned, in this case, the newly-married couple. Communion should be available to the entire congregation.

When Communion is to follow, the Blessing of the Marriage takes place at a later point, the Proclamation of the Marriage being followed by prayers in litany form. To each petition, the congregation responds with a simple *Amen*. The suffrages cover the gift of children, the gift of love, concern for others, and the strengthening of the marriage vows of all those present. The final petition, recalling the bonds of our common humanity "which unite every man to his neighbor, and the living to the dead," prays that these bonds "may be transformed by divine grace, that justice and peace may prevail, and your will be done on earth as it is in heaven." The traditional prayer over the couple and the nuptial Blessing then take place, followed by the exchange of the Peace. The Liturgy continues with the Offertory, and the new husband and wife present the bread and wine and receive communion, their first acts together as a married couple.

A Thanksgiving for the Birth of a Child

In introducing the first attempt, in 1958, to revise "The Thanksgiving of Women after Child-birth/Commonly called 'The Churching of Women'," the Standing Liturgical Commission pointed out[7] the defects of the service in the Prayer Book: its suggestion of a taboo of uncleanness associated with childbirth, and the implied need of some kind of "purification"; an exaggerated emphasis upon the dangers of childbirth; and the "unreality of building an entire service about

---

6. See above page 246.

7. *A Thanksgiving for the Birth of a Child* (*Prayer Book Studies* XI), The Church Pension Fund, New York, 1958.

this theme in the light of present-day conditions where the normative expectancy of the family is hopeful of a happy and successful birth of a new life."[8] A related defect of the present service is the absence of an indication of the point, in a regular service of worship, at which the Thanksgiving is to take place.

In preparing this new revision for trial use by the Church, the Commission's purpose was to express the feelings of exultation and thankfulness felt by the parents when a child is born to them, and to associate the entire family of the Church in this expression of thankfulness and joy, thus bringing a feeling of warmth and community into our congregations.

Prayers with three specific emphases have been included: Thankfulness for the birth of the child, petition for help and guidance in raising the child, and a blessing on the family of the newborn, and on all families.

The rubrics make it clear that one or more of the prayers may be used alone at any time or in the context of a service in the hospital or at home, but preferably in the Church.

When used at the Eucharist, and this is recommended, a suitable place for the Thanksgiving is after the conclusion of the Announcements. The Minister invites the parents of the child, accompanied, if desired, by other members of the family to come for ward and take their place before the Altar. Then all say the appointed Psalm. The Minister may arrange, instead, for ushers or one of the servers to lead the family to the Altar during the singing or recitation of the Psalm. Much depends on the physical arrangement of the Church, the degree of intimacy and informality among the members of the congregation, and other factors best left to the Minister's discretion. A priestly blessing or the exchange of the Peace is a fitting conclusion to the Service.

If used with Morning or Evening Prayer, the Thanksgiving could also be used after the Announcements.

A Form of Commitment to Christian Service

The publication of "Holy Baptism with the Laying-on-of-Hands"[9] raised some questions regarding the advisability of completing the entire process of Christian Initiation at a very early age. There is considerable dissatisfaction with the current practice of a once-for-all renewal of baptismal vows at Confirmation as a prerequisite to Communion at somewhere between the ages of nine and sixteen. To resolve the problem two opposite suggestions have been made. One is to admit young children to Communion before Confirmation, the other is to postpone Confirmation until it can be a fully adult commitment.

---

8. *ibid.* Vol. 3, p. 19.

9. *Prayer Book Studies* 18, prepared by the Standing Liturgical Commission, New York, The Church Hymnal Corporation, 1970.

The Commission has taken the stand that the theological and pastoral integrity of Baptism should not be broken or overshadowed by a separated Confirmation. The Commission's proposal reunites Confirmation with Baptism, in accordance with ancient practice and the theological importance of Baptism as one of the two great Sacraments instituted by Our Lord. The Commission has suggested that personal commitment to one's Baptismal promises should be made not once and for all at Confirmation, but many times over, preferably within the context of a service of Baptism with the Laying-on-of-Hands, which, it is hoped, would become a principal service of the congregation some three or four times a year, one of these at its traditional place in the Vigil Service of Easter Eve.

It has been suggested, however, that in addition to this reaffirmation of its commitment by the entire congregation, provision should be made for a form of individual commitment at critical points in a person's life—a graduation, a change of vocation, the beginning of military service, the undertaking of a course of training, and so on. The form proposed is designed to meet these situations. While it may be used at any time for a personal renewal of one's baptismal promises (in which case the questions in the baptismal office may be asked), the intent of the proposed form is to enable a lay person to affirm and to renew his personal commitment to the service of Christ in the world, for only a baptized person can make a specific personal commitment and recommitment to serve Christ. Such a public commitment becomes, in fact, a reaffirmation of Baptismal promises in the concrete context of Christian service.

The form is extremely simple. It may be extended, as necessary or desirable, by the inclusion of suitable questions and answers and appropriate prayers. It was felt that considerable latitude should be left to the Minister and the person concerned to work together in formulating the terms of such recommitment. Any prescribed form of words that would attempt to cover all contingencies would have to be so vague as to be more confusing than helpful. On the other hand, a conference between the Minister and a lay person intended to clarify the nature of his commitment to Christian service in the world could have great pastoral value.

The Ministration to the Sick and Suffering

As *Prayer Book Studies III* pointed out,[10] our attitudes toward sickness in the twentieth century have changed greatly from those of earlier periods. The grim view of illness as punishment for sin and the concept of the "visitation" as a preparation for death, no longer are sound in the light of the advances of medical knowledge and techniques, particularly in the last fifty years, nor has such an approach any

---

10. *The Order for the Ministration to the Sick* (*Prayer Book Studies III*), prepared by the Standing Liturgical Commission, New York; The Church Pension Fund, 1951.

foundation in Scripture. The purpose of the Order is to seek through God's help the restoration of the patient to health and to soundness of mind and body, and to give him the comfort and spiritual strength to enable him to endure suffering and all the discomforts of illness with hope and with quietness of mind. At the same time it must be recognized that we cannot fully know God's will in these matters, and that we are really asking God to "fulfill now the desires and petitions of his servants *as may be most expedient for them.*"

It needs to be recognized, too, that there is a wide variety of circumstances under which the sick may be ministered to, from a critical case where death may be imminent and the patient barely conscious, to the severely handicapped or chronically ill in body, but sound in mind, to the mentally ill and the retarded, or to groups of the aged whose attention span may not be long, but who cherish the regular ministrations of the Church; from the individual in a hospital room or at home, to a public service of healing. Any adequate service must, therefore, take into account all these possibilities and be flexible enough to meet many conceivable situations. An important consequence is that this calls for a degree of brevity and simplicity, so that the sick person may not be tired by overlong exposition or too active participation. The essential task is to establish the sense of compassion and healing mercy which our Lord showed in the many acts of healing recorded in the Gospels and which were carried on by the Apostles, as set down in the Book of Acts. This function is essentially the same whether in private visits or public services of healing.

With this in mind, the Order for the Ministration to the Sick has been constructed on a modular pattern, as was suggested in *Prayer Book Studies III*, but omitting some of the modules or options provided in that study. Four basic sections of a complete Order have been drawn up, so that any one of them can be used alone or any combination may be made, always with the proviso, that in a combination, the parts shall be included in the order given in this text: Ministry of the Word, Reconciliation, Anointing or laying on of hands, and Communion. How much of each element will be used on any one occasion will, of course, depend on the situation and the judgment of the Minister.

While the Service was being developed some of the Commission's consultants questioned the "coldness" of the form in its earlier versions. In some measure this is unavoidable in a formal service such as this. But it should not be assumed that this is all that happens in the visit to the sick. A heavy responsibility always rests on the Minister to provide by his tone and manner and by his personal comments the warmth and comfort and compassion that will put this Order in the right perspective."[11]

---

11. While it would be wrong to focus attention on healing as the one exclusive purpose of such ministration, and thus to arouse expectations which are not always fulfilled, the facts of Christian experience referred to in *Prayer Book Studies III*, Vol. 1, p. 103, must not be overlooked: that "spiritual help and *therefore* also physical betterment, is to be expected," and that often at least partial and temporary improvement follows the Anointing or laying on of hands, or Communion.

In reworking this material for publication, it became apparent that to include under one heading "The Ministry to the Sick," all the separable sections, namely, the Reconciliation of the Penitent, the Anointing of the Sick, and the form of Communion administered in the home or the hospital, would be to limit severely the use of these forms in other circumstances than those of the sick-room. The Reconciliation of the Penitent should be available for use by the physically healthy, no less than the sick. The Second Exhortation in the Book of Common Prayer urges the Communicant to examine his life, to confess his sins, and to make restitution and satisfaction for any wrong done to his neighbor. The Priest concludes by adding that "if there be any of you, who by this means cannot quiet his own conscience herein, but requireth further comfort and counsel, let him come to me, or to some other Minister of God's Word, and open his grief; that he may receive such godly counsel and advice, as may tend to the quieting of his conscience, and the removal of all scruple and doubtfulness."[12]

Yet the form for such reconciliation of the penitent with God was given only in the context of illness, and thus inevitably conveyed an aura of "last rites."

The Commission believes that there is great value in dissociating this form from the context of illness and the sick-room. By printing it as a separate unit in this book, the form is made available for use at other times and places. At the same time, its availability for use with the sick is in no way impaired.

The same considerations apply to the Anointing of the Sick and the Laying on of hands. *Prayer Book Studies III* cautioned that it was not to be thought of as extreme unction, i.e. to be administered only when death was thought to be imminent. Yet the association of this form with the Visitation of the Sick could not but convey precisely that meaning. By taking this form out of the context of the sick-room and printing it separately the Commission hopes that it may come to be regarded as perfectly appropriate to a public service of healing or other pastoral situations, without minimizing its value as a natural and normal part of a visit to the sick.

Similar considerations apply with even greater force to the Communion of the Sick. There are many occasions when Communion is administered outside the Church, but equally outside the sick room: there are chronic invalids who cannot come to church but who gain strength and comfort from the Sacrament; there are the aged, whether in their own homes or in institutions, who are by no means ill, and for whom Communion is an important part of life; there are those who minister to the shut-in or the sick, nurses, doctors, hospital personnel, and relatives, whose hours of work make it impossible to attend regularly scheduled services in church. Again, by printing the service as a separate unit, the exclusive association of this form with illness is removed, without making the service any less available as the climax of the Visit to the Sick.

---

12. The Book of Common Prayer, p. 88

Thus the separation of the four "modules" originally designed as components of a complete ministry to the sick and suffering, fulfills the role of each as a "module," available for separate use or together in the sequence outlined above.

Ministry of the Word

The first of the modular elements of this Service, the Ministry of the Word, consists of an opening sentence of greeting, a Collect, a passage from Scripture (an Epistle) followed by a Psalm and a reading from the Gospel. Thereafter, three similar units follow, each consisting of a brief passage from an Epistle, a Psalm, and a brief reading from the Gospel. The four sets of Epistle-Psalm-Gospel readings are interchangeable, and may be used in succession, or separately. Any one set may be used as the Ministry of the Word when a celebration of the Holy Eucharist follows; when appropriate, the Proper of the Day may be used instead. It is also possible for only one or two of the passages to be read. The Minister may, at his discretion, choose the Epistle from one set, the Psalm from another, the Gospel from a third. There is nothing fixed or binding about the grouping of these selections.

The passages of Scripture and the Psalms have been chosen to meet many kinds of need and many different occasions. Flexibility, as well as appropriateness, has been the aim.

As a matter of convenience the Revised Standard Version has been used for the Epistles and Gospels, with the exception of James 5:14-16 which is an independent translation by the Commission. The Psalms are taken from the new version of the Psalter prepared by the Commission.[13] The Minister may, at his discretion, use any of the versions of Holy Scripture authorized by Canon 20.

The Reconciliation of a Penitent

Several forms of service are available for use at a public service of penance or reconciliation: in a penitential season or in a corporate act of solemn preparation for the Eucharist, on the eve of a special celebration or at a preparatory service on Sunday morning. The Penitential Order from *The Liturgy of the Lord's Supper*, or any of the forms of General Confession and Absolution provided in *The Holy Eucharist* (*Prayer Book Studies* 21), and in *The Daily Office* (*Prayer Book Studies* 22), are entirely appropriate for such corporate use. They can be used separately or combined with other prayers, such as the Solemn Biddings and Collects in the Proper for Good Friday in *The Church Year* (*Prayer Book Studies* 19), reprinted among the prayers of intercession in *The Holy Eucharist*.

---

13. "*The Psalter: Part I*" (*Prayer Book Studies* 23) The Church Corporation, New York, 1970.

The form of reconciliation here provided is intended for use, not as a corporate service, but on a private occasion of reconciliation, such as is recommended in the Exhortation in the Book of Common Prayer, referred to above.

It has purposely been made brief and to the point. As is stated in the rubric immediately before the form, the secrecy of a confession is absolute, and must under no circumstances be broken. Provision is made for confession to be heard by a deacon or lay person, in extraordinary circumstances of emergency, and in the absence of a Priest. The appropriateness of lay confession was recognized from ancient times in situations of emergency and need, just as the validity of Baptism by a lay person was always recognized in similar circumstances.[14]

The obligation of secrecy is no less incumbent on a deacon or a lay person than on a priest.

The rubrics for the form stress two conditions: the lay person must be asked by the penitent to hear a confession; the lay confessor, in turn, must make it clear to the penitent, so far as is possible under the circumstances, that he is not a priest.

Anointing with Oil and the Laying on of Hands

In the early undivided Church, the use of oil and the laying on of hands was a normal part of the Visitation of the Sick, to be administered to all the sick, and to be repeated as often as necessary. It was only in the Middle Ages that Holy Unction became restricted to *extreme* Unction, as a "Sacrament of the Dying," "bestowed only upon those for whose recovery there was little hope, and restricted to be received only once in the course of a given illness."[15]

An aspect of the therapeutic value of the anointing and the laying on of hands, is the palpable evidence of something being done, an action rather than the recitation of a formula, a form of physical contact between the patient and the priest, which conveys an assurance of concern and is the expression of a shared faith.

The use of oil and the laying on of hands have been separated from the Ministration to the Sick, in order to emphasize their availability for any service of healing, in church or in the home. Provision is made for the blessing of the oil, either by the Bishop or a Priest, in conformity with a long-standing Christian tradition. In this prayer, based on the longer form in *Prayer Book Studies III*, the healing work of the Holy Spirit is prayed for, and the Apostolic practice of anointing the sick is recalled.

If the anointing is to be administered in the course of a public celebration, it should precede the distribution of Holy Communion so as not to imply that

---

14. W. K. Lowther Clark, "Liturgy and Worship," London, S.P.C.K., 1959; page 603 ff.

15. "The Order for the Ministration to the Sick" (*Prayer Book Studies III*) . See also "Liturgy and Worship," by W. K. Lowther Clarke, London, S.P.C.K., 1959, pp. 472 ff. The entire essay by Charles Harris provides an illuminating discussion of all aspects of the Visitation of the Sick.

something greater, or more efficacious, than the Body and Blood is added. The Commission recommends that the anointing take place immediately after the prayers of intercession.

The Order for Private Communions

As was pointed out above, there are many occasions when Communion must be administered outside the Church and also outside the sick room. The name of this service, and its separation from the context of illness, will make it available, it is hoped, in a great variety of pastoral situations.

The form is brief and is based on the form provided in The Book of Common Prayer. It has been expanded somewhat. Two forms of the Prayer of Consecration are printed in full. A short form based on the 1928 language, and the Canon of *The Liturgy of the Lord's Supper* in its contemporary wording from *The Holy Eucharist* (*Prayer Book Studies 21*, p. 32). It is recommended that the Proper of the Day be used, when this can be done without prolonging the service unduly, so that yet another link be established with the worship of the whole Church. It is also desirable, when possible, that the service be used with a group, so that a sense of community may be expressed.

If, because of the condition of any of those present, the Communion service must be made as brief as possible, it is recommended that the service begin at the Offertory.

Provision has been made for the use of the Reserved Sacrament, when desired, in accordance with the Instruction of the House of Bishops, adopted in 1966 at a special meeting in Wheeling, West Virginia, and in conformity with the directions in *The Liturgy of the Lord's Supper*.[16]

It is part of a Priest's pastoral responsibility to instruct his people in the use of private Communion, and to prepare the people with whom the service is to be used.

Prayers for the Dying

A litany and several prayers are included in this section for use in those situations when it is perfectly obvious that any hope of recovery must be abandoned, and the dying needs to be sustained to meet death by the prayers of those present.

This material is printed in a separate section, to remove any implication that every illness leads to death. The Litany and the prayers are based on the corresponding material in the Book of Common Prayer.

---

16. *Special Meeting of the House of Bishops*, Wheeling, West Virginia, 1966: *Journal of the General Convention, 1967, Supplement B*, pages 10 and 18; *Prayer Book Studies XVII*, Vol. 4, p. 293.

The Order for the Burial of the Dead

In *Prayer Book Studies XIII*,[17] the Commission defined the purpose of the revision as an attempt "To provide appropriately for the departed, for the bereaved, and for the total congregation." The principle it then adopted was "that the Office should be designed for the comfort of the living rather than for the benefit of the dead."

The proposed revision offers few radical changes, but endeavors to conserve the real values of the present Order in the Book of Common Prayer.

It is offered in the belief that any Christian rites for the departed should combine the following notes or emphases:

a. glorifying God with Christian faith in eternal life, in the face of death;
b. commending the departed to God;
c. comforting the bereaved; and
d. bearing witness for the benefit of the living to the faith of a Christian community.

The Order attempts to strike a dominant note of joy in the faith that we shall rise again through the power of Christ's resurrection, rather than that of a penitential and mournful contemplation of death, without, however, ignoring the latter's stark reality. In general, the concept of "continual growth in the love and service of God" has been emphasized over that of "rest eternal grant unto them." The latter, concept, however, is also recognized.

Unduly spatial descriptions of the state of the dead have been omitted as far as possible (resulting, for example, in the passing over of 1 Thessalonians 4:13-18, which is the Epistle at the Burial of the Dead on p. 268 of the Book of Common Prayer). In the belief that it is a person who is being commended to the mercy of God, the use of the person's name has been provided for, and references couched in terms of the body/soul dichotomy have been avoided, except for the traditional "May the souls of the faithful departed through the mercy of God rest in peace", where the pull of hallowed antiquity has been allowed to prevail.

The thrust of the present proposal is in the direction of holding the Burial Service in the Church as the fitting farewell of believers to one of their company. The form of the rite has also been consciously altered to lead to the celebration of the Holy Eucharist, with the family, at least, receiving Holy Communion. While the form of the proposed rite leads naturally to the celebration of the Eucharist, provision is made for continuity and completeness when the Order is used without Offertory, Consecration and Communion.

---

17. "The Order for the Burial of the Dead," (*Prayer Book Studies XIII*), prepared by the Standing Liturgical Commission, New York, The Church Pension Fund, 1959.

Since the Commission has decided to recommend the trial use of the Holy Eucharist in two forms, one using the traditional words of the Book of Common Prayer, the other using a contemporary idiom, the present revision is also in two forms. The first is in the style of the Revised Standard Version of the Bible for the Scriptural elements. In the prayers and thanksgivings, it retains the familiar "Thee" and "Thou" forms in addressing God, and some familiar though archaic terminations. This first Service is designed for use with the Communion Service of the Book of Common Prayer, *The Liturgy of the Lord's Supper*, and the First Service in *The Holy Eucharist* (*Prayer Book Studies 21*, p. 32).

The second Service, intended for use with the Second Service in "The Holy Eucharist," uses the New English Bible for both the New and Old Testament passages.[18]

The Psalms in the First Service are from the Prayer Book Psalter with Psalm 23 quoted also in the more widely known King James version. The Psalms in the Second Service are from the Commission's new version of The Psalter.[19] In the prayers and thanksgivings "You" has been substituted for "Thou" and "Thee", and a few other modernizations have been introduced with due regard for tradition.

Indeed, every effort has been made to retain a sensitivity to tradition and to preserve the beauties of the Bible passages and prayers. The familiar passages from 1 Corinthians 15 and Romans 8 have been shortened without, it is hoped, emasculating them. The Commission felt that it had a distinct responsibility to avoid language and innovations which might disturb unduly the sensibilities of older Episcopalians, especially at such a difficult time as the burial service.

The availability of two forms underlines the pastoral responsibility of the Minister in charge of the Service to consult carefully with the members of the family, so as to give them full opportunity of making an informed choice, both as regards the service and as regards the various options within it.

Provision has been made for more congregational participation in the service. And since many of those present may not be Episcopalians, and may not be familiar with the Prayer Book, the Commission intends, if the General Convention should approve the Order for trial use, that it then be printed separately in its entirety, including the relevant sections from the Communion Services authorized for trial use.

Old rubrics have been re-written for clarity, and some new rubrics have been added to prevent confusion and to provide more information about the practices of the Episcopal Church. One rubric rules out the viewing of the body any time during the burial Service and makes a closed coffin mandatory throughout the rite. This would apply whether the service were being held in a church or elsewhere.

---

18. "The New English Bible with the Apocrypha", Oxford University Press and Cambridge University Press, 1970. The passages are reprinted by permission of the Copyright holders.

19. "The Psalter: Part I," p. 178.

The direction that a pall or national flag be placed on the coffin is intended to discourage the heaping of flowers on the casket and thus diminish an unduly sentimental or marked concern for the body. This helps the Minister to bring a Christian emphasis into the Service.

Rubrics intended to clarify the action as it proceeds have been placed at appropriate points within the rite. "Information" rubrics have been gathered together and are to be found in the Additional Directions and Suggestions at the end of the rite.

A sermon or homily is optional to allow the Minister to speak of the Christian view of death, if he and the family so desire, and to relate it to the present occasion. There seems to be a decided trend towards this practice in the Episcopal Church today, and it was felt necessary to provide the proper place in the proposed service for those who desire it.

Questions of practical expediency dictate that some ceremonial be made optional. For example, casting earth on the coffin: there may be no earth available, as at sea, or where the ground may be frozen; or, it may simply be awkward and both impractical and artificial, as in a mausoleum.

This revised Office can be used either for a Burial Service with the body present, or as a Memorial Service. It is drafted to fit any manner of interment.

No special service is provided for the burial of a child as this Order should be satisfactory for either a child or an adult. However, a Psalm, Epistle and Gospel are indicated as being particularly fitting at the burial of a child.

Prayers, some traditional, some of modern style, are appended at the end of the rite for use either at home or at the funeral service, or on other occasions.

Concerning the Service

Christian Marriage is a solemn and public covenant between a man and a woman. In the Episcopal Church it is required that one, at least, of the parties must be a baptized Christian; that the ceremony be attested by at least two witnesses; and that the marriage conform to the laws of the State and the Canons of this Church.

A priest or a bishop normally presides at the Celebration and Blessing of a Marriage, because such Ministers alone have the function of pronouncing the nuptial Blessing, and of celebrating the Holy Eucharist.

When both a bishop and a priest are present and officiating, the bishop should pronounce the Blessing and preside at the Eucharist.

A deacon, or an assisting priest, may deliver the charge and ask for the declaration of intention, read the Gospel, and perform other assisting functions at the Eucharist.

Where it is permitted by civil law that deacons may perform marriages, and no priest or bishop is available, the deacon may use the service which follows, omitting only the priestly Blessing, beginning, "God the Father, God the Son . . ."

It is desirable that Lessons from the Old Testament and the Epistles be read by lay persons and that the newly married couple present the offerings of Bread and wine at the Offertory.

In the opening exhortation (at the symbol of *N.N.*), the full names of the persons to be married are to be declared. Subsequently, only their Christian names are used.

Additional Directions and Suggestions may be found on page 266.

The Celebration and Blessing of a Marriage

At the time appointed, the persons to be married, with their witnesses, assemble with the Minister in the church or some other appropriate place.

During their entrance, a Psalm, Hymn, or Anthem may be sung; or instrumental music may be used.

Then the presiding Minister, facing the People and the persons to be married, with the woman on his right and the man on his left, addresses the congregation and says

Good people, we have come together in the presence of God to witness and proclaim the joining together of this man and this woman in marriage. The bond of marriage was established by God at creation, and our Lord Jesus Christ himself adorned this manner of life by his presence and first miracle at a wedding in Cana of Galilee. It signifies to us the union between Christ and his Church, and Holy Scripture commends it to be honored among all men.

The union of man and woman in heart, body, and mind is intended by God for their mutual joy; for the help and comfort given one another in prosperity and adversity; and, when it is God's will, for the procreation of children and their nurture in the knowledge and love of the Lord. Therefore marriage is not to be entered into unadvisedly or lightly, but reverently, deliberately, and in accord with the purposes for which it was instituted by God.

Into this holy union *N.N.* and *N.N.* come now to be joined. If any of you can show just cause why they may not lawfully be married, speak now, or for ever hold your peace.

Then the Minister says to the persons to be married

I require and charge you both in the Name of God, that if either of you know any reason why you may not be united in marriage lawfully and in accordance with God's Word, you confess it now.

The Minister then says to the man

N., Will you have this woman to be your wife, to live together in a holy marriage? Will you love her, comfort her, honor and keep her, in sickness and in health, and forsaking all others, be faithful to her as long as you both shall live?

The man answers

I will by God's help.

The Minister then says to the woman

N., Will you have this man to be your husband to live together in a holy marriage? Will you love him, comfort him, honor and keep him in sickness and in health, and forsaking all others, be faithful to him as long as you both shall live?

The woman answers

I will by God's help.

The Minister addresses the following question to the wedding party and congregation:

Will you who witness these vows do all in your power to support and uphold this marriage in the years ahead?

Answer

We will.

Here the Minister may ask

Who gives this woman to be married to this man?

The father, or a friend, says

I do.

The Minister receives the woman at her father's or friend's hand and causes the man to take the woman's right hand in his.

The presiding Minister then says to the People

	The Lord be with you.
Answer	And also with you.
Minister	Let us pray.

THE COLLECT

The People standing

Eternal God, creator and sustainer of all men, giver of all grace, author of salvation: Look with favor upon this man and this woman, that they may grow in love and peace together; through Jesus Christ your Son our Lord, who lives and reigns with you in the unity of the Holy Spirit, one God, now and for ever. *Amen.*

Then one or more of the following passages from Holy Scripture is read. If there is to be a Communion, a passage from the Gospels is always included.

THE LESSON	THE GOSPEL
Genesis 2:4-9, 15-24	Mark 10:6-9
Colossians 3:12-17	Matthew 7:21,24-29
Ephesians 5:20-33	Matthew 5:13-16
1 Corinthians 13	John 15:11-17
1 John 4:7-16	

Between the Readings, Psalm 128, 113, or 100, or some other Psalm, Hymn, or Anthem may be sung or said.

After the Readings (or after the homily if there is one), the Service continues with

The Marriage

All stand, and the man facing the woman, and taking her right hand in his, says

I, N., take you, N., to be my wife, to have and to hold from this day forward, for better for worse, for richer for poorer, in sickness and in health, to love and to cherish, until we are parted by death. This is my solemn vow.

Then they loose their hands and the woman, still facing the man, takes his right hand in hers and says

I, N., take you, N., to be my husband, to have and to hold from this day forward, for better for worse, for richer for poorer, in sickness and in health, to love and to cherish, until we are parted by death. This is my solemn vow.

They loose their hands.

The Minister may ask God's blessing on the ring (or rings) as follows:

Bless, O Lord, this ring that *he* who gives it and *she* who wears it may live in your peace, and continue in your favor, all the days of their life; through Jesus Christ our Lord. *Amen.*

The giver places the ring on the ring-finger of the other's hand, and says,

N., I give you this ring as a symbol of my vow, and with all that I am, and all that I have, I honor you, in the Name of God.

Then the Minister joins the right hands of the husband and wife and says

Now that N. and N. have given themselves to each other by solemn vows, with the joining of hands and the giving and receiving of *a ring* (rings), I pronounce that they are husband and wife, in the Name of the Father, and of the Son, and of the Holy Spirit.

Those whom God has joined together let not man put asunder.

The Congregation responds   Amen.

When Communion is to follow, the Service continues on page 265.

When there is no Communion, the Service continues on the following page.

The Blessing of the Marriage

The Minister says

Let us pray together in the words our Savior taught us:

Standing, all say

Our Father in heaven,
    holy be your Name,
    your kingdom come,
    your will be done,
       on earth as in heaven.
Give us today our daily bread.
Forgive us our sins,
    as we forgive those who trespass against us.
Do not bring us to the test
    but deliver us from evil.
For the kingdom, the power, and the glory, are yours
    now and for ever. Amen.

The Minister says this prayer over the couple:

Almighty God, look graciously, we pray, on this man and this woman, and on all whom you make to be one flesh in holy marriage. Make their lives together a sacrament of your love to this broken world, so that unity may overcome estrangement, forgiveness heal guilt, and joy triumph over despair; in the Name of our Lord Jesus Christ, to whom be all honor and glory, now and forever. *Amen.*

He may then add one or more of the following three prayers:

Almighty God, Creator of mankind, the source of all life, grant to *N.* and *N.*, if it be your will, the gift and heritage of children, and the grace to nurture them in the knowledge and love of your Name; through Jesus Christ our Lord. *Amen.*

Almighty God, giver of life and love, bless *N.* and *N.* whom you have now joined in holy matrimony. Grant them wisdom and devotion in the ordering of their common life that each may be to the other a strength in need, a counsellor in perplexity, a comfort in sorrow, and a companion in joy. And so knit their wills together in your will, and their spirits in your spirit, that they may live together in love and in peace all the days of their life, through Jesus Christ our Lord. *Amen.*

Almighty God, by whose love the whole world is created, sustained and redeemed, so fill *N.* and *N.* with the overflowing abundance of your grace that their lives may reflect your compassion for all men. May their love for each other not blind them to the brokenness in the world. As you teach them to bind up each other's wounds, teach them also to heal the hurts of others. As their mutual respect orders their common life within the family, direct them to their share also in the shaping of a society in which human dignity may flourish and abound. At all times and in all seasons may they rejoice to serve you and to give you thanks, through Jesus Christ our Lord. *Amen.*

The following prayer is always added, the couple kneeling:

O God, who consecrated the state of Marriage to be a sign of the spiritual unity between Christ and his Church; Bless these your servants, that they may love, honor, and cherish each other in faithfulness and patience, in wisdom and true godliness, and that their home may be a haven of blessing and of peace; through Jesus Christ our Lord, who lives and reigns with you and the Holy Spirit, one God, now and for ever. *Amen.*

The husband and wife still kneeling, the Priest pronounces this nuptial Blessing:

God the Father, God the Son, God the Holy Spirit, bless, preserve and keep you; the Lord mercifully with his favor look upon you and fill you with all spiritual benediction and grace, that you may faithfully live together in this life, and in the world to come have life everlasting. *Amen.*

The Peace may now be exchanged.

As the wedding party leaves the Church, a Psalm, Hymn, or Anthem may be sung; or instrumental music may be used.

One of the Ministers may dismiss the Congregation.

At the Eucharist: The Blessing of the Marriage

For the Intercession, the Deacon or person appointed says

Almighty God, in whom we live and move and have our being: Look graciously upon the world which you have made, and on the Church for which your Son gave his life; and especially on all whom you make to be one flesh in holy marriage:

Grant that their lives together may be a sacrament of your love to this broken world, so that unity may overcome estrangement, forgiveness heal guilt, and joy overcome despair. *Amen.*

Grant that *N.* and *N.* may so live together, that the strength of their love may enrich our common life and become an example of your faithfulness. *Amen.*

The following suffrage may be omitted:

Grant that they may have children, if it be your will, and may bring them up by your help to know and love you. *Amen.*

Grant them such fulfillment of their mutual affection that they may reach out in concern for others, to the praise of your Name. *Amen.*

Grant that all married persons who have witnessed this exchange of vows may find their union strengthened and their loyalty confirmed. *Amen.*

Grant that the bonds of our common humanity which unite every man to his neighbor, and the living to the dead, may be transformed by your grace, that justice and peace may prevail and your will be done on earth as it is in heaven. *Amen.*

Then, while the congregation remains standing, the husband and wife kneel, and the Priest says the following prayer:

O God, who consecrated the state of Marriage to be a sign of the spiritual unity between Christ and his Church; Bless these your servants, that they may love, honor, and cherish each other in faithfulness and patience, in wisdom and true godliness, and that their home may be a haven of blessing and of peace; through Jesus Christ our Lord, who lives and reigns with you and the Holy Spirit, one God, now and for ever. *Amen.*

The husband and wife still kneeling, the Priest pronounces this nuptial Blessing:

God the Father, God the Son, God the Holy Spirit, bless, preserve and keep you; the Lord mercifully with his favor look upon you and fill you with all spiritual benediction and grace, that you may faithfully live together in this life, and in the world to come have life everlasting. *Amen.*

The Peace is now exchanged.

The Liturgy continues with the Offertory.

The following Proper Preface may be used at the Eucharist:

TRADITIONAL	**CONTEMPORARY**
Because thou has ordained the solemn covenant of love between husband and wife as a witness of the union of thy son Jesus Christ with the holy fellowship of all faithful people:	Because you have ordained the solemn covenant of love between husband and wife as a witness of the union of your son Jesus Christ with the holy fellowship of all faithful people:

Additional Directions and Suggestions

The Celebration and Blessing of a Marriage may be used with any authorized liturgy for the Holy Eucharist. This Order of Service will then replace the Ministry of the Word, and the Eucharist will begin with the Offertory. When this Service is used with the Order for the Holy Communion in the Book of Common Prayer, the Prayer for the Church and the Confession of Sin may be omitted.

After the declaration of intention (betrothal), it is fitting that the man and woman to be married remain where they may conveniently hear the reading of Scripture. They may then approach the altar either for the marriage vows or for the prayers and nuptial Blessing.

It is appropriate that all remain standing until the conclusion of the Collect. Seating may be provided for the wedding party, so that all may be seated for the Lessons and the Homily.

The Apostles' Creed may be recited after the Lessons (or after the Homily, if there is one).

At the Offertory, it is desirable that the bread and wine be offered to the Ministers by the newly married persons. They may then remain before the Lord's Table and receive Holy Communion before other members of the congregation.

At the Peace, the newly married couple shall first greet each other, after which greetings may be exchanged throughout the congregation.

A Thanksgiving for the Birth of a Child

As soon as convenient after the birth of a child, the parents, with other members of the family, should give thanks to Almighty God in his Church.

If this service is used at the hospital or the home, and not in the church, the Minister may omit the Psalm.

At a Sunday Service, after the Announcements, the Minister invites the parents and other members of the family to present themselves before the altar.

The Minister begins with these or similar words:

Since it has pleased our heavenly Father to bestow upon N. and N. the gift of a child, let us, together with them, give thanks to God, and say

[*From Psalm 116*]

I love the Lord, because he has heard
the voice of my entreaty;
    because he has inclined his ear to me
    whenever I called upon him.
Gracious is the Lord, and righteous;
    our God is full of compassion.
How shall I repay the Lord
    for all the good things he has done for me?
I will lift up the cup of salvation,
    and call upon the Name of the Lord,
I will fulfill my vows to the Lord
in the presence of all his people,
    in the courts of the Lord's house,
    in the midst of you, O Jerusalem. [Hallelujah!]
Glory to the Father, and to the Son, and to the Holy Spirit:
    as in the beginning, so now, and for ever. Amen.

Or this Psalm may be said:

[*Psalm 121*]

I will lift up my eyes to the hills.
"Where is my help to come from?"
My help comes from the Lord,
    the Maker of heaven and earth.

He will not let your foot be moved,
>   and he who watches over you will not fall asleep.
>
> Behold, he who keeps watch over Israel
> shall neither slumber nor sleep:
>   he who watches over you is the Lord.
>
> The Lord is your shade at your right hand,
>   so that the sun shall not strike you by day,
>   nor the moon by night.
>
> The Lord shall preserve you from all evil;
>   it is he who shall keep you safe.
>
> The Lord shall watch over your going out
> and your coming in,
>   from this time forth for evermore.
>
> Glory to the Father, and to the Son, and to the Holy Spirit:
>   as in the beginning, so now, and for ever. Amen.

When this office is used separately, the Lord's Prayer is said here.

The Minister then says one or more of the following prayers:

O God, our heavenly Father, we thank you and praise your glorious Name for your blessing upon your servant(s) in your gift to her (*them*) of a child: Grant most merciful Father, that N. (*and her husband*) may diligently lead this child in the way of righteousness, to her (*their*) own great joy, and to the glory of your Name; through Jesus Christ our Lord. *Amen.*

Almighty God, heavenly Father: you have blessed us with the joy and care of children: Give us wisdom and strength to bring them up to love what is true and pure, and honorable, and good, following the example of their Savior Jesus Christ. *Amen.*

Almighty God, our heavenly Father, we commend to your continual care the homes in which your people dwell. Put far from them all bitterness, selfishness, and pride of life. Fill them with faith, courage, knowledge, temperance, patience, godliness. Knit together in constant affection those who in holy marriage have been made one flesh. Turn the hearts of parents to their children, and the hearts of children to their parents; and so enkindle charity among us all, that we may evermore be bound together in your love; through Jesus Christ our Lord. *Amen.*

The Minister may add this or some other Blessing:

Unto God's gracious mercy and protection we commit you. The Lord bless you, and keep you. The Lord make his face to shine upon you, and be gracious unto you. The Lord lift up his countenance upon you, and give you peace, both now and evermore. *Amen.*

Concerning the Service

This form may be used when a person wishes to re-affirm his commitment to the service of Christ in the world, either in general terms, or because he is called to some special responsibility.

The questions and answers in the baptismal service may be used at any time for the renewal of one's baptismal promises. It is preferable, however, that this be done in the context of a public service of Baptism. The renewal of baptismal vows by this means is most appropriate at the Service of Easter Eve.

It is desirable that the statement of purpose, or the questions and answers to be used, be determined in advance during a private consultation between the Minister and the person concerned.

A Form of Commitment to Christian Service

Before the Offertory at the Eucharist, the person, standing before the congregation, states his purpose, either in his own words, or in response to a question or questions.

After this, the Minister says these or similar words:

May the Holy Spirit guide and strengthen you, that in this and all things you may do God's will in the service of the kingdom of his Christ. *Amen.*

In the name of this congregation I commend you to this work, and pledge you our prayerful encouragement and support.

The Minister then says this or some similar prayer, first saying to the Congregation

Let us pray.

Almighty God, look with favor upon this person who has now reaffirmed his commitment to follow Christ and to serve in his name. Give him courage, patience, and vision; and strengthen us all in our Christian vocation of witness to the world, and of service to our fellow men; through Jesus Christ our Lord. *Amen.*

A prayer for the special work in which the person will be engaged may be added.

The Service then continues with the exchange of the Peace and the Offertory.

Concerning the Service

One or more of the four parts of this Service may be used upon a single occasion; but when two or more are used together, they should be used in the order set forth in the Service: Part I being The Ministry of the Word; Part II, Confession and Absolution; Part III, Anointing of the Sick or Laying on of hands; Part IV, Communion of the Sick.

The Ministration should always include the Lord's Prayer and a blessing.

Unless otherwise indicated, any part of this Service may be used by a deacon or by a lay person.

In Part I, the Readings (Epistle-Psalm-Gospel) are intended for use as units, but the Minister may, at his discretion, combine Readings from different groups, or use only one or two from any group.

The Ministration to the Sick and Suffering

Part I. The Ministry of the Word

If a group of people are present, the Minister may begin:

Grace be to you, and peace, from God our Father and from the Lord Jesus Christ.

	The Lord be with you.
Answer	And also with you.

Then he says the Collect below. In the absence of a group, he begins the Collect without introduction.

O God of peace, who taught us that in returning and rest we shall be saved, in quietness and confidence shall be our strength; by the might of your Spirit lift us, we pray, to your presence, where we may be still and know that you are God; through Jesus Christ our Lord. *Amen.*

Then one or more of the following portions of Scriptures are read. In the Psalms, the bracketed verses may be omitted.

The Epistle. 2 Corinthians 1:3-5

Blessed be the God and Father of our Lord Jesus Christ, the Father of mercies and God of all comfort, who comforts us in all our affliction, so that we may be able to comfort those who are in any affliction, with the comfort with which we ourselves are comforted by God. For as we share abundantly in Christ's sufferings, so through Christ we share abundantly in comfort too.

Psalm 103

Bless the Lord, O my soul;
    and all that is within me, bless his holy Name.

Bless the Lord, O my soul;
>   and forget not all his benefits.

He forgives all my sins,
>   and heals all my infirmities;

He redeems my life from the grave,
>   and crowns me with mercy and loving-kindness;

He satisfies me with good things,
>   and my youth is renewed like an eagle's.

[The Lord executes righteousness,
>   and judgment for all who are oppressed.

He made his ways known to Moses;
>   and his works to the children of Israel.

The Lord is full of compassion and mercy,
>   slow to anger and of great kindness.

He will not always accuse us,
>   nor will he keep his anger forever.

He has not dealt with us according to our sins,
>   nor rewarded us according to our wickedness.

For as the heavens are high over the earth,
>   so is his mercy great over those who fear him.

Far as the east is from the west,
>   so far has he removed our sins from us.]

As a father cares for his children,
>   so does the Lord care for those who fear him.

For he himself knows whereof we are made;
>   he remembers that we are but dust.

[The days of man are like the grass:
>   he flourishes like a flower of the field;

When the wind goes over it, it is gone;
>   and its place shall know it no more.

But the merciful goodness of the Lord endures for ever
>   on those who fear him,
>   and his righteousness on children's children;

On those who keep his covenant;
>   and remember his commandments and do them.

The Lord has set his throne in heaven;
>   and his kingship has dominion over all.]

Bless the Lord, you angels of his,
you mighty ones who do his bidding.
>   and hearken to the voice of his word.

Bless the L ORD, all you his hosts,
> you ministers of his who do his will.

Bless the L ORD, all you works of his
in all places of his dominion.
> Bless the L ORD, O my soul.

The Gospel. St. Matthew 9:2-8

They brought to *Jesus* a paralytic, lying on his bed; and when Jesus saw their faith he said to the paralytic, "Take heart, my son; your sins are forgiven." And behold, some of the scribes said to themselves, "This man is blaspheming." But Jesus, knowing their thoughts, said, "Why do you think evil in your hearts? For which is easier, to say, 'Your sins are forgiven,' or to say, 'Rise and walk'? But that you may know that the Son of man has authority on earth to forgive sins"—he then said to the paralytic—"Rise, take up your bed and go home." And he rose and went home. When the crowds saw it, they were afraid, and they glorified God, who had given such authority to men.

* * * * *

The Epistle. Galatians 2:20

I have been crucified with Christ; it is no longer I who live, but Christ who lives in me; and the life I now live in the flesh I live by faith in the Son of God, who loved me and gave himself for me.

Psalm 91

He who dwells in the shelter of the Most High,
> abides under the shadow of the Almighty.

He shall say to the L ORD,
> "You are my refuge and my stronghold,
> my God in whom I put my trust."

He shall deliver you from the snare of the hunter,
> and from the deadly pestilence.

He shall cover you with his pinions,
and you shall find refuge under his wings;
> his faithfulness shall be a shield and buckler.

You shall not be afraid of any terror by night,
> nor of the arrow that flies by day;

Of the plague that stalks in the darkness,
> nor of the sickness that lays waste at mid-day.

[A thousand shall fall at your side,
and ten thousand at your right hand;
> but it shall not come near you.

Your eyes have only to behold,
> to see the reward of the wicked.]

Because you have made the LORD your refuge,
and the Most High your habitation,
> there shall no evil happen to you,
> neither shall any plague come near your dwelling.

For he shall give his angels charge over you,
> to keep you in all your ways.

[They shall bear you in their hands,
> lest you dash your foot against a stone.

You shall tread upon the lion and adder;
> you shall trample the young lion and the serpent
under your feet.]

Because he is bound to me in love,
therefore will I deliver him;
> I will protect him, because he knows my Name.

He shall call upon me, and I will answer him;
> I am with him in trouble;
> I will rescue him and bring him to honor.

With long life will I satisfy him,
> and show him my salvation.

The Gospel. St. Luke 6:6-10

On another sabbath, when *Jesus* entered the synagogue and taught, a man was there whose right hand was withered. And the scribes and the Pharisees watched him, to see whether he would heal on the sabbath, so that they might find an accusation against him. But he knew their thoughts, and he said to the man who had the withered hand, "Come and stand here." And he rose and stood there. And Jesus said to them, "I ask you, is it lawful on the sabbath to do good or to do harm, to save life or to destroy it?" And he looked around on them all, and said to him, "Stretch out your hand." And he did so, and his hand was restored.

* * * * *

The Epistle. Romans 8:15b-18

When we cry, "Abba! Father!" it is the Spirit himself bearing witness with our spirit that we are children of God, and if children, then heirs, heirs of God and fellow heirs with Christ, provided we suffer with him in order that we may also be glorified with him. I consider that the sufferings of this present time are not worth comparing with the glory that is to be revealed to us.

Psalm 27:1-8

The LORD is my light and my salvation;
whom then shall I fear?
    the LORD is the strength of my life;
of whom then shall I be afraid?
When evildoers came upon me to eat up my flesh,
    it was they, my foes and my adversaries, who stumbled and fell.
Though an army should encamp against me,
yet shall not my heart be afraid;
    and though war should rise up against me,
    yet will I put my trust in him.
For one thing have I asked the LORD;
for one thing I seek:
    that I may dwell in the house of the LORD all the days of my life;
To behold the fair beauty of the LORD,
    and to seek him in his temple.
For in the day of trouble he shall keep me safe in his shelter;
    he shall hide me in the secrecy of his dwelling,
    and set me up upon a rock of stone.
Even now he lifts up my head
    above my enemies round about me.
Therefore, I will offer in his dwelling an oblation,
with sounds of great gladness;
    I will sing and make music to the LORD.

The Gospel. St. John 6:47-51

Jesus said, "Truly, truly, I say to you, he who believes has eternal life. Your fathers ate the manna in the wilderness, and they died. This is the bread which comes down from heaven, that a man may eat of it and not die. I am the living bread which came down from heaven; if any one eats of this bread, he will live for ever; and the bread which I shall give for the life of the world is my flesh."

* * * * *

The Epistle. St. James 5:14-16

Is any sick among you? Let him call for the presbyters of the Church; and let them pray over him, anointing him with oil in the Name of the Lord: and the prayer of faith shall save the sick, and the Lord shall raise him up. And if he have committed sins, absolution shall be given him. Confess therefore your sins to one another, and pray for one another, that you may be healed. The prayer of a righteous man has great power.

Psalm 23

The Lord is my shepherd;
> nothing, therefore, shall I lack.

He makes me lie down in green pastures;
> and leads me beside still waters.

He revives my soul,
> and guides me along safe pathways for his Name's sake.

Though I walk through the valley of the shadow of death,
I shall fear no evil;
> for you are with me;
> your rod and your staff, they comfort me,

You spread a table before me,
in the presence of those who trouble me;
> you have anointed my head with oil,
> and my cup is full.

Surely your goodness and mercy shall follow me all the days of my life;
> and I will dwell in the house of the Lord for ever.

The Gospel. St. Mark 6:7, 12-13

Jesus called to him the twelve, and began to send them out two by two, and gave them authority over the unclean spirits. So they went out and preached that men should repent. And they cast out many demons, and anointed with oil many that were sick and healed them.

> *After any lesson the Minister may comment upon it briefly.*

> *Prayers and Thanksgivings may be offered.*

Part II. Confession and Absolution

> *Here may be used the Confession of Sin given below, or any of the forms provided for the Eucharist, or the Form for the Reconciliation of a Penitent (page 277).*

> *Minister and People*

Most merciful God,
we confess that we have sinned against you
in thought, word and deed:
we have not loved you with our whole heart;
we have not loved our neighbors as ourselves.

We pray you of your mercy
> forgive what we have been,
> amend what we are,
> direct what we shall be;
that we may delight in your will,
and walk in your ways,
> through Jesus Christ our Lord. Amen.

The Minister says this prayer

Almighty God have mercy on us, forgive us all our sins, through our Lord Jesus Christ; strengthen us in all goodness, and by the power of the Holy Spirit, keep us in eternal life. *Amen.*

If a Bishop or Priest is present, he may substitute an absolution.

Part III. Anointing or Laying on of Hands

The Form on pages 278-280 of this Book is used.

Part IV. The Communion of the Sick

The Order for Private Communions on pages 280-286 is used, beginning with the Offertory; or, if Communion is to be administered from the Sacrament already consecrated, beginning with the Lord's Prayer.

When necessary, or when desired, it is fitting that the Sacrament be administered by intinction.

Additional Prayers

FOR THE RECOVERY OF A SICK PERSON

O merciful God, giver of life and health; bless we pray you your servant, *N.*, and those who minister to *him* of your healing gifts; that *he* may be restored to health of body and mind; through Jesus Christ our Lord. Amen.

FOR ONE ABOUT TO UNDERGO SURGERY

Almighty God our Heavenly Father, we beseech you graciously to comfort your servant in *his* suffering, and to bless the persons and means made use of for *his* cure. Fill *his* heart with confidence, that though *he* be sometime afraid *he* may yet put his trust in you; through Jesus Christ our Lord. *Amen.*

FOR THOSE IN MENTAL STRESS

Heavenly Father, you know all our needs before we ask: Make this your servant know that you are nearer to *him* than the breath he breathes; grant that in struggles of mind, *he* may turn to your light, and in the midst of turmoil may find that peace which passes all understanding; through Jesus Christ our Lord. Amen.

FOR THOSE WHO SUFFER FROM ADDICTION

Mercifully regard, O Lord, this your servant who is bound with the chains of harmful addiction. Give *him* strength that *he* may be freed from fear and guilt and be restored in you to the liberty of the sons of God; now and forever. Amen.

A THANKSGIVING FOR RECOVERY

Glory be to you, O Lord God, for the deliverance which you have granted this your servant from illness of body and mind. Grant, O Gracious God, that he may employ the powers restored to him to your glory and to the salvation of his soul, for the sake of Jesus Christ. *Amen.*

Concerning the Rite

This form may be used at any private occasion of reconciliation.

The secrecy of a confession is absolute, and must under no circumstances be broken. Under extraordinary circumstances, in the absence of a priest, a deacon or a lay person may hear the confession of another Christian, if he is asked to do so. The deacon or lay confessor must make it clear to the penitent that he is not a priest.

The obligation to maintain the secrecy of a confession is no less absolute for a deacon or a lay person than it is for a priest.

The Reconciliation of a Penitent

The person who comes to confess may begin as follows:

Answer me when I call, O God my protector: you have set me at liberty when I was hard pressed; have mercy on me and hear my prayer.

or Bless me, a sinner.

Priest May the love of God who gave his only Son that none should perish but have eternal life, be in your heart and on your lips to bring you to true repentance; through Jesus Christ our Lord. *Amen.*

Penitent   I confess to Almighty God and before his Church that I have sinned in thought, word, and deed, and in what I have left undone, by my own fault, especially . . . Therefore, I humbly beg forgiveness of God and his Church.

Here the priest may offer counsel, direction, and comfort.

The Absolution

Our Lord Jesus Christ who has left power to his Church to absolve all sinners who truly repent and believe in him, of his great mercy forgive you all your offences; and by his authority committed to me, I absolve you from all your sins: In the Name of the Father, and of the Son, and of the Holy Spirit. *Amen.*

Or

Our Lord Jesus Christ, who offered himself to be sacrificed for us to the Father, and who conferred power on his Church to forgive sins, absolve you through my ministry by the grace of the Holy Spirit, and restore you in the perfect peace of the Church. *Amen.*

The Priest may add the Lord's Prayer, or other suitable prayers, and a Blessing.

The Priest concludes by saying

Go (*or* abide) in peace. The Lord has put away all your sins; and of your charity pray for me who am also a sinner.

Form of Absolution by a Deacon or Lay Person

Our Lord Jesus Christ who offered himself to be sacrificed for us to the Father, forgive your sins by the grace of the Holy Spirit. *Amen.*

In conclusion, the Lord's Prayer may be said together.

The Anointing of the Sick

The Anointing of the Sick may take place in the course of the Ministration to the Sick and Suffering, or at a public celebration of the Eucharist, or separately.

When the Anointing takes place at the Eucharist, it is desirable that it precede the distribution of Holy Communion; and it is recommended that it take place immediately after the Intercession.

In cases of necessity, a Deacon or lay person may perform the Anointing, using oil blessed by a Bishop or Priest.

The Minister says

The Almighty Lord, who is a most strong tower to all who trust in him, be now and evermore your defense, and make you know that the only Name given for health and salvation is the Name of our Lord Jesus Christ.

The Anointing

The Priest anoints the sick person with blessed oil on the forehead, or elsewhere when necessary, saying

N., I anoint you in the name of the Father, and of the Son, and of the Holy Spirit:
As you are outwardly anointed with this holy oil, so may our heavenly Father grant you the inward anointing of the Holy Spirit. Of his great mercy, may he forgive you your sins, release you from suffering, and restore you to wholeness and strength. May he deliver you from all evil, preserve you in all goodness, and bring you to everlasting life; through Jesus Christ our Lord. *Amen.*

The Laying on of Hands

If the laying on of hands is used in connection with, or instead of, the Anointing, the following may be said:

(N.) I lay my hand upon you in the name of the Father, and of the Son, and of the Holy Spirit: Beseeching the mercy of our Lord Jesus Christ, that, putting to flight all sickness of body and spirit, he may give you that victory of life and peace which will help you to serve him both now and evermore. Amen.

A Form for the Blessing of Oil

The oil for the Anointing of the Sick is blessed by a Bishop or Priest, using the form below. The oil may be blessed immediately before the Anointing; or if it is intended for use on subsequent occasions it may be blessed at the Eucharist, immediately before the Lord's Prayer.

Priest	The Lord be with you.
Answer	And also with you.
Priest	Let us pray.

O Lord, Holy Father, giver of health and salvation: Send your Holy Spirit, we beseech you, to sanctify this oil; that as your holy Apostles anointed many that were sick, and healed them; so those who in faith and repentance receive this holy unction may be made whole; through Jesus Christ our Lord, who lives and reigns with you and the Holy Spirit, one God, for ever and ever. *Amen.*

Concerning the Service

This form is intended for use with those who for reasonable cause cannot be present at a regular public celebration of the Eucharist. Especially when persons are unable to be present for extended periods of time, it is desirable that the Priest arrange to celebrate with them privately, on a regular basis.

It is desirable that fellow-parishioners, relatives, and friends be present, when possible, to communicate with them.

At other times, or when desired, it is fitting that they be communicated from the Reserved Sacrament.

The Collect and Lessons may be taken from the Proper of the Day, or from those appointed for Special Occasions.

If it is necessary to shorten the service, the Priest may begin the celebration at the Offertory.

The Order for Private Communions

The Minister may begin the Service with the salutation The Lord be with you, *and with this or some other Collect:*

Almighty God, to you all hearts are open, all desires known, and from you no secrets are hid: Cleanse the thoughts of our hearts by the inspiration of your Holy Spirit, that we may perfectly love you, and worthily magnify your holy Name; through Christ our Lord. *Amen.*

One or more passages from Scripture may be read: a brief commentary may follow.

The Apostles' Creed may be said.

A Confession and Absolution may be used.

Minister

Let us confess our sins against God and our neighbor.

A period of silence may be observed.

Minister and People

Most merciful God,
we confess that we have sinned against you
in thought, word and deed:
we have not loved you with our whole heart;
we have not loved our neighbors as ourselves.
We pray you of your mercy
> forgive what we have been,
> amend what we are,
> direct what we shall be;
that we may delight in your will,
and walk in your ways,
through Jesus Christ our Lord. Amen.

The Absolution

Almighty God have mercy on you, forgive you all your sins, through our Lord Jesus Christ; strengthen you in all goodness, and by the power of the Holy Spirit, keep you in eternal life. *Amen.*

> *Appropriate Intercessions and Thanksgivings may be offered.*

> *[If Communion is to be administered from the Reserved Sacrament, the Lord's Prayer is now said, the Minister first saying,* Let us pray in the words our Savior Christ hath *(has)* taught us. *The Ministration of the Sacrament follows immediately. See page 286.]*

At the Offertory and Consecration

> *The bread and cup of wine to be consecrated are placed on a suitable table. The Priest says one of the following Eucharistic Prayers:*

I

Priest	The Lord be with you.
People	And with thy spirit.
Priest	Lift up your hearts.
People	We lift them up unto the Lord.
Priest	Let us give thanks unto our Lord God.
People	It is meet and right so to do.

Priest

It is very meet, right, and our bounden duty, that we should at all times, and in all places, give thanks unto thee, O Lord, Holy Father, Almighty, Everlasting God.

A proper Preface may be said.

Therefore with Angels and Archangels, and with all the company of heaven, we laud and magnify thy glorious Name; evermore praising thee, and saying,

Priest and People

HOLY, HOLY, HOLY, Lord God of Hosts:
Heaven and earth are full of thy glory.
Glory be to thee, O Lord Most High.

Here may be added

Blessed is He that cometh in the Name of the Lord:
Hosanna in the highest!

Then the Priest continues

All glory be to thee, Almighty God, our heavenly Father, for that thou, of thy tender mercy, didst give thine only Son Jesus Christ to suffer death upon the Cross for our redemption; who made there, by his one oblation of himself once offered, a full, perfect, and sufficient sacrifice for the sins of the whole world; and did institute, and in his holy Gospel command us to continue, a perpetual memory of that his precious death and sacrifice, until his coming again:

> *At the following words concerning the Bread, the Priest is to hold it, or lay his hand upon it. And at the words concerning the Cup, he is to hold, or lay his hand upon, the Cup and any other vessel containing wine to be consecrated.*

For in the night in which he was betrayed, he took bread; and when he had given thanks, he brake it, and gave it to his disciples, saying, "Take, eat: This is my Body which is given for you. Do this in remembrance of me."

Likewise, after supper, he took the cup; and when he had given thanks, he gave it to them, saying, "Drink this, all of you: For this is my Blood of the New Covenant, which is shed for you, and for many, for the remission of sins. Do this, as oft as ye shall drink it, in remembrance of me."

Wherefore, O Lord and heavenly Father, we, thy humble servants, do celebrate and make here before thy Divine Majesty, with these thy holy Gifts, which we now offer unto thee, the memorial thy Son hath commanded us to make; having in remembrance his blessed passion and precious death, his mighty resurrection and glorious ascension; rendering unto thee most hearty thanks for the innumerable benefits procured unto us by the same.

And we most humbly beseech thee, O merciful Father, to hear us; and, of thy almighty goodness, vouchsafe to bless and sanctify, with thy Word and Holy Spirit, these Gifts of bread and wine; that we, receiving them according to thy Son our Savior Jesus Christ's holy institution, may be partakers of his most blessed Body and Blood.

And we earnestly desire thy fatherly goodness, mercifully to accept this our sacrifice of praise and thanksgiving; through Jesus Christ our Lord; by whom, and with whom, in the unity of the Holy Ghost, all honor and glory be unto thee, O Father Almighty, world without end.
Amen.
And now, as our Savior Christ hath taught us, we are bold to say,

People and Priest

Our Father, who art in heaven,
    hallowed be thy Name,
    thy Kingdom come,
    thy will be done,
        on earth as it is in heaven.
Give us this day our daily bread.

And forgive us our trespasses,
as we forgive those who trespass against us.

And lead us not into temptation,
but deliver us from evil.

For thine is the kingdom, and the power,
and the glory, for ever and ever. *Amen.*

The Priest then breaks the consecrated Bread, and communicates himself and the other persons present.

The Service continues on page 286.

II

Priest	The Lord be with you.
People	And also with you.
Priest	Lift up your hearts.
People	We lift them up to the Lord.
Priest	Let us give thanks to the Lord our God.
People	It is right to give him thanks and praise.

Priest

It is right, and a good and joyful thing, always and everywhere to give thanks to you, Father Almighty, Creator of heaven and earth:

A Proper Preface may be said.

Therefore we praise you,
joining our voices with angels and archangels
and with all the company of heaven,
who for ever sing this hymn
to proclaim the glory of your Name:

Priest and People

Holy, holy, holy Lord, God of power and might,
heaven and earth are full of your glory.
    Hosanna in the highest.
Blessed is he who comes in the name of the Lord.
    Hosanna in the highest.

Then the Priest continues

All glory is yours, Almighty God, Holy Father:
You made us in your own image;
and when we had fallen into sin,
you gave your only-begotten Son Jesus Christ,
to take our nature upon him,
and to suffer death upon the Cross for our redemption.
He made there, by his one oblation of himself,
a full and perfect sacrifice for the whole world;
And instituted and commanded us to continue
this memorial of his precious death and sacrifice,
until his coming again.

At the following words concerning the Bread, the Priest is to hold it, or lay his hand upon it. And at the words concerning the Cup, he is to hold, or lay his hand upon, the Cup and any other vessel containing wine to be consecrated.

For in the night in which he was betrayed, he took bread;
and when he had given thanks to you,
he broke it, and gave it to his disciples, and said,
"Take, eat: This is my Body which is given for you.
Do this in remembrance of me."

After supper, he took the cup;
and when he had given thanks, he gave it to them and said,
"Drink this, all of you: For this is my Blood of the New Covenant
which is poured out for you and for many
for the forgiveness of sins.
Do this, as often as you drink it, in remembrance of me."

Therefore, O Lord and Holy Father, we your people
celebrate here before your Divine Majesty,
with these holy Gifts which we offer to you,
the memorial of the blessed Passion
and precious Death of your dear Son,
his mighty Resurrection and glorious Ascension,
looking for his Coming again in power and great glory.
And with these Gifts, O Lord, we offer to you ourselves,
for this is our duty and service.
And we pray you, in your goodness and mercy, to accept,
through the eternal mediation of our Savior Jesus Christ,
this our sacrifice of praise and thanksgiving.

Gracious Father, in your almighty power,
bless and sanctify us and these holy Mysteries
with your Life-giving Word and Holy Spirit;
fill with your grace all who partake
of the Body and Blood of our Lord Jesus Christ;
makes us one Body that he may dwell in us and we in him.
And grant that with boldness
we may confess your Name in constancy of faith,
and at the last Day enter with all your Saints
into the joy of your eternal kingdom:

Through Jesus Christ our Lord,
by whom, and with whom, and in whom,
in the unity of the Holy Spirit
all honor and glory is yours,
O Father Almighty,
now and for ever.
Amen.

As our Savior Christ has taught us, we now pray,

People and Priest

Our Father in heaven,
> holy be your Name,
> your kingdom come,
> your will be done,
>> on earth as in heaven.
Give us today our daily bread.
Forgive us our sins,
> as we forgive those who trespass against us.
Do not bring us to the test
> but deliver us from evil.
For the kingdom, the power, and the glory, are yours
> now and for ever. Amen.

The Priest then breaks the consecrated Bread, and communicates himself and the other persons present.

The Ministration of the Sacrament

The Sacrament is ministered with these or other words:

The Body [*and Blood*] of our Lord Jesus Christ keep you unto everlasting life.

or

The Body of Christ, the Bread of heaven.
The Blood of Christ, the Cup of salvation.

After Communion, a suitable prayer may be said.

The Service concludes with this or some other Blessing:

The Peace of God, which passeth all understanding, keep your hearts and minds in the knowledge and love of God, and of his Son Jesus Christ our Lord: And the Blessing of God Almighty, the Father, the Son, and the Holy Ghost, be amongst you, and remain with you always. *Amen.*

Prayers for the Dying

A Prayer for a Person near Death

Almighty God, look on this your servant, lying in great weakness, and comfort Him with the promise of life everlasting given in the resurrection of your Son, Jesus Christ our Lord. *Amen.*

Litany for the Dying

God the Father,
Have mercy upon your servant.
God the Son,
Have mercy upon your servant.
God the Holy Spirit,
Have mercy upon your servant.
Holy Trinity, one God,
Have mercy upon your servant.

From all evil, from all sin, from all tribulation,
Good Lord, deliver him.
By your holy Incarnation, by your Cross and Passion, by your precious Death and Burial,
Good Lord, deliver him.
By your glorious Resurrection and Ascension, and by the coming of the Holy Spirit,
Good Lord, deliver him.
We sinners beseech you to hear us, Lord Christ: That it may please you to deliver your servant from fear and loneliness, from the power of evil, and from eternal death,
We beseech you to hear us, good Lord.
That it may please you mercifully to pardon all his sins.
We beseech you to hear us, good Lord.
That it may please you to grant him a place of refreshment and everlasting blessedness;
We beseech you to hear us, good Lord.
That it may please you to give him joy and gladness in your kingdom, with your saints in light;
We beseech you to hear us, good Lord.
Lamb of God, you take away the sins of the world:
Have mercy on him.
Lamb of God, you take away the sins of the world:
Have mercy on him. Lamb of God, you take away the sins of the world:
Grant him your peace. Lord, have mercy.
Christ, have mercy.
Lord, have mercy.

Our Father, who art in heaven ...

or

Our Father in heaven,
> holy be your Name,
> your kingdom come,
> your will be done,
>> on earth as in heaven.
Give us today our daily bread.
Forgive us our sins,
> as we forgive those who trespass against us.
Do not bring us to the test
but deliver us from evil.

Let us pray.

Deliver your servant, O Sovereign Lord, from all evil, and set him free from every bond; that he may rest with all your saints in the eternal habitations; where with the Father and the Holy Spirit you live and reign, one God, for ever and ever. *Amen.*

A Commendation at the Time of Death

Depart, O Christian soul, out of this world,
In the name of God the Father Almighty who created you.
In the name of Jesus Christ who redeemed you.
In the name of the Holy Spirit who sanctifies you.
May your rest be this day in peace, and your dwelling place in the Paradise of God.

A Commendatory Prayer

Into your hands, O merciful Saviour, we commend your servant *N*. Acknowledge, we humbly beseech you, a sheep of your own fold, a lamb of your own flock, a sinner of your own redeeming. Receive *him* into the arms of your mercy, into the blessed rest of everlasting peace, and into the glorious company of the saints in light. Amen.

May *his* soul and the souls of all the faithful, through the mercy of God, rest in peace. *Amen.*

Concerning the Service

The death of a member of the Church should be reported to the Minister as soon as possible, and arrangements for the funeral should be made in consultation with him.

Baptized Christians are properly buried from the church, except for weighty reasons; and the service in the church should be held at a time when the congregation has opportunity to be present. The word "Body" is used to denote the mortal remains of the departed, whether in a coffin, or prepared for burial at sea, or in an urn after cremation. The coffin is to be closed before the service begins, and shall remain closed throughout the service. It should be covered with a pall or a national flag.

If necessary, or if desired, the whole or a part of the service at the grave may be said in the church.

At the Burial of a Child, the passages from Lamentations, First John, and St. John 6, together with Psalm 23, are recommended.

It is customary that the Minister meet the Body, and go before it into the church or towards the grave.

The Anthems at the beginning of the service are said or sung:
1. As the Body is borne into the church
or 2. During the entrance of the Ministers
or 3. By the Minister, standing in his accustomed place.

The text of the Burial Anthems given in the Book of Common Prayer may be substituted for those in this Service when a musical setting composed for the Prayer Book text is used.

The Order for the Burial of the Dead

First Service

All stand while the following Anthems are sung or said:

I am the Resurrection and the Life, says the Lord.
    He who believes in me shall live,
        even though he die.
Those who live and believe in me
    shall not die for ever.

I know that my Redeemer lives,
    and that he will rise up and stand
    here on the earth, at the Last Day;
and though my flesh shall have turned to dust,
    yet shall I see God.
I shall see him for myself;
    these eyes shall behold him;
    he will not be a stranger.

For none of us has life in himself,
    and none becomes his own master when he dies.
For if we have life, we are alive in the Lord,
    and if we die, we die in the Lord.
So, then, whether we live or die,
    we are the Lord's possession.

Blessed are the dead who die in the Lord!
So it is, says the Spirit,
    they may now rest from their labors,
    for they take with them the record of their deeds.

The Minister then says

Blessed be God: Father, Son, and Holy Spirit.

People	And blessed be his Kingdom, now and forever. Amen
Minister	The Lord be with you.
Answer	And with your spirit.
Minister	Let us pray.

THE COLLECT

O God, whose mercies cannot be numbered: Accept our prayers on behalf of thy servant, *N.*, and grant *him* an entrance into the land of light and joy, in the fellowship of thy saints; through Jesus Christ thy Son our Lord, who liveth and reigneth with thee and the Holy Spirit, one God, now and for ever. *Amen.*

THE COLLECT AT THE BURIAL OF A CHILD

O God, whose most dear Son took little children into his arms and blessed them: Give us grace to entrust the soul of this child to thy never-failing care and love, and bring us all to thy heavenly kingdom; through Jesus Christ our Lord, who liveth and reigneth with thee and the Holy Spirit, one God, now and for ever. *Amen.*

The People sit.

The Reader or Readers appointed announce and read one or two of the following Lessons:

From the Old Testament

Wisdom 3:1-5, 9

The souls of the righteous are in the hand of God, and no torment will ever touch them. In the eyes of the foolish they seemed to have died, and their departure was thought to be an affliction, and their going from us to be their destruction; but they are at peace. For though in the sight of men they were punished, their hope is full of immortality. Having been disciplined a little, they will receive great good, because God tested them and found them worthy of himself. Those who trust in him will understand truth, and the faithful will abide with him in love, because grace and mercy are upon his elect, and he watches over his holy ones.

Isaiah 61:1-3

The Spirit of the Lord God is upon me, because the Lord has anointed me to bring good tidings to the afflicted; he has sent me to bind up the brokenhearted, to proclaim liberty to the captives, and the opening of the prison to those who are bound; to proclaim the year of the Lord's favor, and the day of vengeance of our God; to comfort all who mourn; to grant to those who mourn in Zion—to give them a garland instead of ashes, the oil of gladness instead of mourning, the mantle of praise instead of a faint spirit; that they may be called oaks of righteousness, the planting of the Lord, that he may be glorified.

Lamentations 3:22-26, 31-33

The steadfast love of the Lord never ceases,
>his mercies never come to an end;
they are new every morning;
>great is thy faithfulness.
"The Lord is my portion," says my soul,
>"therefore I will hope in him."

The Lord is good to those who wait for him,
>to the soul that seeks him.
It is good that one should wait quietly for the salvation of the Lord.

For the Lord will not cast off for ever,
but, though he cause grief, he will have compassion
>according to the abundance of his steadfast love;
for he does not willingly afflict or grieve the sons of men.

From the Epistles

1 Corinthians 15:20-26, 35-38, 42-44, 53-58

Christ has been raised from the dead, the first fruits of those who have fallen asleep. For as by a man came death, by a man has come also the resurrection of the dead. For as in Adam all die, so also in Christ shall all be made alive.

But each in his own order: Christ the first fruits, then at his coming those who belong to Christ. Then comes the end, when he delivers the kingdom to God the Father after destroying every rule and every authority and power. For he must reign until he has put all his enemies under his feet. The last enemy to be destroyed is death.

But some one will ask, "How are the dead raised? With what kind of body do they come?" You foolish man! What you sow does not come to life unless it dies. And what you sow is not the body which is to be, but a bare kernel, perhaps of wheat or of some other grain. But God gives it a body as he has chosen, and to each kind of seed its own body.

So is it with the resurrection of the dead. What is sown is perishable, what is raised is imperishable. It is sown in dishonor, it is raised in glory. It is sown in weakness, it is raised in power. It is sown a physical body, it is raised a spiritual body.

For this perishable nature must put on the imperishable, and this mortal nature must put on immortality. When the perishable puts on the imperishable, and the mortal puts on immortality, then shall come to pass the saying that is written: "Death is swallowed up in victory." "O death, where is thy victory? O death, where is thy sting?"

The sting of death is sin, and the power of sin is the law. But thanks be to God, who gives us the victory through our Lord Jesus Christ.

Therefore, my beloved brethren, be steadfast, immovable, always abounding in the work of the Lord, knowing that in the Lord your labor is not in vain.

Romans 8:14-19, 34-35, 37-39

All who are led by the Spirit of God are sons of God. For you did not receive the spirit of slavery to fall back into fear, but you have received the spirit of sonship. When we cry, "Abba! Father!" it is the Spirit himself bearing witness with our spirit that we are children of God, and if children, then heirs, heirs of God and fellow heirs with Christ, provided we suffer with him in order that we may also be glorified with him.

I consider that the sufferings of this present time are not worth comparing with the glory that is to be revealed to us. For the creation waits with eager longing for the revealing of the sons of God.

It is Christ Jesus, who died, yes, who was raised from the dead, who is at the right hand of God, who indeed intercedes for us. Who shall separate us from the love of Christ? Shall tribulation, or distress, or persecution, or famine, or nakedness, or peril, or sword?

No, in all these things we are more than conquerors through him who loved us. For I am sure that neither death, nor life, nor angels, nor principalities, nor things present, nor things to come, nor powers, nor height, nor depth, nor anything else in all creation, will be able to separate us from the love of God in Christ Jesus our Lord.

1 John 3:1-2

See what love the Father has given us, that we should be called children of God; and so we are. The reason why the world does not know us is that it did not know him. Beloved, we are God's children now; it does not yet appear what we shall be, but we know that when he appears we shall be like him, for we shall see him as he is.

One of the following Psalms, or a suitable Hymn or Canticle, may be said or sung after each of the preceding Readings.

Psalm 23

The Lord is my shepherd;
    therefore can I lack nothing.

He shall feed me in a green pasture,
    and leads me forth beside the waters of comfort.
He shall convert my soul,
    and bring me forth in the paths of righteousness
    for his Name's sake.

Yea though I walk through the valley
of the shadow of death,
I shall fear no evil;
    for thou art with me;
    thy rod and thy staff comfort me,

Thou spread a table before me,
in the presence of them that trouble me;
    thou hast anointed my head with oil,
    and my cup shall be` full.

Surely thy lovingkindness and mercy
shall follow me all the days of my life;
    and I shall dwell in the house of the Lord for ever.

Psalm 23 (King James Version)

The LORD is my shepherd;
    I shall not want.

He maketh me to lie down in green pastures,
    and leadeth me beside the still waters.

He restoreth my soul,
    he leadeth me in the paths of righteousness
    for his Name's sake.

Yea, though I walk through the valley of the shadow of death,
I shall fear no evil;
    for thou art with me;
    thy rod and thy staff they comfort me.

Thou preparest a table before me,
in the presence of mine enemies;
    thou anointest my head with oil;
    my cup runneth over.

Surely goodness and mercy
shall follow me all the days of my life;
    and I will dwell in the house of the LORD for ever.

Psalm 121

I will lift up mine eyes unto the hills;
    from whence cometh my help?
My help cometh even from the LORD,
    who hath made heaven and earth.
He will not suffer thy foot to be moved;
    and he that keepeth thee will not sleep.
Behold, he that keepeth Israel
    shall neither slumber nor sleep.
The LORD himself is thy keeper;
    the LORD is thy defence upon thy right hand;
So that the sun shall not burn thee by day,
    neither the moon by night.
The LORD shall preserve thee from all evil;
    yea, it is even he that shall keep thy soul.
The LORD shall preserve thy going out, and thy coming in,
    from this time forth for evermore.

Psalm 130

Out of the deep have I called unto thee, O Lord;
    Lord, hear my voice.
O let thine ears consider well
    the voice of my complaint.
If thou, Lord, wilt be extreme to mark what is done amiss,
    O Lord who may abide it?
For there is mercy with thee;
    therefore shalt thou be feared.
I look for the Lord; my soul doth wait for him;
    in his word is my trust.
My soul fleeth unto the Lord before the morning watch;
    I say, before the morning watch.
O Israel, trust in the Lord;
for with the Lord there is mercy,
    and with him is plenteous redemption.
And he shall redeem Israel
    from all his sins.

The following Psalms* are also appropriate

        65:1-8
        139:1-11
        116:1-9
        116:9-16

* The verse references are to The Book of Common Prayer.

The Gospel

Then, all standing, the Minister appointed reads the Gospel, first saying

The Holy Gospel of our Lord Jesus Christ, according to _____.

    The People respond   Glory be to thee, O Lord.

    At the end of the Gospel, the Minister says

The Gospel of the Lord.

    The People respond   Praise be to thee, O Christ.

St. John 6:37-40

Jesus said, "All that the Father gives me will come to me; and him who comes to me I will not cast out. For I have come down from heaven, not to do my own will, but the will of him who sent me; and this is the will of him who sent me, that I should lose nothing of all that he has given me, but raise it up at the last day. For this is the will of my Father, that every one who sees the Son and believes in him should have eternal life; and I will raise him up at the last day."

or

St. John 11:21-27

Martha said to Jesus, "Lord, if you had been here, my brother would not have died. And even now I know that whatever you ask from God, God will give you." Jesus said to her, "Your brother will rise again." Martha said to him, "I know that he will rise again in the resurrection at the last day." Jesus said to her, "I am the resurrection and the life; he who believes in me, though he die, yet shall he live, and whoever lives and believes in me shall never die. Do you believe this?" She said to him, "Yes, Lord; I believe that you are the Christ, the Son of God, he who is coming into the world."

or

St. John 14:1-6

Jesus said, "Let not your hearts be troubled; believe in God, believe also in me. In my Father's house are many rooms; if it were not so, would I have told you that I go to prepare a place for you? And when I go and prepare a place for you, I will come again and will take you to myself, that where I am you may be also. And you know the way where I am going." Thomas said to him, "Lord, we do not know where you are going; how can we know the way?" Jesus said to him, "I am the way, and the truth, and the life; no one comes to the Father, but by me."

Here a Sermon or Homily may be preached, the People being seated.

THE APOSTLES' CREED *may be said here, the People standing:*

I believe in God the Father Almighty, Maker of heaven and earth:
 And in Jesus Christ his only Son our Lord: Who was conceived by the Holy Ghost, Born of the Virgin Mary:
 Suffered under Pontius Pilate, Was crucified, dead, and buried: He descended into hell; The third day he rose again from the dead: He ascended into heaven, And sitteth on the right hand of God the Father Almighty: From thence he shall come to judge the quick and the dead.

I believe in the Holy Ghost: The holy Catholic Church; The Communion of Saints: The Forgiveness of sins: The Resurrection of the body: And the Life everlasting. Amen.

When there is to be a Communion, the Service continues on page 298.

When there is no Communion, the Service is concluded as follows:

Minister   In the words our Savior taught us, let us say together,

Our Father, who art in heaven, Hallowed be thy Name. Thy kingdom come. Thy will be done, On earth as it is in heaven. Give us this day our daily bread. And forgive us our trespasses, As we forgive those who trespass against us. And lead us not into temptation; But deliver us from evil. For thine is the kingdom, and the power, and the glory, for ever and ever. Amen.

Minister

Almighty God, with whom do live the spirits of those who depart hence in the Lord, and with whom the souls of the faithful, after they are delivered from the burden of the flesh, are in joy and felicity: We give thee hearty thanks for the good examples of all those thy servants, who, having finished their course in faith, do now rest from their labors. And we beseech thee, that we, with all those who are departed in the true faith of thy holy Name, may have our perfect consummation and bliss, both in body and soul, in thy eternal and everlasting glory; through Jesus Christ our Lord. *Amen.*

Almighty God, Father of mercies and giver of comfort; Deal graciously, we pray, with all who mourn, that, casting all their care on thee, they may know the consolation of thy love; through Jesus Christ our Lord. *Amen.*

Other authorized prayers may follow.

Then the Minister, standing and facing the Body, says

Unto God's gracious mercy and protection we commit *him*. The Lord bless *him* and keep *him*. The Lord make his face to shine upon *him*, and be gracious unto *him*. The Lord lift up his countenance upon *him*, and give *him* peace, both now and evermore. *Amen.*

Or else, the Service of Committal takes place at this point.

A Priest (or the Bishop) may then bless the People.

A Canticle or Hymn may be sung or said as the Body is borne from the Church (see pages 302 for Canticles).

If the Body is not then to be taken to the grave, the Deacon, or other Minister, dismisses the People:

Let us go forth in the Name of Christ.
Thanks be to God.

At the Eucharist

When Communion follows, this Prayer of Intercession may be used:

The Prayer of Intercession

(People Standing)

In Peace, let us pray to the Lord.

For the peace from above, for the salvation of mankind: that righteousness, mercy, and truth may prevail among all peoples and nations.
Hear us, good Lord.

For the well-being of thy holy Catholic Church in every place: that thou wilt confirm it in the truth of thy holy Word, and grant to all Christians to live in unity, love, and concord.
Hear us, good Lord.

Deal graciously, Lord, with all those who mourn, that, casting every care on thee they may know the consolation of thy love.
Hear us, good Lord.

Have mercy upon us, most merciful Lord; and in thy compassion forgive us all our sins and failures, known and unknown, things done and left undone; and so uphold us by thy Spirit, that we may end our days in peace, trusting in thy mercy at the day of judgment.
Have mercy upon us.

We commend to thy keeping all thy servants departed this life in thy faith and fear, and especially thy servant, *N*.: that thou wilt grant them continual growth in thy love and service. May we with them and with all thy saints be partakers of thine everlasting kingdom; through Jesus Christ, our only Mediator and Advocate.
To thee be honor, glory, and dominion, now and forever. Amen.

The Service then continues with the Offertory.

After the postcommunion Prayer, the Minister, standing before the Body, says

Unto God's gracious mercy and protection we commit *him*. The Lord bless *him* and keep *him*. The Lord make his face to shine upon *him*, and be gracious unto *him*. The Lord lift up his countenance upon *him*, and give *him* peace, both now and evermore. *Amen.*

Or else, the Service of Committal takes place at this point.

A Priest (or the Bishop) may then bless the People.

A Canticle or Hymn may be sung or said as the Body is borne from the Church (see pages 302 for Canticles).

Let us go forth in the Name of Christ.
Thanks be to God.

At the Grave

The following Anthems are sung or said:

In the midst of life we are in death;
    of whom may we seek for succor,
    but of thee, O Lord,
    who for our sins art justly displeased?
Yet, O Lord God most holy, O Lord most mighty,
O holy and most merciful Savior:
    Deliver us not into the bitter pains of eternal death.
Thou knowest, Lord, the secrets of our hearts;
    shut not thy merciful ears to our prayer;
But spare us, Lord most holy, O God most mighty,
O holy and merciful Savior,
thou most worthy Judge eternal:
    Suffer us not, at our last hour,
    for any pains of death, to fall from thee.

or these Anthems

Jesus said:
"All whom the Father gives me
    shall come to me;
and him who comes to me
    I will not cast out."
He who raised Christ Jesus from the dead
will give new life to our mortal bodies also,
    through his Spirit which dwells in us.

Therefore my heart is glad
> and my soul rejoices;
> my body shall rest in hope.
Thou shalt show me the path of life;
> in thy presence there is fulness of joy,
> and at thy right hand there is pleasure for evermore.

The Words of Committal

The Minister then says these words, during which earth may be cast upon the coffin.

Unto Almighty God we commend our *brother N.*, as we commit *his* Body to the ground *; earth to earth, ashes to ashes, dust to dust; in sure and certain hope of the resurrection to eternal life; through our Lord Jesus Christ.

> *or* the deep, *or* the elements, *or* this resting place

Lord have mercy.
Christ have mercy.
Lord have mercy.

> *The LORD'S PRAYER may be said.*

> *Then the Minister says one or more of the Prayers on pages 300-302, after which he may say*

Rest eternal grant to *him*, O Lord:
And let light perpetual shine upon him.
May his soul and the souls of all the faithful,
through the mercy of God, rest in peace. *Amen.*

> *He concludes the Service as follows:*

The God of peace, who brought again from the dead our Lord Jesus Christ, the great Shepherd of the sheep, through the blood of the everlasting covenant: Make you perfect in every good work to do his will, working in you that which is well pleasing in his sight; through Jesus Christ, to whom be glory for ever and ever. *Amen.*

Additional Prayers, and Canticles

Almighty God, with whom do live the spirits of those who depart hence in the Lord, and with whom the souls of the faithful, after they are delivered from the burden of the flesh, are in joy and felicity: We give thee hearty thanks for the good examples of all those thy servants, who, having finished their course in faith, do now rest from their labors. And we beseech thee, that we, with all those who are departed in the true faith of thy holy Name, may have our perfect consummation and bliss, both in body and soul, in thy eternal and everlasting glory; through Jesus Christ our Lord. *Amen.*

O Lord Jesus Christ, who by thy death didst take away the sting of death: Grant unto us thy servants so to follow in faith where thou hast led the way, that we may at length fall asleep peacefully in thee, and awake up after thy likeness; through thy mercy, who livest with the Father and the Holy Spirit, one God, now and for ever. *Amen.*

O God, whose days are without end, and whose mercies cannot be numbered: Make us, we beseech thee, deeply sensible of the shortness and uncertainty of human life; and let thy Holy Spirit lead us in holiness and righteousness all our days; that, when we shall have served thee in our generation, we may be gathered unto our fathers: having the testimony of a good conscience; in the communion of the Catholic Church; in the confidence of a certain faith; in the comfort of a reasonable, religious and holy hope; in favor with thee our God, and in perfect charity with the world. All which we ask through Jesus Christ our Lord. *Amen.*

O Heavenly Father, who hast given us a true faith and a sure hope: Help us, we pray, in the midst of things we cannot understand, to believe and trust in thy fatherly care—in the communion of saints, the forgiveness of sins, and the resurrection to life everlasting; and strengthen, we beseech thee, this faith and hope in us all the days of our life; through the love of thy Son, our Savior Jesus Christ. *Amen.*

O Merciful God, the Father of our Lord Jesus Christ who is the Resurrection and the Life; in whom whosoever believeth shall live, though he die; and whosoever liveth and believeth in him shall not die eternally; who also hath taught us by his holy Apostle Saint Paul not to be sorry, as men without hope, for those who sleep in him: We humbly beseech thee, O Father, to raise us from the death of sin unto the life of righteousness; that when we shall depart this life we may rest in him; and that at the general Resurrection, we may be found acceptable in thy sight; and receive that blessing which thy well-beloved Son shall then pronounce to all who love and fear thee, saying, "Come, ye blessed of my Father, receive the kingdom prepared for you from the beginning of the world." Grant this, we beseech thee, O merciful Father, through Jesus Christ, our Mediator and Redeemer. Amen.

Grant, O Lord, to all who are bereaved the spirit of faith and courage, that they may have strength to meet the days to come with steadfastness and patience; not sorrowing as those without hope, but in thankful remembrance of all the manifestations of thy great goodness, and in the joyful expectation of eternal life with those they love. And this we ask in the name of Jesus Christ our Savior. *Amen.*

Almighty God, Father of mercies and giver of comfort; Deal graciously, we pray, with all who mourn, that, casting all their care on thee, they may know the consolation of thy love; through Jesus Christ our Lord. *Amen.*

The Song of Zechariah (Benedictus)
(Luke 1:69-79)

Blessed be the Lord God of Israel;
    for he hath visited and redeemed his people;
And hath raised up a mighty salvation for us,
    in the house of his servant David;
As he spake by the mouth of his holy Prophets,
    which have been since the world began;
That we should be saved from our enemies,
    and from the hand of all that hate us.

To perform the mercy promised to our forefathers,
    and to remember his holy covenant;
To perform the oath which he sware to our forefather Abraham,
    that he would give us;
That we being delivered out of the hand of our enemies
    might serve him without fear;
In holiness and righteousness before him,
    all the days of our life.

And thou, child, shalt be called the prophet of the Highest:
    for thou shalt go before the face of the Lord to prepare his ways;
To give knowledge of salvation unto his people
    for the remission of their sins,
Through the tender mercy of our God;
    whereby the day-spring from on high hath visited us;
To give light to them that sit in darkness,
and in the shadow of death,
    and to guide our feet into the way of peace.

The Song of Simeon (Nunc dimittis)
(Luke 2:29-32)

Lord, now lettest thou thy servant depart in peace,
    according to thy word.
For mine eyes have seen thy salvation,
    which thou hast prepared before the face of all people;
To be a light to lighten the Gentiles,
    and to be the glory of thy people Israel.

The Consecration of a Grave
FROM THE BOOK OF OFFICES, 1960

If the Grave is in a place that has not previously been set apart for Christian burial, the Priest may use the following form, either before the service at the grave or at some other convenient time:

In the place where Jesus was crucified there was a garden, and in the garden a new sepulcher wherein was never man yet laid.

The eternal God is thy refuge.
And underneath are the everlasting arms.

Let us pray.
O God, whose blessed Son was laid in a sepulcher in the garden: Bless, we beseech thee, this grave, that he whose Body is [is to be} buried here may dwell with Christ in paradise, and may come to thy heavenly Kingdom; through the same Jesus Christ, our Lord. *Amen.*

Concerning the Service

The death of a member of the Church should be reported to the Minister as soon as possible, and arrangements for the funeral should be made in consultation with him.

Baptized Christians are properly buried from the church, except for weighty reasons; and the service in the church should be held at a time when the congregation has opportunity to be present.

The word "Body" is used to denote the mortal remains of the departed, whether in a coffin, or prepared for burial at sea, or in an urn after cremation. The coffin is to be closed before the service begins, and shall remain closed throughout the service. It should be covered with a pall or a national flag.

If necessary, or if desired, the whole or a part of the service at the grave may be said in the church.

At the Burial of a Child, the passages from Lamentations, First John, and St. John 6, together with Psalm 23, are recommended.

It is customary that the Minister meet the Body, and go before it into the church or towards the grave.

The Anthems at the beginning of the service are said or sung:
  1. As the Body is borne into the church
  or 2. During the entrance of the Ministers
  or 3. By the Minister, standing in his accustomed place. The text of the Burial Anthems given in the Book of Common Prayer may be substituted for those in this Service when a musical setting composed for the Prayer Book text is used.

Second Service

All stand while the following Anthems are sung or said:

I am Resurrection and I am Life, says the Lord.
    Whoever has faith in me shall have life,
    even though he die.
And everyone who has life,
and has committed himself to me in faith,
    shall not die for ever.

I know for sure that my Redeemer lives
    and that at the Last he will stand upon the earth.
After my awaking, he will raise me up;
    and in my body I shall see God.
I myself shall see, and my eyes behold him
    who is my Friend and not a Stranger.

For none of us has life in himself,
    and none becomes his own master when he dies.
For if we have life, we are alive in the Lord,
    and if we die, we die in the Lord.
So, then, whether we live or die,
    we are the Lord's possession.

How blest, from now on,
    are those who die in the Lord!
So it is, says the Spirit,
for the record of their deeds goes with them,
    that they may have rest from their weary toil.

The Minister then says

	Blessed be God: Father, Son, and Holy Spirit.
People	And blessed be his Kingdom, now and for ever. Amen.
Minister	The Lord be with you.
Answer	And also with you.
Minister	Let us pray.

THE COLLECT

O God, whose mercies cannot be numbered: Accept our prayers on behalf of your servant, *N.*, and grant *him* an entrance into the land of light and joy, in the fellowship of your saints; through Jesus Christ our Lord, who lives and reigns with you and the Holy Spirit, one God, now and for ever. *Amen.*

THE COLLECT AT THE BURIAL OF A CHILD

O God, whose most dear Son took little children into his arms and blessed them: Give us grace to entrust the soul of this child to your never-failing care and love, and bring us all to your heavenly kingdom; through Jesus Christ our Lord, who lives and reigns with you and the Holy Spirit, one God, now and for ever. *Amen.*

The People sit.

The Reader or Readers appointed announce and read one or two of the following Lessons:

From the Old Testament

Wisdom 3:1-5, 9

The souls of the just are in God's hand, and torment shall not touch them. In the eyes of foolish men they seemed to be dead; their departure was reckoned as defeat, and their going from us as disaster. But they are at peace, for though in the sight of men they may be punished, they have a sure hope of immortality; and after a little chastisement they will receive great blessings, because God has tested them and found them worthy to be his. Those who have put their trust in him shall understand that he is true, and the faithful shall attend upon him in love; they are his chosen, and grace and mercy shall be theirs.

Isaiah 61:1-3

The spirit of the Lord God is upon me
because the Lord has anointed me;
he has sent me to bring good news to the humble,
    to bind up the broken-hearted,
to proclaim liberty to captives
    and release to those in prison;
to proclaim a year of the Lord's favor
    and a day of the vengeance of our God;
    to comfort all who mourn,
to give them garlands instead of ashes,
    oil of gladness instead of mourners' tears,
    a garment of splendor for the heavy heart.
They shall be called Trees of Righteousness,
    planted by the Lord for his glory.

Lamentations 3:22-26, 31-33

The Lord's true love is surely not spent,
    nor has his compassion failed;
    they are new every morning,
    so great is his constancy.
The Lord, I say, is all that I have;
    therefore I will wait for him patiently.
The Lord is good to those who look for him,
    to all who seek him;
it is good to wait in patience and sigh
    for deliverance by the Lord.
For the Lord will not cast off.
    his servants for ever.
He may punish cruelly, yet he will have compassion
    in the fullness of his love;
he does not willingly afflict
    or punish any mortal man.

From the Epistles

1 Corinthians 15:20-26, 35-38, 42-44, 53-58

Christ was raised to life—the firstfruits of the harvest of the dead. For since it was a man who brought death into the world, a man also brought resurrection of the dead. As in Adam all men die, so in Christ all will be brought to life; but each in his own proper place: Christ the firstfruits, and afterwards, at his coming, those who belong to Christ. Then comes the end, when he delivers up the kingdom to God the Father, after abolishing every kind of domination, authority, and power. For he is destined to reign until God has put all enemies under his feet; and the last enemy to be abolished is death.

But you may ask, how are the dead raised? In what kind of body? How foolish! The seed you sow does not come to life unless it has first died; and what you sow is not the body that shall be, but a naked grain, perhaps of wheat, or of some other kind; and God clothes it with the body of his choice, each seed with its own particular body.

So it is with the resurrection of the dead. What is sown in the earth as a perishable thing is raised imperishable. Sown in humiliation, it is raised in glory; sown in weakness, it is raised in power; sown as an animal body, it is raised as a spiritual body.

This perishable being must be clothed with the imperishable, and what is mortal must be clothed with immortality. And when our mortality has been clothed with immortality, then the saying of Scripture will come true: "Death is swallowed up; victory is won!" "O Death, where is your victory? O Death, where is your sting?" The sting of death is sin, and sin gains its power from the law; but God be praised, he gives us the victory through our Lord Jesus Christ.

Therefore, my beloved brothers, stand firm and immovable, and work for the Lord always, work without limit, since you know that in the Lord your labor cannot be lost.

Romans: 8:14-19, 34-35, 37-39

All who are moved by the Spirit of God are sons of God. The Spirit you have received is not a spirit of slavery leading you back into a life of fear, but a Spirit that makes us sons, enabling us to cry "Abba! Father!" In that cry the Spirit of God joins with our spirit in testifying that we are God's children; and if children, then heirs. We are God's heirs and Christ's fellow-heirs, if we share his sufferings now in order to share his splendor hereafter.

For I reckon that the sufferings we now endure bear no comparison with the splendor, as yet unrevealed, which is in store for us. For the created universe waits with eager expectation for God's sons to be revealed.

It is Christ—Christ who died, and, more than that, was raised from the dead—who is at God's right hand, and indeed pleads our cause. Then what can separate us from the love of Christ? Can affliction or hardship? Can persecution, hunger, nakedness, peril, or the sword? In spite of all, overwhelming victory is ours through him who loved us. For I am convinced that there is nothing in death or life, in the realm of spirits or superhuman powers, in the world as it is or the world as it shall be, in the forces of the universe, in heights or depths—nothing in all creation that can separate us from the love of God in Christ Jesus our Lord.

1 John 3:1-2

How great is the love that the Father has shown to us! We were called God's children, and such we are; and the reason why the godless world does not recognize us is that it has not known him. Here and now, dear friends, we are God's children; what we shall be has not yet been disclosed, but we know that when it is disclosed, we shall be like him, because we shall see him as he is.

One of the following Psalms, or a suitable Hymn or Canticle, may be said or sung after each of the preceding Readings.

Psalm 23

The LORD is my shepherd;
    nothing, therefore, shall I lack.
He makes me lie down in green pastures;
    and leads me beside still waters.

He revives my soul,
>   and guides me along safe pathways
>   for his Name's sake.
Though I walk through the valley of the shadow of death,
I shall fear no evil;
>   for you are with me;
>   your rod and your staff, they comfort me,
You spread a table before me,
in the presence of those who trouble me;
>   you have anointed my head with oil,
>   and my cup is full.
Surely your goodness and mercy
shall follow me all the days of my life;
>   and I will dwell in the house of the LORD for ever.

Psalm 121

I will lift up my eyes to the hills.
>   "Where is my help to come from?"
My help comes from the LORD,
>   the Maker of heaven and earth.
He will not let your foot be moved,
>   and he who watches over you will not fall asleep.
Behold, he who keeps watch over Israel
shall neither slumber nor sleep:
>   he who watches over you is the LORD.
The LORD is your shade at your right hand,
>   so that the sun shall not strike you by day,
>   nor the moon by night.
The LORD shall preserve you from all evil;
>   it is he who shall keep you safe.
The LORD shall watch over your going out
and your coming in,
>   from this time forth for evermore.

Psalm 130

Out of the depths have I called to you, O LORD;
LORD, hear my voice;
>   let your ears consider well the voice of my supplication.
If you, LORD, were to note what is done amiss,
O LORD, who could survive?
>   but there is forgiveness with you;

therefore you shall be feared.
I wait for the LORD; my soul waits for him;
    in his word is my hope.
My soul waits for the LORD,
more than watchmen for the morning,
    more than watchmen for the morning.
O Israel, wait for the LORD;
    for with the LORD there is mercy;
With him there is plenteous redemption;
    and he shall redeem Israel from all his sins.

The following Psalms* are also appropriate

    65:1-8
    139:1-11
    116:1-8
    116:8-16

* The verse references are to *The Psalms: Part I* (*Prayer Book Studies* 23).

The Gospel

Then, all standing, the Minister appointed reads the Gospel, first saying

The Holy Gospel of our Lord Jesus Christ, according to _____.

The People respond   Glory to you, Lord Christ.

At the end of the Gospel, the Minister says

The Gospel of the Lord.

The People respond   Praise to you, Lord Christ.

        St. John 6:37-40

Jesus said, "All that the Father gives me will come to me, and the man who comes to me I will never turn away. I have come down from heaven, not to do my own will, but the will of him who sent me. It is his will that I should not lose even one of all that he has given me, but raise them all up on the last day. For it is my Father's will that everyone who looks upon the Son and puts his faith in him shall possess eternal life; and I will raise him up on the last day."

or

St. John 11:21-27

Martha said to Jesus, "If you had been here, sir, my brother would not have died. Even now I know that whatever you ask of God, God will grant you." Jesus said, "Your brother will rise again." "I know that he will rise again", said Martha, "at the resurrection on the last day." Jesus said, "I am the resurrection and I am life. If a man has faith in me, even though he die, he shall come to life; and no one who is alive and has faith shall ever die. Do you believe this?" "Lord, I do," she answered; "I now believe that you are the Messiah, the Son of God who was to come into the world."

or

St. John 14:1-6

Jesus said, "Set your troubled hearts at rest. Trust in God always; trust also in me. There are many dwelling-places in my Father's house; if it were not so I should have told you; for I am going there on purpose to prepare a place for you. And if I go and prepare a place for you, I shall come again and receive you to myself, so that where I am you may be also; and my way there is known to you." Thomas said, "Lord, we do not know where you are going, so how can we know the way?" Jesus replied, "I am the way; I am the truth and I am life; no one comes to the Father except by me."

Here a Sermon or Homily may be preached, the People being seated.

THE APOSTLES CREED *may be said here, the People standing:*

I believe in God, the Father almighty,
    creator of heaven and earth.
I believe in Jesus Christ, his only Son, our Lord.
    He was conceived by the power of the Holy Spirit
        and born of the Virgin Mary.
    He suffered under Pontius Pilate,
        was crucified, died, and was buried.
    He descended to the dead.
    On the third day he rose again.
    He ascended into heaven,
        and is seated at the right hand of the Father.
    He will come again to judge the living and the dead.

I believe in the Holy Spirit,
    the holy catholic Church,
    the communion of saints,

the forgiveness of sins,
the resurrection of the body,
and the life everlasting.

The version of the Creed in the Book of Common Prayer may be used instead.

When there is to be a Communion, the Service continues on page 312.

When there is no Communion, the Service is concluded as follows:

The Minister says

Let us pray together in the words our Savior taught us:

Standing, all say

Our Father in heaven,
   holy be your Name,
   your kingdom come,
   your will be done,
      on earth as in heaven.
Give us today our daily bread.
Forgive us our sins,
   as we forgive those who trespass against us.
Do not bring us to the test
   but deliver us from evil.
For the kingdom, the power, and the glory, are yours
   now and for ever. Amen.

The version of the Lord's Prayer in the Book of Common Prayer may be used instead.

Minister

Almighty God, with whom still live the spirits of those who die in the Lord, and with whom the souls of the faithful, after they are delivered from the burden of the flesh, are in joy and felicity: We give you heartfelt thanks for the good examples of all your servants, who, having finished their course in faith, now rest from their labors. May we, with all those who have died in the true faith of your holy Name, find perfect fulfillment and bliss, both in body and soul, in your eternal and everlasting glory; through Jesus Christ our Lord. *Amen.*

   Almighty God, Father of mercies and giver of comfort: Deal graciously, we pray, with all who mourn, that, casting all their care on you, they may know the consolation of your love; through Jesus Christ our Lord. *Amen.*

Other authorized prayers may follow.

Then the Minister, standing and facing the Body, says

To God's loving care and protection we entrust *him*. The Lord bless *him*, and keep *him* safe; the Lord show *him* his glory, and be gracious to *him*; the Lord look upon *him* with favor, and give *him* peace; now, and for ever. *Amen.*

Or else, the Service of Committal takes place at this point. A Priest (or the Bishop) may then bless the People.

A Canticle or Hymn may be sung or said as the Body is borne from the Church (see pages 317-318 for Canticles).

If the Body is not then to be taken to the grave, the Deacon, or other Minister, dismisses the People:

Let us go forth in the Name of Christ.
Thanks be to God.

At the Eucharist

When Communion follows, this Prayer of Intercession may be used:

The Prayer of Intercession

(People Standing)

In Peace, let us pray to the Lord.

For the peace from above, for the salvation of mankind: that righteousness, mercy, and truth may prevail among all peoples and nations.

Hear us, good Lord.

For the well-being of your holy Catholic Church in every place: that you will confirm it in the truth of your holy Word, and grant to all Christians to live in unity, love, and concord.

Hear us, good Lord.

Deal graciously, Lord, with all who mourn, that, casting every care on you, they may know the consolation of your love.

Hear us, good Lord.

Have mercy upon us, most merciful Lord; and in your compassion forgive us all our sins and failures, known and unknown, things done and left undone; and so uphold us by your Spirit, that we may end our days in peace, trusting in your mercy at the day of judgment.

Have mercy upon us.

We commend to your keeping all who have departed this life in your faith and fear, and especially your servant, *N.*: that you will grant them continual growth in thy love and service. May we with them and with all your saints be partakers of your everlasting kingdom; through your Son Jesus Christ, our only Mediator and Advocate.

To you be honor, glory, and dominion,
now and for ever. Amen.

The Service then continues with the Offertory.

After the postcommunion Prayer, the Minister, standing before the Body, says

To God's loving care and protection we entrust *him*. The Lord bless *him*, and keep *him* safe; the Lord show *him* his glory, and be gracious to *him*; the Lord look upon *him* with favor, and give *him* peace; now, and for ever. *Amen.*

Or else, the Service of Committal takes place at this point. A Priest (or the Bishop) may then bless the People.

A Canticle or Hymn may be sung or said as the Body is borne from the Church (see pages 317-318 for Canticles).

If the Body is not then to be taken to the grave, the Deacon, or other Minister, dismisses the People:

Let us go forth in the Name of Christ.
Thanks be to God.

At the Grave

The following Anthems are sung or said:

In the midst of life, we are in death.
    To whom can we turn for help,
      but to you, only, Lord,
    who by our sins are justly angered.
Holy God, Holy and mighty, Holy and merciful Savior:
    Deliver us not into the bitter pain of eternal death.
You, Lord, know the secrets of our hearts.
    Close not your ears to our prayers;
    but spare us, worthy and eternal Judge.

Holy Lord, Holy and mighty, Holy and merciful Savior:
>   Let not the pains of death at our last hour
>   turn us away from you.

or these Anthems

Jesus said:
"Everyone whom the Father gives me
>   will come to me;
I will never turn away anyone
>   who believes in me."
He who raised Christ Jesus from the dead
will also give new life to our mortal bodies,
>   through his indwelling Spirit.
Because of this, my heart is glad,
>   and my spirit sings for joy;
>   my body shall rest in hope.
You will show me the path of life;
you will fill me with joy in your presence,
and with pleasures at your right hand, for ever.

The Words of Committal

The Minister then says these words, during which the earth may be cast upon the coffin.

To Almighty God we commend our *brother, N.*, as we commit *his* Body to *the ground**; earth to earth, ashes to ashes, dust to dust; in sure and certain hope of the resurrection to eternal life, through our Lord Jesus Christ.

> * *or,* the deep, *or* the elements, *or* this resting place.

Lord have mercy.
Christ have mercy.
Lord have mercy.

> *The LORD'S PRAYER may be said.*

> *Then the Minister says one or more of the Prayers on pages 315-317; after which he may say*

Give him eternal rest, O Lord:
Let your light shine upon him for ever.

May his soul and the souls of all the faithful, through the mercy of God, rest in peace. *Amen.*

He concludes the Service as follows:

The God of peace, who brought again from the dead our Lord Jesus Christ, the great Shepherd of the sheep, through the blood of the everlasting covenant: Make you perfect in every good work to do his will, working in you that which is well pleasing in his sight; through Jesus Christ, to whom be glory for ever and ever. *Amen.*

Additional Prayers and Canticles

Almighty God, with whom still live the spirits of those who die in the Lord, and with whom the souls of the faithful, after they are delivered from the burden of the flesh, are in joy and felicity: We give you heartfelt thanks for the good examples of all your servants, who, having finished their course in faith, now rest from their labors. May we, with all those who have died in the true faith of your holy Name, find perfect fulfillment and bliss, both in body and soul, in your eternal and everlasting glory; through Jesus Christ our Lord. *Amen.*

Lord Jesus Christ, who by your death have taken away the sting of death: Grant us so to follow in faith where you have led the way, that we may at length fall asleep peacefully in you, and wake up after your likeness; through your mercy, O Christ, who with the Father and the Holy Spirit live and reign, one God, for ever and ever. *Amen.*

O God, whose days are without end, and whose mercies cannot be numbered: Make us, we pray, deeply sensible of the shortness and uncertainty of human life; and let your Holy Spirit lead us in holiness and righteousness all our days; so that, when we shall have served you in our generation, we may be gathered to our fathers: having the testimony of a good conscience; in the communion of the Catholic Church; in the confidence of a certain faith; in the comfort of a rational, religious and holy hope; in favor with you our God, and in perfect charity with the world. All which we ask through Jesus Christ our Lord. *Amen.*

Heavenly Father, giver of a true faith and a sure hope: Help us, we pray, in the midst of things we cannot understand, to believe and trust in your fatherly care—in the communion of saints, the forgiveness of sins, and the resurrection to life everlasting; and strengthen, we pray, this faith and hope in us all the days of our life; through Jesus Christ our Lord. *Amen.*

Father of all, we pray to you for those we love, but see no longer. Grant them your peace; let light perpetual shine upon them; and in your loving wisdom and almighty power, work in them the good purpose of your perfect will; through Jesus Christ our Lord. *Amen.*

Merciful God, Father of our Lord Jesus Christ who is the Resurrection and the Life, in whom whosoever believes shall live, even though he die, and whosoever lives and believes in him shall not die eternally; who also has taught us by his holy Apostle Saint Paul not to be sorry, as men without hope, for those who sleep in him: We humbly beseech you, O Father, to raise us from the death of sin to the life of righteousness; that when we shall depart this life we may rest in him, and that at the general Resurrection we may be found acceptable in your sight; and receive that blessing which your well-beloved Son shall then pronounce to all who love and fear you, saying, "Come you blessed of my Father, receive the kingdom prepared for you from the beginning of the world." Grant this, we beseech you, merciful Father, through Jesus Christ, our Mediator and Redeemer. *Amen.*

Grant, O Lord, to all who are bereaved the spirit of faith and courage, that they have strength to meet the days to come with steadfastness and patience; not sorrowing as those without hope, but in thankful remembrance of all the manifestations of your great goodness, and in the joyful expectation of eternal life with those they love. And this we ask in the Name of Jesus Christ our Savior. *Amen.*

Almighty God, Father of mercies and giver of comfort: Deal graciously, we pray, with all who mourn, that, casting all their care on you, they may know the consolation of your love; through Jesus Christ our Lord. *Amen.*

* Lord God, you were happy to give us
the light of our eyes
and let us be born.
You did not make us
for darkness and death,
but so that we should, with all our hearts,
live and come closer to you.
Be merciful to us then
and take us by the hand
and lead us to life
today and for ever.

For a dead person

* We thank you, God,
for this *man* who was so near and dear to us
and who has now been taken from us.
We thank you
for the friendship that went out from *him*
and the peace *he* brought.
We thank you
that through suffering *he* learned obedience

and that *he* became a person others could love
while *he* was with us here on earth.

For ourselves, who are still living

* Let us pray for ourselves,
who are severely tested by this death,
that we do not try to minimize this loss
or seek refuge from it in words
and also that we do not brood over it
so that it overwhelms us
and isolates us from others.
May God grant us new courage
and confidence to face life.

* From "Your Word is Near" by Huub Oosterhuis, Newman Press, New York, N.Y. Reprinted by permission.

The Song of Zechariah (Benedictus)
(Luke 1:69-79)

Blessed be the Lord, the God of Israel;
    he has come to his people and set them free.
He has raised up for us a mighty savior,
    born of the house of his servant David.
Through his holy prophets he promised of old,
that he would save us from our enemies,
    from the hands of all who hate us.

He promised to show mercy to our fathers and to remember his holy covenant.
This was the oath he swore to our father Abraham,
    to set us free from our enemies' hand,
free to worship him without fear,
    holy and righteous in his sight,
    all the days of our life.
And you, my child, shall be called the prophet of the Most High,
    for you will go before the Lord to prepare his way,
to give his people knowledge of salvation
    by forgiveness of their sins.
In the tender compassion of our God
    the dawn from on high shall break upon us.
to shine on those who dwell in darkness and the shadow of death,
    and to guide our feet on the road to peace.

The Song of Simeon (Nunc dimittis)
(Luke 2:29-32)

Lord, you have fulfilled your word;
> now let your servant depart in peace.

With my own eyes I have seen the salvation,
> which you have prepared in the sight of every people:

A Light to reveal you to the nations,
> and the glory of your people Israel.

The Consecration of a Grave

ADAPTED FROM THE BOOK OF OFFICES, 1960

If the Grave is in a place that has not previously been set apart for Christian burial, the Priest may use the following form, either before the Service at the Grave, or at some other convenient time:

In the place where Jesus was crucified there was a garden, and in the garden a new sepulcher in which no man had been buried before.

The eternal God is your dwelling-place;
And underneath are the everlasting arms.

Let us pray.
O God, whose blessed Son was laid in a sepulcher in the garden: Bless, we pray, this grave, that *he* whose body is [is to be] buried here may dwell with Christ in paradise, and may come to your heavenly Kingdom; through the same Jesus Christ, our LORD. *Amen.*

www.ingramcontent.com/pod-product-compliance
Lightning Source LLC
Chambersburg PA
CBHW070746020526
44116CB00032B/1988